NL28
OLYMPIC FIRE
Future Games

NAI
MVRDV
Berlage Institute
AVBR
NOC*NSF

NAi Publishers

Foreword	NOC*NSF	4
Games That Think Big	OLE BOUMAN	6
Can the Netherlands Dream of a Sports-Minded and Healthy Society?	WINY MAAS	10
What is Sport?		22
'Spatial planning should take a sporting attitude'	Riek Bakker	36
What is the Olympic Spirit?		38
'Green Games are good for both the athletes and the crowd'	Agnes van den Berg	60
What Can We Learn From Previous Olympics?		64
'We have space and we need more urbanisation. What more can you ask for?'	John Bos	102
'Create enough grass plots and sports clubs in neighbourhoods'	Jet Bussemaker	104
What Can We Expect in the Future?		106
'The Olympic Games as a motor for urban renewal'	Kees Christiaanse	118
'Amsterdam has a name of tolerance to live up to'	Cohen and Gehrels	120
Why the Netherlands?		122
'Games in the heart of Europe, powered by energy from the new Falling Lake'	Rudolf Das	138
What is the Current State of NL Sport Facilities?		142
'Why would I care what a hall looks like?'	Anton Geesink	158
'No reason to get excited'	Jaap van Ginneken	160
What is the Olympic Programme & Schedule?		162
'We must use the Games to put the Randstad on the world map'	Hans Mommaas	194
'Ecologically sound Games in 2028: it goes without saying'	Liesbeth van Tongeren	196
What Kind of Olympic Games Can We Imagine?		200
'If it is only about sports, than we should not want to organise the Games	Henk Ovink	300
'No guts, no glory'	Ivo Opstelten	302
What Kind of Stadiums Can We Imagine?		304
'We will have to "cast" sports and landscapes'	Dirk Sijmons	324
'I wouldn't be surprised at all if the Olympic Games withered away'	Abram de Swaan	326
'Olympic Village in the city centre adds to the atmosphere'	Stephan Veen	328
What is Next?	OLE BOUMAN	330

Foreword

What began as a small affair in Athens in 1896 has by now, more than one hundred years later, grown into an event without parallel in the world: the International Olympic and Paralympic Games. A celebration of sports, it is the supreme moment in which athletes perform at the highest of levels, accomplishing feats which often have never before been achieved by themselves or others. Wanting to give their all, wanting and daring to measure themselves against others – this is what is most important. To do this, athletes put everything else aside for years. They dream of reaching the top once in their lifetimes and receiving the crown of laurel to the thundering applause of the audience – a moment they will never, ever forget, one that will be permanently engraved in their memories.

Just as winning a gold medal is reserved for only a few athletes, only a few cities can claim with pride that they have hosted the Olympic Games. The cities belonging to this select group know that the Olympic power, the Olympic fire, has inspired them and given them energy – just like the athletes – to go beyond their limits, enter into competition with others and transcend themselves. Wherever they take place, the Olympic Games leave a huge footprint: they can change the appearance of a city, as in Barcelona; improve its infrastructure, as in Munich and Athens; or put a city and country on the global map, as occurred with Sydney and Australia. This transformation is the magic of the Olympic Games.

The Olympic Games stand for daring, ambition, and repeatedly getting the best of out oneself. In this same Olympic spirit, the Netherlands Olympic Committee*Netherlands Sport Federation (NOC*NSF) has collaborated with sports, governmental and business organisations to develop the Olympic Plan. The idea is to turn the Netherlands into a Land of Sports at the Olympic level, where lots of people engage in sports, many sporting events are organised and sports make an important contribution to society;

a land where the Olympic fire burns in the hearts of everyone. An ambitious plan, indeed, but one with which NOC*NSF dares to face the future and boldly tread new paths. The goal will be achieved in 2016, when the Netherlands will be a true Land of Sports and the Olympic fire will burn in the heart of many a Dutch person. At that point the Netherlands can seriously consider becoming a candidate for the Olympic Games and then perhaps we will succeed in once again organising, after 100 years, the Olympic Games in the Netherlands in 2028.

Architecture is an important factor in the Olympic Plan – after all, stadiums and venues are where it's all happening! This is not only true for top sports and athletes; it is also true for those who like to practice a sport because it does them good, gives them pleasure and satisfaction. The Plan reaches even further, though, because a stadium is not enough. The crux of the matter is having cities and regions that are sports-minded. This is why the sports world is calling upon architects and designers to come up with creative ideas to bring sports closer to the Dutch people. Make it easy for the public to do sports and let the Dutch be proud of their cities!

NOC*NSF is pleased that the NAI, the MVRDV architecture firm, the Berlage Institute, and the Rotterdam Academy of Architecture and Urban Design have been the first to pick up the glove and suit action to word. The Ministries of Health, Welfare and Sport; Economic Affairs; and Housing, Spatial Planning and the Environment; the Cities of Amsterdam and Rotterdam and the Province of Flevoland have quickly shown their appreciation for this initiative by making this exhibition possible. With daring and ambition, let all parties show how creatively the Netherlands can play ball with the future.

André Bolhuis
Member of the Board
NOC*NSF

Marcel Sturkenboom
Sports Director
NOC*NSF

Games That Think Big

Resting makes you rusty. Practice makes Perfect. Strength through Willpower. If at first you don't succeed, try, try again. In that order.

Anyone who has ever set themselves a distant goal knows from experience that each and every one of these nuggets of wisdom is true. So it is only logical that many of these proverbs should come from the vocabulary of sports, for nowhere is the culture of postponed gratification so strongly developed as it is among athletes, who are willing to put their hearts and souls into goals that are sometimes very far in the future: the mountain bike finals, the national squad, the world record, Olympic Gold. Many a clubhouse and canteen is decorated with maxims expressing this mentality. Sometimes the entire club is named after the triumph over the sin known as giving up: De Volharding (The Perseverers); Door Training Sterk (Strength through Training); the NAC (Never Quit, Always Carry On Combination).

Some claim, in reference to the manner in which struggle and competition are channelised through socially acceptable activities, that sports are a civilised form of waging war within society. This notion primarily exists amongst those who do not practice a sport themselves. For athletes know – and this too is a cliché – that all of that sacrifice is primarily inspired by an urge to triumph over oneself. The greater the effort and the longer the agony, the less pleasure you have in defeating someone else, and the more satisfaction you have in your own achievement. As the athlete approaches 'citius, altius, fortius', it is not hatred that grows but respect. At this point, therefore, sports are not concerned with war but self-improvement. Through the training of the body and the testing of the competition, the athlete above all demonstrates the strength of his or her will to achieve. Competitors become colleagues. Only the highest goals can motivate people to ask the utmost of themselves. Conversely, people who do not set themselves a goal get stuck in a rut…rest… grow rusty.

Here sports begin to resemble architecture, which has exemplified the strength of ambition much longer than sport. Like the athlete, the architect has a distant goal in view. That goal may be years away and the road full of obstacles, but the results are worth the effort. The design is the fruit of imaginative power, but the building itself is at least equally the result of the capacity to persist and persevere. This aspect of good architecture is seldom acknowledged. Much more often do you hear about the very unusual design of a successful building than about the remarkable fact that the design was followed to its completion. Yet these are opposite sides of the same success. It might be best to consider the triumph of beautiful architecture as not only a triumph over matter but also ourselves. We must dare to think big when it comes to big buildings, and therefore must dare to set goals. People who do not set themselves goals get stuck in a rut. Resting makes you rusty.

Suppose we build something for the world of sports. Architecture and sport, the two ideal forms of ambition, thus come together in one common undertaking. And imagine that this means constructing something for the Olympic Games: then first and foremost we need Olympic fire. Not the fire which symbolises the Olympic idea, but the fire which inspires it. Minima magnus scintilla nascitur ignis: a small spark starts a big fire. Before we can start accumulating the medals, before we can start thinking about the stadiums in which those metals can be earned, yes, even before we can start designing the roads which lead to them, we must first of all ask ourselves whether we have enough willpower to embark upon those roads. These are big words – not for nothing are we talking about the biggest peaceful collective event ever known to mankind. Are we capable of imagining a horizon which lies further away than the end of an administrative period, appears to be beyond the end of our active lives, and lies further off than almost every other goal we usually set in order to make sense of our lives? Can we play around with a big idea that does not so much give immediate results but opens up potential? Do we know how to deal with a value that we share with all humanity? Can we find inspiration in a project that serves as a guideline for our actions? And do we dare to set a deadline for our success? In other words, are we capable of accomplishing something which is much more than a project to impress the world? Are we capable of triumphing over ourselves?

The Netherlands Architecture Institute has set itself the goal of coupling assignment with design, social urgencies with available talent. In terms of Games that Think Big, however, the assignment is perhaps as important as the design. Or rather, only the design can embody the assignment and make it tangible. Only the design can sharpen the minds, foster the speculative power and boost the courage that is indispensable for tackling this assignment. The NAI is throwing itself with Olympic fire into an exploration of the possibilities of raising ourselves to Olympian heights. This exploration will also map out all that is necessary, desirable and possible in terms of architecture, town and country planning, infrastructure and administration.

What's more, the NAI is not doing this alone. We are fortunate to be collaborating with the Netherlands Olympic Committee*Netherlands Sport Federation (NOC*NSF); the Ministries of Health, Welfare and Sport (VWS), and Housing, Spatial Planning and the Environment (VROM); the province of Flevoland; the cities of Amsterdam and Rotterdam; MVRDV; the Berlage Institute; the Rotterdam Academy of Architecture and Urban Design; and many other parties. Without them, this exercise in big thinking would never have taken shape.

Ole Bouman
Director of the NAI

CAN THE NETHERLANDS DREAM OF A SPORTS-MINDED AND HEALTHY SOCIETY?

NL 2028: THE DUTCH BID

Winy Maas

1. CITY OF SPORTS

DAILY SPORTS!
Nowadays, at the beginning of a new millennium, our high standard of living combined with stressful, competitive work patterns, improved medical science and a greater Body Mass Index has increased the importance of healthcare, leisure and sports in our daily lives. The threats of obesity, cholesterol, heart problems and other diseases, and the financial consequences for our healthcare systems have encouraged interest in sports, which in turn highlights the need for more and better sports facilities.

WHY PLACE THEM ON THE PERIPHERY?
Strikingly enough, most of those facilities are not very well integrated within the urban fabric; we generally find them on the peripheries of our cities. The behaviour (or misbehaviour) of supporters, easy accessibility and the desire to keep large mobs away from dense urban areas has led to stadiums being banned to the outskirts. Every amateur sports field is doomed to be located in a sad place left over during the planning process. The amount of time I have spent on windy fields in some strange corner of a city in view of an airport, next to a highway, is endless. The architecture of most of these facilities is minimal, let alone if it can even be considered architecture. Fences and canals surround the fields as if they are prisons. Swimming pools are located in utilitarian, dark buildings, since the budgets don't allow for true quality. Why, oh why, can't we give sports facilities a more prominent place in our cities? Is it really true that we should be glad that they even exist at all?

IN THE CENTRE!

Maybe if sports gain renewed importance and they become an integrated part of daily life, a more centrally located programme can be imagined and a better quality of architecture will become possible. That might draw more attention, more users and more spectators. And maybe then, simply because of the increase in numbers, the quality of the sports will improve, leading to more top talents. This in turn will attract more attention and even more participants.

Of course, there are several interesting and exemplary directions to follow in that respect. The new sports club culture is leading to centrally located buildings. The boom in golf clubs (some like it, others hate it) has led to the integration of golf courses in new housing zones: golfing communities. The desire for nearby tennis clubs has lead to the situating of tennis clubs in apartment buildings. Skating plazas, such as the one in the centre of Rotterdam, attract many visitors and inspire many to join in; the extensive use and success of the national parks…and so forth.

CITY OF SPORTS

But can we go even further? Why not advocate a more sports-minded city? One that not only has a mix of sports amenities, but is based on them! A *cité sportive*, not only financed by the public sector but also by health insurance companies and the health industry. A truly healthy city!

2. THE OLYMPIC GAMES AND LATER USE: AN URBAN TOOL

THE GAMES?

'City of Sports' implies initiating a discussion on the location of sports facilities. Should they be spread out or all in one central location? And should this be in the country or the city? Which is best? This discussion might be furthered by organising bigger sports events like the Olympic Games. Such events help to develop top talents, stimulate enthusiasm among inhabitants and inspire young people.

But what does the choice of bidding for the Olympic Games imply? What mix of sports facilities is required in the future? Is the current mix all that good? Or would it be better to think of locating the Games somewhere else? Where, then? How far in advance do we need to get ourselves organised? And when are investments in the Games useful? How can we convince the sceptics? Let's analyse the pros and cons….

THE BARCELONA EXPERIENCE

Over the last twenty years the Olympic Games have shifted focus, highlighted by Barcelona in 1992: they have proven to be a motor for urban development as much as they are a sporting event – both directly (investing in them can entail a series of urban improvements) and indirectly (they can call attention to other investments and attractions). Post-Games use has become as important as its initiator, the Games themselves.

This offers fascinating possibilities. What kind of urban processes should we ultimately aim for? What should be repaired and how can that be included in the strategy of the bidding process? London's decision to use the plans for the Olympic Games to help regenerate its poor East London district is exemplary. And the practice of bringing in star architects can be considered emblematic. The Beijing Games are a prime example of this.

But what sort of plans will appeal in the future selection process?

URBAN THEMES

Urban themes help in winning the competition to host the Games – undeniably. But what kind of themes will attract attention in the future? What will attract the most global recognition? If the Olympic Spirit still embodies the Good and the Universal, then this will definitely lead to Games which protect the Earth, which help to increase and spread economic development, eradicate poverty and so on. In that respect, one can wonder if very site-specific

Games still have a future. The bids of Madrid and Paris were examples of this trend. Urbanism of the Games thus gets a wider meaning or agenda. It makes it possible to discuss larger themes, creates an Olympic Spirit and in its competitive élan, urbanism becomes an Olympic sport in itself!

SPACE OF THE EVENT
Although use after the Games is important, the design for the Olympic event itself seems essential. The design should provide the best environment for a series of athletic highlights, for setting records. It should support those achievements by creating the best possible atmosphere: enthusiastic crowds, great ambience, beautiful amenities and architecture.

BROTHERHOOD
Besides that, the Olympic Games have an extra message to bring across: the 'brotherhood of man' and 'friendship'. How can we use, improve upon and embody this message in the proposal? How can we create greater happiness during the Games?
This obviously depends on the situation, on the extent of people's enthusiasm. 'Improvement' seems to be the key word here; the world expects the Games to address more and more social and political issues, developments aimed at eradicating poverty, creating more freedom, more equality, higher living standards, cleaner and nicer cities, and so forth. And the more the 'poor' are included, the better, wider and more authentic the message can be.
Perhaps the solution is even more centralised and compact Games, where one can see the supporting crowds and the events can easily be staged against a spectacular backdrop; Games that are completely integrated in the city. In Sydney the Games are remembered not for the Village but for the people partying in Darling Harbour, with the Opera and the Harbour Bridge as a backdrop.

LATER USE
Later use will have a stronger role to play in this respect. How can we include this in our planning? Let's start by looking at the situation in

reverse. First, consider what we want to achieve as a city; second, whether this is universally acknowledged, and then the design of the Games can evolve from there. So: what later uses can be imagined? What sort of programmes can be used afterwards? Housing? Retail? What are the benefits, both in terms of specifics (what kind of new stadiums are really useful and how?) and urban planning (what does this give to a city: an improved poor area, a bridge, an urban node?). This completely dispels the fear of white elephants.

3. THE NETHERLANDS

TOP SPORTS

In the Netherlands the demand for top sports facilities has grown since the year 2000. This not only helps the top sports, but also can make the Dutch population more enthusiastic for sports in general. Successes in sports attract people and convince them to do sports as well, thus making the Dutch more healthy. In addition, they act as a national advertisement, drawing attention to the country and improving the tourist industry and export trade.

The country obviously has facilities, some good, others poor. However, they are not on the level of big events such as the Olympic Games or the World Football Championships, for instance. They are not concentrated and at times are simply badly located and hard to reach. (Famous names such as Alkmaar and Papendal are typical examples.)

Developing a potential bid for the Olympic Games in the Netherlands can focus on planning for such facilities. This makes it imaginable to already start investing in stadiums, infrastructure and other elements and in return making a successful Olympic Bid or the organisation of other large sports events more likely. One can say that the concept of a possible bid for the Games can be used to already create some of the desired elements. The dream of a more healthy and sports-minded city thus becomes more real.

2028
Could the realisation of this dream perhaps coincide with the anniversary of the last time the Games took place in the Netherlands? Is celebrating the fact that they took place Amsterdam 100 years ago a good reason to host the Games? Those Games left the city with a monumental stadium as well as a great neighbourhood, the now famous and gentrified Amsterdam Zuid, designed by Berlage. Isn't that reason enough in itself?

BUT...
In the 1980s, the city of Amsterdam made a bid for the 1992 Olympic Games. During that process a group of residents started a campaign against it, questioning the benefits of Games that would only lead to white elephants. The campaign harmed the bidding process to such an extent that Amsterdam's bid was unsuccessful. As a result of that experience, many local and national politicians have shied away from the idea of a bid because action groups might reject it. But is this still the case? Is the opposition still there? Are we not overestimating such sentiments? Does the majority see the need for international exposure and vitalisation? If objections exist, how can they be overcome? What alternatives can lead to a successful strategy? Can Amsterdam overcome such opposition? Should it be Amsterdam, anyway? Maybe the residents of other Dutch cities would react more maturely?
One can conclude from these public discussions that the host city and the Netherlands should get something out of the Games, that they should not lead to unusable white elephants and that they can be used to create a great legacy. How can we do that?

DUTCH LETHARGY
Lethargy coincides with another strong development in the Netherlands since the turn of the millennium. The 1990s are seen as a Golden Age, with great social, technological, economic and – yes – architectural successes. Prior to that, the Dutch had produced great collective works with fantastic innovations: the Delta Works after the flood in 1953, the 'plot exchange policy' in the 80s for the planning of

new areas, the new high-speed railways and the Rotterdam world port all indicate the potential and necessity of a small country to organise itself.

Somewhere around 9/11, however, the Dutch Golden Age came to an end. After the murder of Pim Fortuyn, a striving populist politician, fear suddenly took hold of the country. Fear that the economy would stop growing, that investments would become insecure. Investors stopped investing in new developments. Risk aversion led to much 'safer' architecture and urbanism – retro houses, 30s neighbourhoods – killing the frivolous, experimental architectural spirit of the country that had attracted so much attention, so many visitors. Now we can see the results of this tendency; the desire for nostalgia kills curiosity, an elementary aspect of innovation.

NL?
The unification of Europe made the situation even clearer; borders dissolved and big companies left. Where is the Netherlands now? Does it still exist, and if so, what is it?

This is a highly contemporary issue. How can a region (not a country) stand out and continue to do so? How can it specialise in order to assume a highly specific role and position in the world economy?

This negates the power of the nation. It blocks ambitions, puts the country in an embarrassing, indefensible state of lethargy.

NL NOW?
And is that over now? Can the country be reborn? Can the Netherlands become aggressive and assertive again? Does the country have the ability to think about its future again, about its need for organisation? Can the Olympic Games be a test case for that?

NL WHEN?
But when can we expect the Netherlands to have a chance in the bidding process? Isn't there a continental sequence? Shouldn't Africa, Arabia, Asia and South America go first? If so, then 2016, 2020,

2024 and even 2028 might already be taken. Political and societal circumstances will influence that decision.

What can we learn from the past? What were the reasons for choosing a city in the past? What ideologies were predominant? How are choices connected with the Zeitgeist? What reasons and ideologies can be expected for choosing future Games? What speculative prognoses can be made? What kind of extrapolations and scenarios can be foreseen? What motives can be expected in the near future? In short, what's next? A north/south dialogue? Perhaps rising economies like Brazil, India, the Middle East, Eastern Europe can become showcases of how they want to 'behave'? And if Western Europe gains a position, what then? Why should it deserve that? What can Europe give to the world?

How can the Netherlands use its relative prosperity? What should it invest in? Art? An answer to demographic aging? How to decrease the size of the population nicely? How to improve a city? How to make it greener? Livelier? Safer? More social? More energy-efficient? Adopt a specific game, maybe?

WHY NL?

And then the Netherlands. Why the NL? Why should one choose the NL? A deep analysis seems necessary, an analysis that not only can be used for a possible bid, but also for more general self-criticism. What should the NL put forward? What is attractive? In other words, what is the potential of the NL? What should the NL 'say'? What design for the new Olympic city can help in this process?

Water management, perhaps? The Netherlands has to deal with water because of its topography and is situated in a moderate climate zone. Can it claim a role in this amongst a wider community? And cultural mix? The Netherlands' once famous transparency, the mixing of cultures, the perceived openness can become a role model.

Or should the bid focus on density? The Netherlands is densely built and can turn this factor into an innovative experimental show case: dense cityscaping, dense agriculture, dense forestry and green management.

Due to this density the Netherlands has a reputation for urban planning, as witnessed by the Delta Works, the new polders, agricultural transformations, urban extensions and inner-city renewals.

Can it prolong this specialism, if it can be considered that? If so, we must create an exemplary proposal for the Games instead of one that simply includes the required stadiums without any ambition or agenda.

NL CHANGES?

It is also possible that the Netherlands will be dramatically different in ten years' time. Will it be a country with only old people? One that has no factories anymore? No landscapes? Or a nation that has a strong new generation, maybe coming from somewhere else, and that has created a new economy with overwhelming energy and production?

PROPOSALS

Let's look at some ideas for putting the Netherlands on the map again.

PROGRAMME

All of these ideas have been based on the programmes currently projected for the Olympic Games. A total of 3.4 million m^2, or 276 million m^3 – the size of an average provincial city – has to be built. Wow. Where can we put this? What is already available in the NL? But how good is it? How can it be used afterwards?

IDEALS

What ideals can be imagined for such an operation? Let's give them a name, a slogan, which makes them more comprehensible. What kind of ideals are they? Spatial, political, ideological? And then, where should we locate these in the NL?

And so, looking ahead to the Netherlands in 2028, it is easy to imagine the ascendance of the Water cleaning Games, which use the programme of the Olympics as a water cleaner and buffer; or the Dyke Games, since they help protect the low countries; or the A4 Games, which help improve the infrastructure of the densest country on earth; or the Light & cheap Games as an example of recycling; the Agro Games, which use the Olympics programme as a future green home; or the Downtown Games, which densify and intensify the cities of Rotterdam and Amsterdam; or the Stacking Games, which show that the Games can beat Dubai; and what to think of the Island-airport Games, which protect the country with a new buffer; or the Transit Games, which make a new, more environmentally sound use of the airport feasible through intensification; or the Dune Games, which encourage the use of dunes as a natural protective device for the Netherlands; or, last but not least, the Travel Games, which make it imaginable that the Dutch Games can be used by the next countries to host the Olympics.

BLACK ELEPHANTS

One could imagine that the main stadium deserves special attention. Everyone asks, can a 110,000 seater still be used afterwards in these democratic times? Well, what can we imagine? Can't we use such giants as housing blocks afterwards? Or multi-entertainment complexes? Or park and ride facilities? Or as coastal protection? That way they could support the strategies mentioned above.

WHAT NOW?

All of these proposals describe ideas for the Games that may benefit the country. What is the future of the Games? How can these proposals facilitate new demands? They all refer to later use and the message this communicates to the world. Should the Games benefit the host city only, or the entire Netherlands, too? And what about others? What's best?

WHAT IS SPORT?

SPORT IS GAMES AND PLAY

The phenomena of games and play are inherent to human behaviour. Games are as old as human culture itself. Any type of game or play, from simple fun to gambling to serious sports competition, has always been a crucial factor both in the development of human culture and that of the individual from childhood to adulthood. Games and play are fundamental components in the evolution of human life and society: from homo sapiens, homo faber and homo ludens to homo athletica. Games and play are the closest most human beings come to contemplation, the highest form of human activity. In requiring all of our energy and skill to perform as best we can, a game takes us out of ourselves. The game, the sport, is worth playing for its own sake. Yet, this activity – the race, the championship, the jump, the goal – stands out as a thing of light and glory in comparison to the dullness of ordinary activities. This light or glory is not merely self-generated but reflects something that exists at all times, something that points to a higher origin of all things, including human things. We are captivated by the absoluteness of games, by their focus and ambition, their strict structure of rules and limitations of time and space. We are delighted by the judge or referee who guarantees that a game be what it is, that it be played in its own way and its own time. Sport simply represents the purest form of imparting order to human existence.

SPORT IS AN INSTITUTION

Sports began in pre-modern society as participatory contests of strength, skill, and speed that were unorganized local competitions with simple rules. With the rise of the modern nation, however, sports became highly organized with formal rules and national competitions. Sports grew more complex, sophisticated, commercial and institutionalized. Institutionalization made the organisational and technical aspects of a sport more important and formalized the learning of game skills. The sports institution found its role by representing a sport and officially carrying out and protecting its rules. In other words, sports have become standardized, regulated and popularized.

As a result of commercialization and popularization, expert athletes have become celebrities who entertain the paying spectators. With the establishment of sports federations and clubs that accommodate people from all walks of life, countless markets have sprung up around sports activities to fulfil the desires of professional and amateur athletes, supporters and spectators. Since the establishment of sports institutions and the modern Olympic Games, sports have become more and more popular.

SPORT IS URBAN SPECTACLE

The Olympic Games are the most global of spectacles, accenting a specific urban locality, where the limits, abilities and endurance of the human body and mind are tested in public and broadcast to a cross-cultural audience. The host city becomes almost transcendental as a result of the choreographed opening and closing ceremonies of the Olympic Games and the obeisance given to heroic athletes. The Olympic Games held in large venues reflect the complexity of our current social system, expressed at various levels: individual versus individual, team versus team, city versus city, nation versus nation, devotee versus devotee.

In itself, any sport spectacle certainly brings benefits to modern urban life. Life in the city is driven by a broad consensus that regular physical activity is essential for the physical, mental and psychological well-being of every modern human being. Having facilities available for sports and participating in them can boost the health of urban dwellers, improve their performance and may even help decrease the crime rate.

SPORT IS A TOOL

The International Olympic Committee (IOC), which has organized the modern Olympic Games every four years since 1896, embodies the most extreme form of institutionalized sport. The modern Olympic Games are the ultimate way of promoting sports and a healthy life style within the urban environment and facilitating international markets. The organisational power of the IOC, its long-term bidding procedure, and, ultimately, 'legacy' have raised sports to the level of the sublime.

Winning bids typically come from the biggest and richest cities. Nevertheless, small cities struggling for improvement keep bidding with little or no chance of winning, because the process itself can be a factor in solving various kinds of urban and social issues. From identity and infrastructure to urban regeneration and New Town developments, bidding has proven to be a major city-making tool. The Olympic Games have become a super tool for city marketing and branding, a political and economical machine controlled entirely by the IOC. By the sheer scale of its revenues, the IOC is worth considering as a powerful political and economic entity, one which plays an increasingly meaningful role in our society, which soon will be post-national. The present tendency, obviously, is the increasing cost of hosting the Games. This turns the event into a luxurious operation, making it ever more difficult for poor countries to host the Olympic Games.

SPORT IS A LIFESTYLE

Sports are everywhere. Millions all over the world enjoy sports. Spectators, investors, competitors, male, female, young, old and every race on Earth are all affected by sports.

Sport is a social phenomenon that is strongly related to the social and cultural contexts in which we live. Specific sports are inherently connected with ideologies as well as with major spheres of society such as the family, the economy, media, politics, education, national identity and religion. Sport adds flavour to our national identity and is a dominant theme in our everyday conversation. Sport has become its own medium of communication and has important ramifications for international and multicultural relationships. The variety of possibilities in the world of sports is increasing; young and old are finding forms of sport which they can coordinate with other affairs and thus incorporate in their lives. For example, there are health and fitness-oriented sports, body-style sports, adventure and recreational sports. This variety of sporting activities is equally accessible to every group within society.

Since everyone is free to choose their own favourite sports, participation is increasing. Playing sports has become a regular part of our daily lives and helps enrich them. Today, sport has become a popular collective tool for improving health. The 'sportification' of human life has begun.

SPORT IS MEDIA

Because of the mediatisation of sports through radio, television, newspapers, the Internet, etc. sport has become a part of human culture to an extent that was once inconceivable. Sport can be considered the religion of our times. Coverage of sports in newspapers has increased and now occupies more space than politics and the economy. Whether the quality of sports has improved accordingly is another matter.

'Spatial planning should take a sporting attitude'

Riek Bakker interviewed by Mieke Dings

Riek Bakker is an urban development specialist who runs her own consultancy agency, Riek Bakker Consultancy. She has previously worked on the master plans for Leidsche Rijn [a new urban development near Utrecht – MD] and the Noordelijke IJ-oever [redevelopment of Amsterdam's harbour district – MD] on behalf of the agency BVR, which she co-founded.

Involvement with the Olympic Games 2028: I am a member of the quality team that supports the spatial studies for the Olympic Games coordinated by Twynstra Gudde Consultants and Managers.

Practicing an Olympic sport? I do swim, but not fast enough to qualify for the Olympics.

Most impressive or best remembered Olympic Games: What never ceases to amaze me is that as soon as the Games are on the horizon, everyone starts calling for a boycott. I can remember this even from when I was little, how we were always wondering why the athletes had to be burdened with all these political issues. It goes against the Olympic spirit, and I ask myself: Why don't politicians and social organisations take a firmer stand in this?

Most memorable sports moment: Ellen van Langen winning a gold medal in 1992. She was so overcome with joy that it was truly touching.

What are the ideal Olympic Games 2028 for an urban planner?
Sport is priority number one. I am used to looking carefully at goals and priorities in my work. In this case it is sports. If we want the bid for the Games to be successful, I think we'll have to work very hard to convince the International Olympic Committee that we are capable of organising them. There are secondary goals, too, which may serve to make the country rally behind the Games, because I don't think the Dutch are particularly eager. Back in 1992 public resistance against the bid was out of all proportion. So the second priority is to look for side effects that may help win over public opinion. Things like the development of the Randstad [the urban agglomeration in Western Holland – MD], and improvement of the general infrastructure. We are all irritated by traffic jams and overcrowded trains, and infrastructure is one thing we desperately need for the Games.
In the third place, I feel that the Games could help us to be proud of our nation again – sincerely proud that we, as a small country, are capable of managing this. I think that many people really want to feel proud again, but not in the sense of Wilders and Verdonk [two right-wing politicians with a nationalistic streak – MD]. We have to get back to that feeling of watching sports on TV on Sunday nights with our dinner plates in our laps. This sports feeling must come first and that is why I don't really want to go into all kinds of options in spatial planning yet. Those options may attract investors later on and make people enthusiastic later on, but at the moment people can't really relate to them.

So, all these eager urban planners and architects should hold their peace for a while?
I think so, yes. Within my own field of expertise I can tell how everyone is seeing opportunities to use the Games for improving the infrastructure everywhere and for planning facilities on locations that really need improving. And of course the Games offer these opportunities, but we mustn't forget that that is not what it's all about. My colleagues and I have been working for many years to make the Netherlands better and make them look better, and we still find it very difficult to get things done. There are reasons for that; spatial planning has never been a priority for any Cabinet. It is always treated as an afterthought. Relatively little money is involved and almost none for green issues. The Dutch themselves are not particularly keen either on all sorts of plans to get spatial planning out of the rut, I think. So let's not reverse things by already focusing on spatial issues now. That's what happened with Amsterdam 1992, and it went wrong.

Were you involved with the preparations for Amsterdam 1992?
Not at first, no. At a later stage, when Saar Boerlage [urban and rural planner, and political activist – MD] started to make a lot of noise that was directed against the Olympic Games, I was asked to lend a hand. But she had cooked up such a storm that I was afraid it would be too much for me. So I told them that I couldn't be of help. Besides, Boerlage voiced a criticism that was widely shared. The people in Amsterdam didn't want all this turmoil for just three weeks of sporting events. And that's what went wrong: the city of Amsterdam didn't present a sports ideal, it presented spatial interventions, and that was the last thing people wanted.

Will it be very different now?
Yes, because now we have started thinking about it in time. We need to give sports a boost and we need to demonstrate that we are capable of doing so by organising other events. This will lead to a sports drive. We cannot boast of a long list of previous events we have organised and that is one of the reasons why the general public thinks our country is much too small to be a player on a global scale. The ambitions of the pioneers of today must first be adopted by the general public as well. Only then can we start looking at which spatial options are viable.

Surely you must want to look ahead just a little bit?
Of course. Spatial planning may benefit from the Games on a conceptual level as well. For instance, for the tourist infrastructure we could, just like in Belgium, have a nice railway system along the coast that connects every community to the beach, with many stops along the way. Such a rather unusual infrastructure, which is quite favourable for recreation and tourism, can be combined with our need to firmly protect our country against the rising sea level and climatic changes. If we manage to combine these elements, we stand a much better chance.

You have done some large projects in several cities, so you are familiar with the world of public administration. What has to happen there in order to be ready for 2028?
First of all, administrators must start putting sports on the map. That includes building facilities right now, for the short term. They should start investing in such a way that the idea of the Olympic Games 2028 becomes irreversible. Administrative willpower, courage and decisiveness are essential for the development of new sports locations. And in this respect I have my doubts about the Randstad.

Because in the past the Randstad has not exactly shown much administrative dash?
Quite. If you really want to do it properly, you should turn to the Cabinet for special legislation to make it all possible. This legislation should specify what the Netherlands wishes to achieve in the field of sports and how people can be persuaded to collaborate. We will have to start now with waking up the administrators, because if we have to build everything by the democratic book of rules, it is going to take us a very long time.

Do you think that the sports world will start being more energetic about this?
I don't know, but they will have to be. If not, what are we doing here?

How old will you be in 2028?
Oh dear, I'll be 83.

Where would you prefer to be watching the Olympic Games then?
At the moment I am working in Limburg [Holland's most southern province – MD]. There, near Roermond, are the Maas Lakes. People always talk about the lakes in Friesland [Holland's most northern province – MD], but if you look at how much 'undeveloped' water there is in Limburg, I would say: Limburg, go for it! Open up those lakes, made them look nice and I will take my place in the stands to look at the rowing races.

Can you think of a motto to make us enthusiastic about sports?
Not really, but I was raised in the firm belief that the sporting spirit means that you don't keep everything for yourself but instead you want to share with others and take care of each other. My mother was a gym teacher and she always encouraged us to go out and then come back home again together. Go for it, come on! That's the sort of sporting spirit we could use now.

WHAT OLYMP SPIRIT

OLYMPIC FIRE 39

What is the Olympic Spirit? | OLYMPIC FIRE | 45

RENEWAL

| 48 | OLYMPIC FIRE | What is the Olympic Spirit? |

COMMERC

'Green Games are good for both the athletes and the crowd'

Agnes van den Berg interviewed by Mieke Dings

Agnes van den Berg is an environmental psychologist with Alterra, a knowledge centre for green space. She specialises in research into how we experience nature (the field in which she obtained her Ph.D.) and has collaborated on a number of reports, including Spelen in het Groen (Playing in the Green) (Alterra 2007) and Van buiten word je beter (Outside You Are Better) (Alterra 2001).

Involvement with Olympic Games 2028: None.

Practicing an Olympic sport: At the moment I am not doing any sports, but I used to row in university, and at a rather high level too.

Most impressive Olympic Games: Actually, I don't really like the competitiveness of top-level sports.
So I never watch the Games on TV either. Whenever I see any of it by chance, I'm always happy to see something other than football. Then I'm easily captivated and I'll watch and know everything about, say, high jumping.

Memorable sports moment: Not really, because I never follow the Games. Still, even I was aware of Inge de Bruyn's achievement in Sydney (2000) with her 'toppiejoppie'.

The Summer Games have always been oriented towards cities, even though it has been established that nature can have a soothing and stress-reducing effect. Wouldn't the athletes' achievements improve if the Games were held in nature? Is there any evidence for a relationship between achievement and environment?
I think it would be a very good idea to organise the Games in nature for a change. It is quite likely that 'natural' games would have a favourable effect. I have found at least three published studies about the added value of sports in natural surroundings versus sports in non-natural surroundings. The first one, an American study, did not show significant results because they didn't have a sufficient number of test subjects. The problem is that sports already have a favourable effect in themselves, so it is very difficult to measure the added benefit of the environment.
In the second study the test subjects were shown images of pleasant and unpleasant urban or rural surroundings while they were running indoors on a treadmill. The British researchers measured health by looking at blood pressure, self-esteem and mood. They found that the unpleasant images had a less favourable effect than the pleasant ones. So environment definitely does have an effect. The only drawback here was that the images of the urban environments were still quite rural.

Not enough reason to hold the games in nature, then…
No. But there's more. The most interesting study took place in the 1980s and dealt with speed differences between test subjects who had to run laps on an indoor athletic track for two weeks and others who were doing the same outdoors. Both groups were running the same distance simultaneously. The study clearly showed that the test subjects running outside were faster and that they also managed to maintain their speed over time. Also, fewer of them gave up compared to the indoor athletes, even though they in fact had to run a rougher and more difficult track. This study almost conclusively proves that performing sports outdoors enhances speed. It also strongly indicates that a natural environment has positive effects because it may improve sporting achievements and physical reactions. Finally, there is a very recent Japanese study which has not yet been published. Here one group would run in the woods and another group in the city. The researchers - in true Japanese fashion - took blood samples from all participants before and after to measure cortisole levels [a hormone that is released by stress – MD] and other relevant values. They again found that exercising had an

effect in itself, but they also found that practicing sports in nature definitely had an added psychological value. Interestingly enough, previous experience with nature was an important factor in this. Test subjects who had gone to the woods as children benefited more from doing sports in nature than those who had hardly ever been to the woods before.

How do you explain this added value of exercising in nature?
In terms of theory, I can think of a number of elements that explain why nature has a favourable influence. One element, and this is also clear from the third study, is that besides reducing stress, exercising in nature also reduces pain. Tolerance for pain increases. It has been proven that nature distracts from pain. There have been experiments where people put their hands in ice cold water while some of them had a view of nature and others did not. The people with a view of nature were able to keep their hands in the ice water longer and so they had a higher pain tolerance. This is a relevant fact for (top) athletes, who undoubtedly have to deal with pain now and again. But the stress-reducing effect of nature is also relevant for them. Most athletes feel some sort of stress right before a match. That is not all bad, because it keeps them alert and concentrated. However, the stress may also be too much, and then nature might offer just enough relaxation. Research shows that all individual cases are different, though.

Does it make any difference what kind of nature it is? For instance, will athletes from the Netherlands perform better in a polder landscape?
We don't know, but pain and stress are reduced in all sorts of nature, unless it contains a really negative element such as a threat or decay. It doesn't have to be really beautiful nature or meet specific requirements. As long as we feel safe, nature will do its work. So my prediction is that it would not be unfair to have the Games in the Netherlands. I would sooner assume that the familiarity of the surroundings plays a part in how we experience the city. People generally appreciate an urban environment better if they have some sort of connection with it.

Up until now the Games have taken place mainly in 'closed' stadiums and sports halls. Isn't it about time to open them up?
I think that would be a very good idea. The Olympic Villages are now often closed off from the outside world and their layout is not exactly 'natural' either. This of course has everything to do with logistics and security. So maybe it is not realistic to have the Games in nature, but it would be relatively easy to construct a village in such a way that both the athletes and the audience have a view of nature.

Do images of athletes in nature encourage viewers to visit nature as well?
I couldn't say. That is more an issue of the influence of mass media on the audience. Intuitively, I would think that that's how it works. Whenever we see appealing pictures, we want to go there ourselves. It is true though, that people who see such images also get their share of the favourable effects of nature. The Australian study already showed that images of surroundings can have various effects. Seeing nature is soothing. This is because nature automatically draws our attention while not demanding any effort or brain power from us. That is why nature is such a good remedy when our brain is suffering from temporary overload, which happens a lot, for instance, when we have to perform tasks that require a lot of concentration for a long period of time. If there is no variety in those tasks our regular mental capacity becomes depleted and we have to rely on our spare capacity, which has its limits as well, however, and this may cause mental exhaustion. Taking short breaks in between tasks can prevent overload, and then nature is one of the best ways to relax. Even just looking out the window every once in a while can be helpful. Besides, nature also has an important symbolic function, one that gives meaning to life, and this becomes more important as people grow older. I think that, subconsciously or not, many men and women who do outdoor sports enjoy this function of nature.

The 2028 Games offer an opportunity to address spatial issues in the Netherlands. What, in your view as an environmental psychologist, are the most urgent issues?
The spatial issue that I'm working on myself is green living. The Olympic Village is perfect for designing and promoting this issue. I immediately thought of Flevoland, [a newly reclaimed polder] as a suitable location. It may

not be the region with the most beautiful and varied nature, but it is relatively close to Amsterdam and it has ample space. The living and working climate of course always improves a little by hosting the games, and then green can have an added value. It would be wonderful to build a truly beautiful village, a model village that integrates sports facilities in the living environment after the games as well. That would fulfil one of the political ambitions to more often combine exercise with nature, both for children and their parents.

Does nature itself encourage sports activity?
There is no evidence of that. However, one of my colleagues, Sjerp de Vries, is conducting a study into the effect of more green in cities on the amount that people exercise. With grown-ups this is hard to determine, because if there is no green in the immediate vicinity they can take a car and drive to someplace where there is, but with children it's different. Several well-controlled studies, including ones that used acceleration meters, have shown that the presence of parks stimulates physical activity in children and juveniles. In America it has even been shown that every additional park in the city has an added stimulating effect. As children have a lot of free time and are not very mobile yet, it seems logical that they are attracted to the green spaces in the neighbourhood. In England so-called 'green gyms' are very hot at the moment. These are exercise programmes in nature for people who are overweight. The people who started these gyms know from experience that the dropout rate is much less when exercise takes place in nature. So nature has a sustaining effect on people to exercise more in the long run. That is worth looking into.

How old will you be in 2028 and where will you be watching the Olympic Games then?
60. Gosh, that sounds old. Probably I will not be watching at all because I will prefer doing something else.

Can you think of a sports quote or slogan to make the country rally behind the idea of hosting the Olympic Games 2028?
I once worked on a report entitled Outside you are better. I would now like to say: Outside you're a better sports person!

WHAT C LEARN F THE PRE OLYMPI

CAN WE
FROM
ROM
VIOUS
CS?

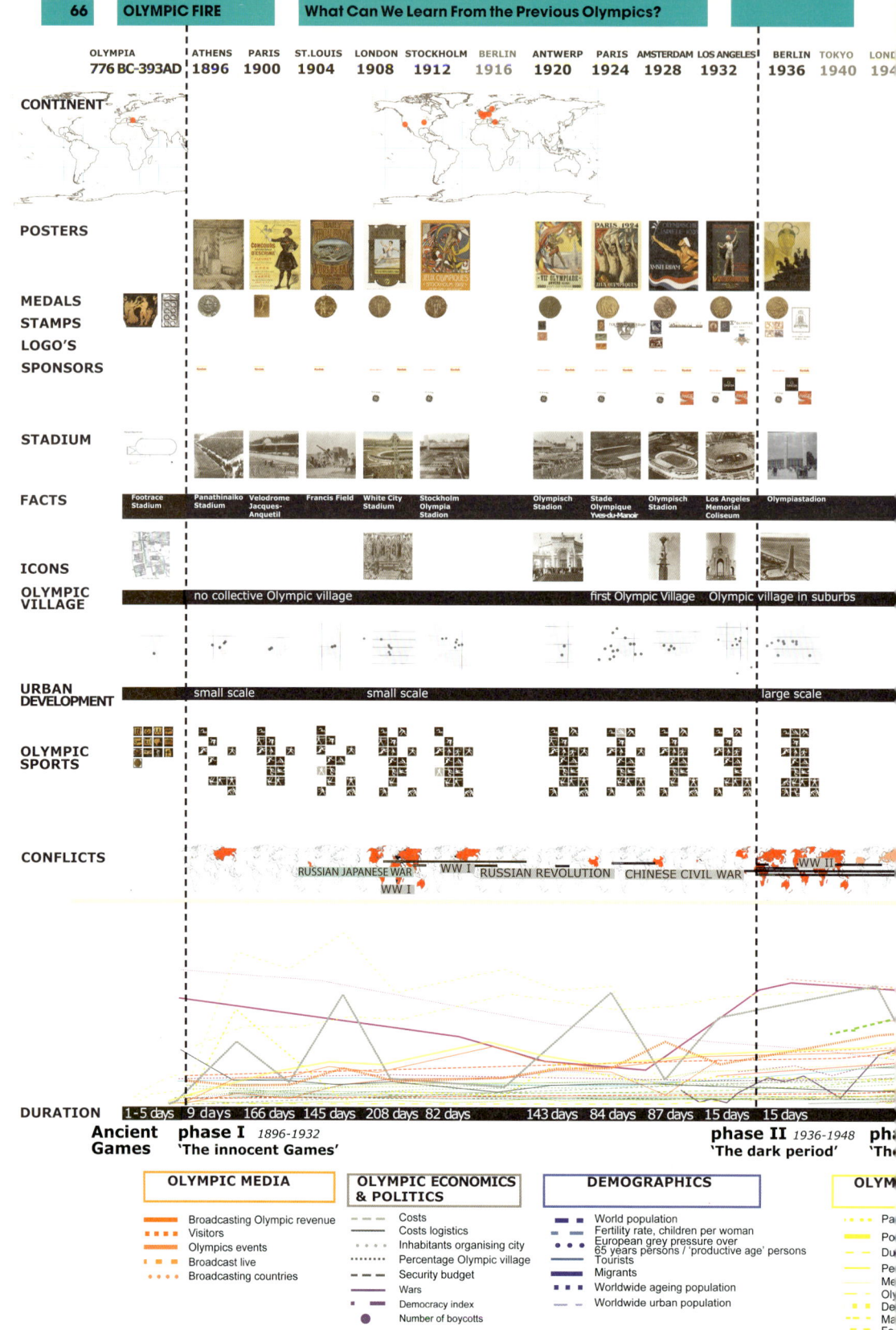

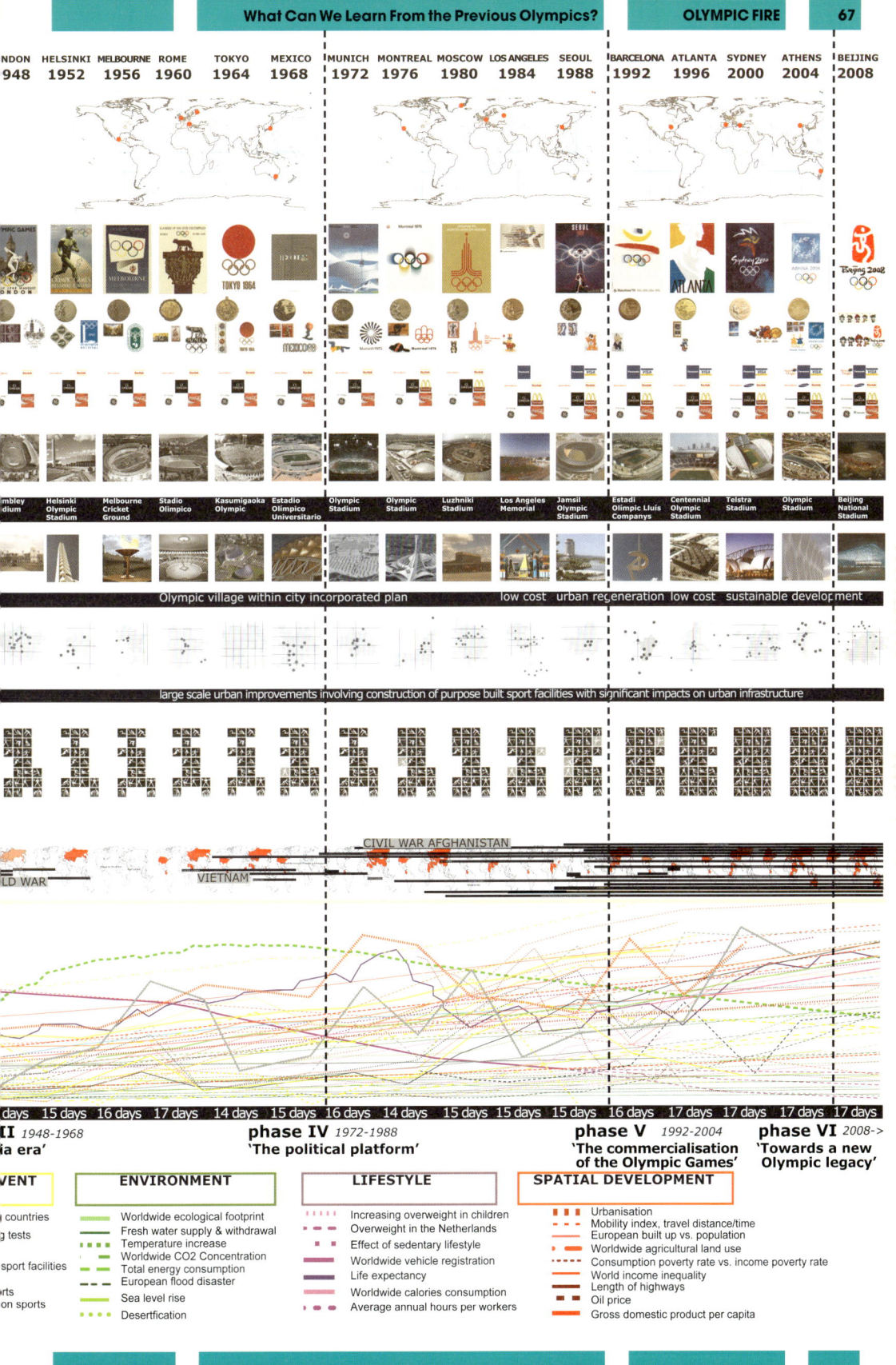

776 BC Olympia

Why Olympia?: **The Games were held in honour of Zeus at Olympia due to the fact that it was the home of the Greek Gods and the Temple of Zeus was located there.**
Number of represented sports: **1 (footrace)**
Number of represented nations: **1 (Greece)**
Olympic Medals: **Olympic champions received olive wreaths, palm branches or woollen ribbons; some winners were entitled to have a statue of themselves erected at Olympia**

Duration of Olympic event: **1 day in 776 BC; in 425 BC the duration was set to 5 days, because the number of disciplines had increased**

Main stadium: **Footrace stadium**

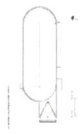

Completion date: **776 BC**
Capacity: **40,000 - 50,000 seats (only male spectators)**
Special factors:
- **The Games were held in four year intervals, and later the Greek method of counting the years even referred to these Games, using the term Olympiad for the period between two Games.**
- **No women were allowed to join the Olympics, not as an athlete nor as a spectator.**
- **The first Games lasted 1 day with only men who spoke Greek participating a stadium race over 190 meters, measured after the feet of Hercules, was the only Olympic sport at the first ancient Games.**

776 BC – 393 AD: The Olympics are of Great Antiquity

In order to understand the legacy of the Olympic Games, we need to briefly refer to ancient Greek history. The original Olympics were one of four games established by the ancient Greeks in 776 BC and were held once every four years in Olympia, located in the Elis region of Greece. Olympia was one of the oldest religious centres in the ancient Greek world. Since athletic contests were one of the ways in which the ancient Greeks honoured their gods, it was logical to hold a recurring athletic competition at the site of the major temple of Zeus. Thus the temple was the main focal point whereas the stadium and other training facilities were situated around it. The period of four years between these events was called an Olympiad, when preparations were made for the next. The other three Games were the Pythian, Isthmian and Nemean Games offering music and singing contests and featuring minor athletic events. The Olympic Games reached the height of their popularity in the 5th and 4th centuries BC and came to an end because of the suppression by the Roman Emperor Theodosius I, in AD 393.

The Olympic Games became the most sacred and popular of the four Games. The first Olympic event was the footrace. By Classical times, there were 18 contests, including boxing, wrestling, horse races, and the pentathlon, as well as additional running events. After the first 13 Olympic Games, the general competition of the Olympics included footraces, jumping, discus and javelin throwing, wrestling, boxing and chariot races. Except for the chariot race, all of the events were performed in the nude. Everyone was allowed to compete at the Olympic Games, with the exception of foreigners, women and slaves.

While the Olympics were an exhibition of men's prodigious strength and courage, the other Games were not so much focused on showing off physical ability and endurance. At the Olympic Games most of the participants were professionals who trained full-time for this event.

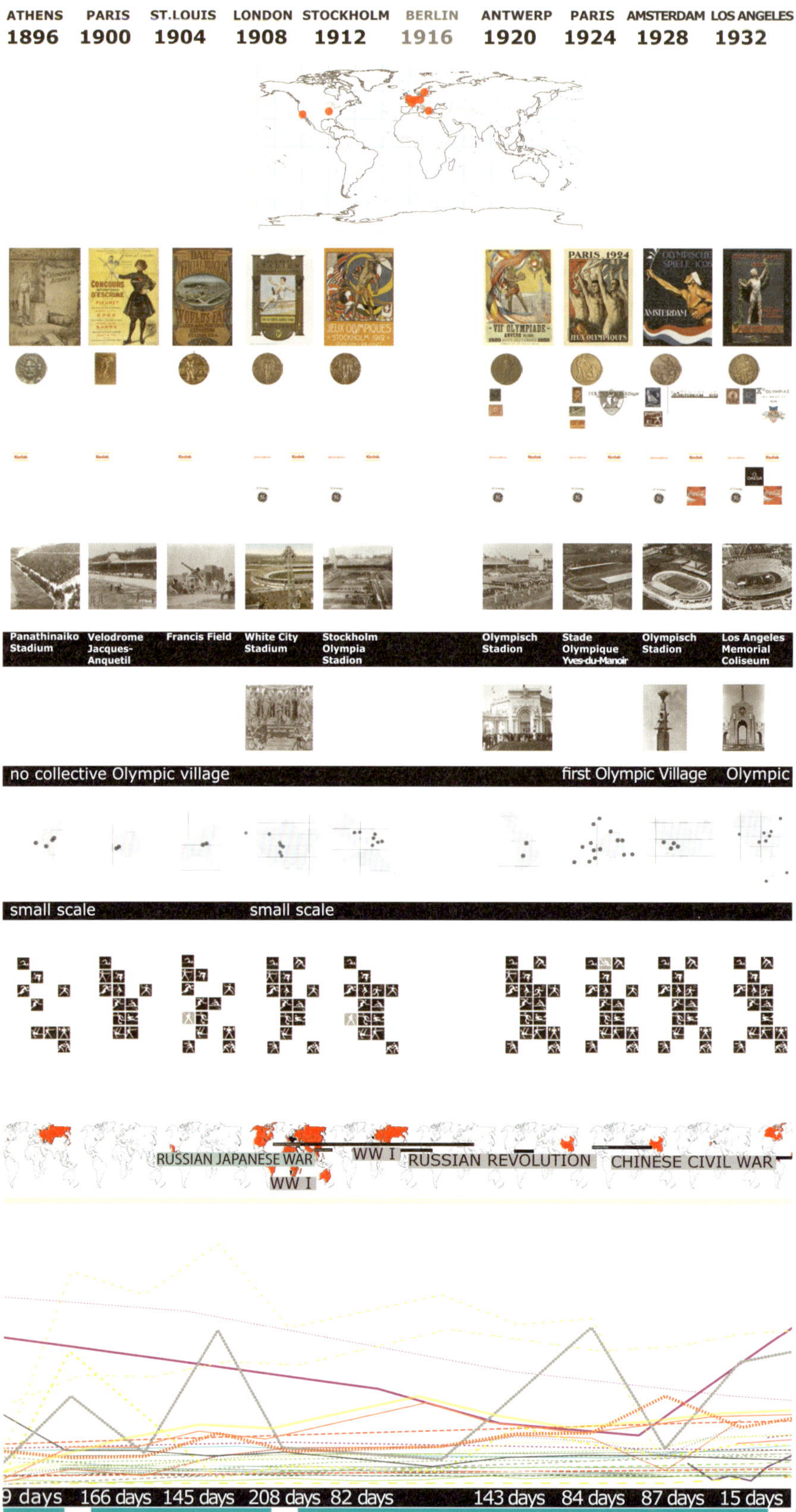

70 OLYMPIC FIRE — What Can We Learn From the Previous Olympics?

ATHENS	PARIS	ST. LOUIS	LONDON	STOCKHOLM	BERLIN	ANTWERP	PARIS	AMSTERDAM	LOS ANGELES
1896	1900	1904	1908	1912	1916	1920	1924	1928	1932

| Panathinaiko Stadium | Velodrome Jacques-Anquetil | Francis Field | White City Stadium | Stockholm Olympia Stadion | | Olympisch Stadion | Stade Olympique Yves-du-Manoir | Olympisch Stadion | Los Angeles Memorial Coliseum |

no collective Olympic village | first Olympic Village | Olympic

small scale | small scale

RUSSIAN JAPANESE WAR | WW I | RUSSIAN REVOLUTION | CHINESE CIVIL WAR
WW I

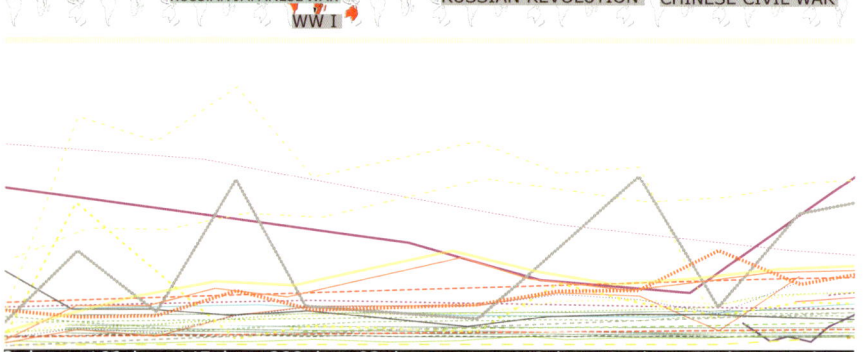

| 9 days | 166 days | 145 days | 208 days | 82 days | | 143 days | 84 days | 87 days | 15 days |

1896-1932: The Modernisation of the Ancient Olympics

Derived from the ancient Greek Olympics, the Modern Olympics officially started in 1896, initiated by a Frenchman named Baron Pierre de Coubertin. De Coubertin's self-appointed mission was to get French people interested in sports. He strongly believed that sports were a perfect way of harmoniously enhancing the physical and mental education of youths and forming a bond between different cultures. This inspired him to found a sports organisation called 'Union des Sociétés Francaises des Sports Athlétiques' (USFSA) in 1890. Two years later, at a meeting of the Union des Sports Athlétiques in Paris on November 25, 1892, De Coubertin publicly presented his idea of reviving the Olympic Games, unfortunately without success. Another two years later, De Coubertin organised a meeting with 79 delegates representing nine countries. At this meeting he once again presented his plan to revive the Olympic Games, this time with success. The delegates at the conference voted unanimously for the Olympic Games, provided that De Coubertin would put together an international committee to organise them. Finally, in 1894, De Coubertin founded the International Olympic Committee (IOC; Comité Internationale Olympique) with Demetrious Vikelas from Greece as its executive president to organise the first modern Olympic Games. Athens was chosen for the revival of the Olympic Games and the planning was begun. With the legal validation of the IOC, De Coubertin saw his philosophy of life actualised, that is to bring cooperation to a peaceful world by means of a big sports event where human beings from different countries meet each other now and then in order to learn to respect one another. Seeing as the first modern Olympic Games were initiated in an era concerned with social segregation, its goals implicitly contributed to a better world. The legacy of the Olympic Games should be continued; they have a powerful role to play in society, being truly engaged and making a meaningful contribution to the world by giving endless credit to friendship and solidarity.

1896 Athens

Why Athens? **Because Greece was the country In which the ancient Olympics began, the Games were hosted by its capital, Athens.**
Number of athletes: **241**
Number of represented sports: **43**
Number of represented nations: **14**
Number of medals: **gold 43, silver 43, bronze 36**

Olympic Medals

Number of main sponsors: **1, Kodak**
Duration of Olympic event: **9 days**
Location of venues

Main stadium: **Panathinaiko Stadium**

Completion date: **329 BCE, restored in 140 AD, 1870 and 1895**
Architect: **Restoration Architects 1895: Anastasios Mataxas, Ernst Ziller**
Capacity: **80,000 seats**
Later use: **sport stadium**
Special factors:
- **1st modern Olympic Games**
- **the Greeks tried to have Greece be the permanent site of the Olympics; the IOC rejected the request due to the lack of a unanimous decision in its favour**

1900 Paris

Why Paris? **The modern Olympic Games were reinstated by the Frenchman Pierre de Coubertin who wished to boost the confidence of France and stimulate sport skills among the French. Against De Coubertin's wishes, the IOC had decided to begin the modern Olympics in Athens, Greece. Therefore the second Games, in the year 1900, became the Paris Olympic Games.**
Number of athletes: **997**
Number of represented sports: **95**
Number of represented nations: **24**
Number of medals: **gold 90, silver 90, bronze 88**

Olympic Medals

Number of main sponsors: **1, Kodak**
Duration of Olympic event: **166 days**
Location of venues

Main stadium: **La Cipale, Vélodrome Municipal Vincennes**

Completion date: **1894**
Capacity: **20,000 seats**
Later use: **Vélodrome Jacques-Anquetil and football and rugby matches**
Special factors:
- **the French Government took over the organisation and planning of the Olympics**
- **the Olympics were poorly organised and publicised due to the fact that the French government was hosting the World Exhibition at the same time**
- **there was no opening or closing ceremony**
- **women were allowed to participate in a number of sports**
- **the Olympics took place in different locations in Paris**

1904 St. Louis

Why St. Louis? **Chicago had won the original bid to host the Games, but the Louisiana Purchase Exposition would not accept the fact that another international event was to be held at the same time. The organisation began to plan its own sports activities, informing the Chicago OCOG that the Exposition intended to eclipse the Olympic Games unless the Games were moved to St. Louis. Pierre de Coubertin, the founder of the modern Olympic movement, gave in and awarded the Games to St. Louis.**
Number of athletes: **651**
Number of represented sports: **91**
Number of represented nations: **12**
Number of medals: **gold 96, silver 92, bronze 92**

Olympic Medals

Number of main sponsors: **1**
Duration of Olympic event: **145 days**
Location of venues

Main stadium: **Francis Field**

Completion date: **1902**
Architect: **David Rowland Francis**
Capacity: **19,000 seats; after Games, 4000**
Later use: **sports events; the stadium has been upgraded to include many of the characteristics of modern stadiums**
Special factors:
- the difficult and often unpleasant journey from Europe to the USA was the reason for the low number of participating countries
- the Games in St. Louis were a side event of the World Fair
- the Games took place over a period of five months
- in a number of sports, because there were no competitors from other nations, the U.S. national championship was combined with the Olympic championship

1908 London

Why London? **These Games were originally scheduled to be held in Rome. The Italian authorities were preparing the infrastructure for the Games when Mount Vesuvius erupted on April 7, 1906, devastating the nearby city of Naples. Funds intended for the Olympics were now used for the reconstruction of Naples, so another venue was required. London was selected, and the Games were held in the district of White City, alongside the French-British Exhibition.**
Number of athletes: **2,008**
Number of represented sports **110**
Number of represented nations: **22**
Number of medals: **gold 110, silver 107, bronze 106**

Olympic Medals

Number of main sponsors: **3**
Duration of Olympic event: **208 days**
Location of venues

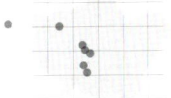

Main stadium: **White City Stadium**

Completion date: **1908**
Capacity: **80,000 seats**
Later use: **the stadium was demolished in 1985 to make way for the new BBC building called White City.**
Special factors:
- for the first time, there was an opening ceremony similar to the ones we now have
- the Games were held in White City alongside the French-British Exhibition, which at the time was the more noteworthy event
- the 1908 Olympics prompted the establishment of standard rules for sports and the selection of judges from different countries, rather than just the host country
- the distance from the start of the Marathon to the finish at the stadium was established at these Games to be 42,195 m
- these Games were the first to include winter events, such as originally proposed for the Games; the events on ice occurred months apart from most of the others

1912 Stockholm

Why Stockholm? **There was probably no special reason for the Games to be held in Stockholm. It is possible that the Swedish Government was keen on organising the Olympics because of their ambition to join the Olympic Movement.**
Number of athletes: **2,407**
Number of represented sports: **102**
Number of represented nations: **28**
Number of medals: **gold 103, silver 104, bronze 103**

Olympic Medals

Number of main sponsors: **3**
Duration of Olympic event: **82 days**
Location of venues

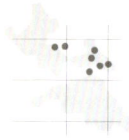

Main stadium: **Stockholm Olympiastadion**

Completion date: **1912**
Capacity: **15,000 seats, smallest stadium of the Olympic Games; after the Olympics, it was reduced to one level.**
Later use: **the Stockholm Olympic Stadium has hosted numerous sports events, notably football and athletics**
Special factors:
- the Swedish organised the best Olympics since their inception in 1896
- for the first time, competitors in the Games came from all five continents
- for the first time, the athletes were housed in comfortable houses
- after the Games, the International Olympic Committee decided to limit the power of host nations in deciding the Olympic programme

1916 Berlin

Why Berlin? **The 1916 Summer Olympics were to be held in Berlin, Germany. At the outbreak of World War I in 1914, organisation for the Games continued, as no one foresaw the war dragging on for four years.**
Special factors:
- **the games were cancelled because of the First World War**

1920 Antwerp

Why Antwerp? **The 1920 Games were awarded to Antwerp to honour the suffering that had been inflicted on the Belgian people during WW I. Budapest had initially won the bid to host the Games, beating Amsterdam and Lyon to it, but as the Austro-Hungarian Empire had been Germany's ally in the war, the Games were relocated in April 1919.**
Number of athletes: **2,626**
Number of represented sports: **154**
Number of represented nations: **29**
Number of medals: **gold 156, silver 146, bronze 135**

Olympic Medals

Number of main sponsors: **3**
Duration of Olympic event: **143 days**
Location of venues

Main stadium: **Olympisch Stadion**

Completion date: 1920
Capacity: **20,000 seats**
Later use: **sports and events; it is currently used as the home ground of K.F.C. Germinal Beerschot**
Special factors:
- the Games were organised in Belgium as a gesture of compassion with the country's suffering during the First World War
- the Olympic hymn and the Olympic flag with the five coloured rings were officially introduced
- for the first time, white doves were released during the opening ceremony as a sign of peace
- for the first time, only the National Olympic Committee could enrol participants

1924 Paris

Why Paris? **The Games were held in Paris, possibly to honour Pierre de Coubertin in his home town.**
Number of athletes: **3,089**
Number of represented sports: **126**
Number of represented nations: **44**
Number of medals: **gold 126, silver 127, bronze 125**

Olympic Medals

Olympic Logo

Number of main sponsors: **3**
Duration of Olympic event: **84 days**
Location of venues

Main stadium: **Stade Olympique Yves-du-Manoir**

Completion date: **1904, remodelled for the Olympics in 1924**
Capacity: **45,000 seats; after the Olympic Games, 60,000**
Later use: **it remained France's largest stadium until the renovated 'Parc des Princes' was inaugurated in 1972; the stadium is not frequently used**
Special factors:
- for the first time, over 1,000 journalists covered the Olympic Games
- Germany was excluded due to the First World War
- in apparent contrast to the ideas of De Coubertin, signs of fierce nationalism were exhibited and officials were also often involved
- at the 1924 Paris Games, the Olympic motto, "Citius, Altius, Fortius" (Swifter, Higher, Stronger) was introduced, as was the closing ceremony ritual of raising three flags
- first discussions on an Olympic Village for the athletes; in reality, a pretentious name for the primitive barracks in which athletes were housed

1928 Amsterdam

Why Amsterdam? **Amsterdam had made bids for the 1920 and 1924 Olympic Games, but had to let Belgium – which had suffered greatly in the war – and De Coubertin's Paris go first, before finally being chosen.**
Number of athletes: **2,883**
Number of represented sports: **109**
Number of represented nations: **46**
Number of medals: **gold 110, silver 108, bronze 109**
Olympic Medals

Number of main sponsors: **4**
Duration of Olympic event: **87 days**
Location of venues

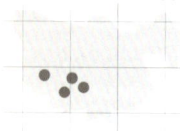

Main stadium: **Olympisch Stadion**

Completion date: **1924**
Architect: **Jan Wils**
Capacity: **34,000 seats; after the Games the capacity was enlarged to 64,000; it is one of the finest examples of the architecture of the Amsterdam School, complementing the surrounding neighbourhood designed by H.P. Berlage; the design won the Olympic gold medal in the architecture competition at the 1928 Olympics**
Later use: **since 2005 the stadium has been home to a sports museum, the Olympic Experience Amsterdam**
Special factors:
- Amsterdam owes its hosting of the 1928 Games to the good friendship of two barons: IOC president Pierre de Coubertin and the Dutch IOC member Van Tuyll van Serooskerken
- many people in the Netherlands were not happy about it; Parliament did not want to subsidise the Olympics; the NOC organised a charity and collected half a million guilders from Amsterdam citizens
- for the first time, the Olympic fire was lit
- for the first time, the parade of nations started with Greece, the origin of the Olympics, and ended with the host country; a tradition which continues today
- the number of female athletes more than doubled, as women were finally allowed to compete in gymnastics and athletics

1932 Los Angeles

Why Los Angeles? **No other city made a bid to host these Olympics during the worldwide Great Depression**
Number of athletes: **1,332**
Number of represented sports: **117**
Number of represented nations: **37**
Number of medals: **gold 116, silver 116, bronze 114**
Olympic Medals

Olympic Logo

Number of main sponsors: **5**
Duration of Olympic event: **15 days**
Location of venues

Main stadium: **Los Angeles Memorial Coliseum**

Completion date: **1932**
Architect: **John Parkinson**
Capacity: **76,000 seats in 1932; 92,000 seats in 1995; the Coliseum Olympic stadium stupefied the whole world by its proportions and the quality of its equipment**
Later use: **sports and events**
Special factors:
- because the 1932 Olympics were held in the middle of the Great Depression and in the comparatively remote city of Los Angeles, half as many athletes took part as in 1928
- the 1932 Olympics were the first to last only 16 days, a schedule that is still used today; from 1900 to 1928 the Summer Olympics had never been shorter than 79 days
- the Olympic Village was only for male athletes; female athletes were housed at the Chapman Park Hotel

BERLIN	TOKYO	LONDON
1936	1940	1944

1936-1944: The Olympics are Abused by Political Interests of Nazi Germany

Olympiastadion

village in suburbs

large scale

WW II

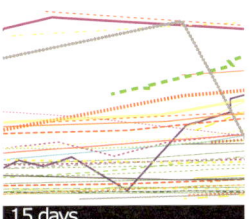
15 days

The Olympic Games of 1936 were a turning point in history. Adolf Hitler used them as a tool for propagating his national-socialist ideology: At the traditional opening ceremonies a number of Nazi symbols were displayed beside the Olympic symbols. For the first time, the Olympic flame was transported by torch, in a relay race from Greece to the Reichssportfeld in Berlin, linking the classical world to the new. All Olympic accommodations were decorated with dozens of swastika-covered Nazi flags. The cinematographer Leni Riefenstahl was famously appointed to make a film of the event, and while Olympia can be labelled as propaganda, it also pioneered a number of techniques that are still used to film sports events. To obtain as many victories as possible and confirm Aryan superiority, the German government gave its athletes anabolic steroids and testosterones. Such assertiveness and ambition was also apparent in the immense infrastructure constructed for the Olympics. This dark period in the history of the Olympics had a dubious social impact. For the first time, primary Olympian goals had clearly been overshadowed by political ones.

1936 Berlin

Why Berlin? **The 1936 Olympic Games were intentionally awarded to Germany so that the republic could show that it had regained its status among European nations.**
Number of athletes: **3,963**
Number of represented sports: **129**
Number of represented nations: **49**
Number of medals: **gold 130, silver 128, bronze 130**
Olympic Medals

Olympic Logo

Number of main sponsors: **5**
Duration of Olympic event: **15 days**
Location of venues

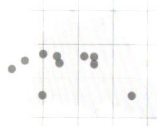

Main stadium: **Olympia Stadion**

Completion date: **1915**
Architects: **Otto March & Werner March**
Capacity: **75,000 seats**
Later use: **sports and events; after the war, the British military occupation force used it for its headquarters until 1994**
Special factors:
- aside from its use as an Olympic stadium, the Olympia Stadion has a rich tradition in football; it is the home base of Berlin's Hertha BSC club
- Hitler used the Olympics as a propaganda tool
- the African-American Jesse Owens was the star of the Games, since his successes proved the Nazi theories of race to be inconsistent
- due to the Nazi rejection of all Jewish participants, many countries spoke out in favour of boycotting the Games; there was a strong lobby, especially in the US; the Netherlands was not enthusiastic about the Nazi decision either; in the end, though, all countries participated; swastika flags and armed soldiers were everywhere
- for the first time in Olympic history the Olympic fire was lit in Olympia, Greece and carried to Berlin on foot
- the 1936 Olympics were also the first to be broadcast on an early type of television

1940 Tokyo

Why Tokyo and then Helsinki? **The 1940 Summer Olympics – which were to be officially known as the Games of the XII Olympiad and originally scheduled to be celebrated between 21 September and 6 October 1940 in Tokyo, Empire of Japan – were cancelled. The IOC denied Tokyo the Games because of the outbreak of the Second Sino-Japanese War in 1937. They were then awarded to runner-up Helsinki, Finland, and were scheduled to be celebrated between 20 July and 4 August, 1940. However, when World War II broke out, the Summer Games were postponed indefinitely – to be resumed in London in 1948.**
Special factors:
- Tokyo experimented with Television Relay Broadcasting of these Games. This was seen as a springboard for the development of live Olympic broadcasting
- several countries planned to boycott the Games because of the war between Japan and China
- Japan decided the Games would be a distraction to their military goals and cancelled the Games
- Helsinki then stepped in to host the 1940 Games, meanwhile constructing the main stadium and promoting the Games via the media
- the rescheduled Games in Helsinki were cancelled as well, when Soviet troops invaded Finland

1944 London

Special factors:
- **the continuation of World War II led to the Olympic Games of 1944 being cancelled**
- **these Games would have celebrated the 50th anniversary of the Modern Olympics**
- **a small ceremony and sports competition were held in Lausanne, Switzerland, to celebrate the 50th anniversary of the Olympic Games**

80 OLYMPIC FIRE — What Can We Learn From the Previous Olympics?

LONDON	HELSINKI	MELBOURNE	ROME	TOKYO	MEXICO
1948	1952	1956	1960	1964	1968

| Wembley Stadium | Helsinki Olympic Stadium | Melbourne Cricket Ground | Stadio Olimpico | Kasumigaoka Olympic | Estadio Olímpico Universitario |

Olympic village within city ind

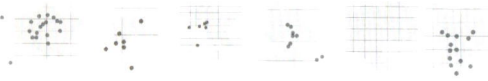

large scale urban improvements i

COLD WAR   VIETNAM

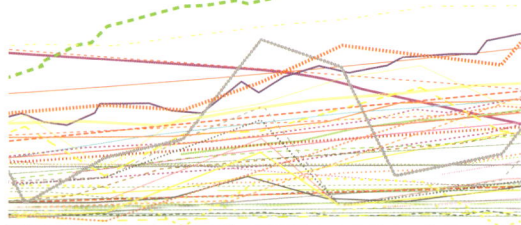

| 15 days | 15 days | 16 days | 17 days | 14 days | 15 days |

1948-1968: The Olympics are Reanimated by the Media

The outbreak of World War II caused the Olympics to be cancelled twice. The media era was rung in by the first television broadcasting of the Olympics in 1936 and the rapid technological progress during the war. This new visibility to the world strengthened the link between the host city and Olympic ideology. The fast increase of media distribution had a huge impact on the Olympics: revenues and expenses increased, but also the number of boycotts. In 1956, the IOC's ideology of world peace and 'keeping politics outside the Olympic arena' appeared far from reality when it decided to continue the Olympics despite the fact that some of the participating countries - Israel, France, Great-Britain and Egypt - were at war with each other over the Suez Canal. Economics and representation also became increasingly important after the example set by Tokyo in 1964, the first Olympics to be held in Asia. The drive of the city to put itself on the world map became a tremendous logic in itself and with a budget of twenty-six million dollars, the organisation was impeccable. The sports accommodations were perfect, there was an impressive stadium, a giant Olympic swimming pool and a splendid Olympic village. These Olympics were a 'turning point'. They caused a decrease in the amount of bids submitted because countries began to realize the financial risks and uncertain benefits.

1948 London

Why London? **The Games were awarded as honorary compensation for the 1944 bid, after the end of WWII.**
Number of athletes: **4,104**
Number of represented sports: **136**
Number of represented nations: **59**
Number of medals: **gold 138, silver 135, bronze 135**

Olympic Medals

Olympic Logo

Number of main sponsors: **5**
Duration of Olympic event: **15 days**
Location of venues

Main stadium: **Wembley Stadium**

Completion date: **1924**
Architects: **Sir John Simpson & Maxwell Ayrton**
Capacity: **127,000 seats**.
Later use: **demolished in 2003**
Special factors:
- after a hiatus of 12 years caused by the Second World War, these were the first Summer Olympics since 1936
- there was no Olympic Village, due to severe shortages in the United Kingdom after the Second World War
 - the participants stayed in university buildings and military sheds; food was still being rationed
- Germany and Japan were excluded from participating; the Soviet Union was not represented because it hesitated to join the Olympic movement
- the 1948 London Games were the first to be shown on home television
- London was the first Olympics to have a political defector: Marie Provaznikova won a gold medal with the Czechoslovakian gymnastics team and then refused to return home, citing 'lack of freedom' there after the country's inclusion in the Soviet bloc

1952 Helsinki

Why Helsinki? **Helsinki had been awarded the 1940 Summer Olympics but these had been cancelled because of World War II.**
Number of athletes: **4,955**
Number of represented sports: **149**
Number of represented nations: **69**
Number of medals: **gold 149, silver 152, bronze 158**

Olympic Medals

Olympic Logo

Number of main sponsors: **5**
Duration of Olympic event: **15 days**
Location of venues

Main stadium: **Helsinki Olympic Stadium**

Completion date: **1938**
Architects: **Yrjö Lindegen & Toivo Jäntti**
Capacity: **70,000 seats (1952); after the Games, 40,000 seats**
Later use: **mainly used for hosting sports events and big concerts**
Special factors:
- the 1940 Olympics scheduled to be held in Helsinki were cancelled, but the Olympic facilities had remained intact
- the Soviet Union stepped into the Olympic arena
- the Cold War between East and West was now also fought in the sports arena
- for the first time, mixed events took place in the equestrian competitions

1956 Melbourne

Why Melbourne? **Australia was the first economically developing and the first southern hemisphere nation to host the Olympics.**
Number of athletes: **3,314**
Number of represented sports: **145**
Number of represented nations: **72**
Number of medals: **gold 153, silver 153, bronze 163**

Olympic Medals

Olympic Logo

Number of main sponsors: **5**
Duration of Olympic event: **16 days**
Location of venues

Main stadium: **Melbourne Cricket Ground**

Completion date: **1861; restored in 1956**
Capacity: **100,000 seats**
Later use: **the open-air stadium is one of the world's most famous cricket venues, and is still used for other sports and events**
Special factors:
- because of the long-term quarantine period for foreign horses in Australia, the equestrian part of the Olympics did not take place in Melbourne, but in Stockholm, in the summer of 1956
- the Soviet Union invaded Hungary after civil protest there
- the Netherlands, Switzerland and Spain did not take part in the Olympics
- for the People's Republic of China, the participation of Taiwan was a reason to stay away from the Games

1960 Rome

Why Rome? **The Rome Games became a showcase for Italy and furthered its rehabilitation after WWII and made up for its failure to host the 1908 Games, following the eruption of Mount Vesuvius in 1906.**
Number of athletes: **5,338**
Number of represented sports: **150**
Number of represented nations: **83**
Number of medals: **gold 152, silver 149, bronze 160**

Olympic Medals

Olympic Logo

Number of main sponsors: **5**
Duration of Olympic event: **17 days**
Location of venues

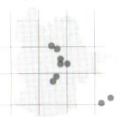

Main stadium: **Stadio Olimpico**

Completion date: **1936**
Architect: **Luigi Moretti**
Capacity: **55,000 seats (1960); after the Olympic Games, 90,000 seats**
Later use: **the stadium is the home of both A.S. Roma and S.S. Lazio, as well as of the Italian national football team; it is still used for sports and events**
Special factors:
- the 'eternal city' was a mix of past and present for the athletes
- the Olympics were transmitted live on 100 television channels in 18 European countries, with a time difference in America, Canada, Japan
- these were the last Games in which South Africa was allowed to participate, due to the 'apartheid' boycott, for a period of 32 years

1964 Tokyo

Why Tokyo? **The first Asian city to host the Olympics, Tokyo spent 3 billion dollars rebuilding the city to show off its post-war success.**
Number of athletes: **5,151**
Number of represented sports: **163**
Number of represented nations: **93**
Number of medals: **gold 163, silver 167, bronze 174**

Olympic Medals

Olympic Logo

Number of main sponsors: **5**
Duration of Olympic event: **14 days**
Location of venues

Main stadium: **Kasumigaoka Olympic Stadium**

Completion date: **1958**
Capacity: **60,000 seats**
Later use: **sports and events**
Special factors:
- the 1964 Summer Games marked the first time the Olympics were held by a non-Western nation
- South Africa was barred from taking part, due to its refusal to racially desegregate its sports
- the Olympic fire was brought to the stadium by Josjinori Sakai, an athlete born on the day that the American nuclear bomb was dropped on Hiroshima
- the first appearance of a team sport for women: volleyball

1968 Mexico

Why Mexico City? **The only Games ever held in Latin America, and the second ever not to be held in Europe, Australia, or the USA.**
Number of athletes: **5,516**
Number of represented sports: **172**
Number of represented nations: **112**
Number of medals: **gold 174, silver 170, bronze 183**

Olympic Medals

Olympic Logo

Number of main sponsors: **5**
Duration of Olympic event: **15 days**
Location of venues

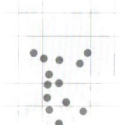

Main stadium: **Estadio Olímpico Universitario**

Completion date: **1952**
Architects: **Luis Martínez del Campo, Rafael Mijares & Pedro Ramírez Vásquez**
Capacity: **58,000 seats**
Later use: **sport and events; this sports facility is part of the 'University City', the main campus of the largest university of Latin America**
Special factors:
- the high altitude of Mexico City (2240 m) made it difficult for many endurance athletes to adapt to the oxygen-deprived air
- all women were given a gender test
- the Games also had the first drug disqualification
- more than 300 student protesters were killed by army and police
- the American black athletes Tommie Smith and John Carlos caused a great upheaval; after they had respectively won gold and bronze for the 200 meters, they came to the stage barefoot and during the national anthem raised a gloved fist as a protest against the poverty and discrimination of black people in the USA; both athletes were barred from the Olympic Village after this Black Power demonstration

86 OLYMPIC FIRE — What Can We Learn From the Previous Olympics?

MUNICH	MONTREAL	MOSCOW	LOS ANGELES	SEOUL
1972	1976	1980	1984	1988

| Olympic Stadium | Olympic Stadium | Luzhniki Stadium | Los Angeles Memorial | Jamsil Olympic Stadium |

orporated plan — low cost — urban re

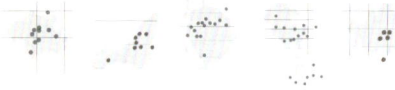

volving construction of purpose built sport facilities with s

CIVIL WAR AFGHANISTAN

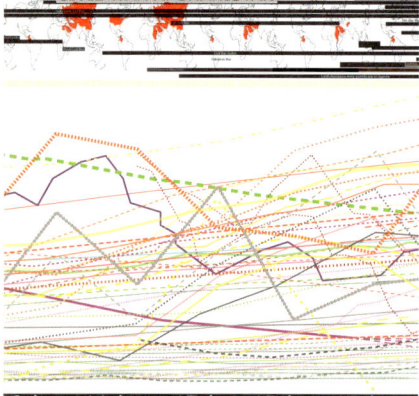

| 16 days | 14 days | 15 days | 15 days | 15 days |

1972-1988: The Olympics are Politicised

The Cold War and the economic downturn due to the oil boycott threw a shadow over the Olympics. The Munich Olympics were meant to portray a positive image of Germany, but this was negatively influenced by the Israeli hostage drama in which 17 people died. The IOC president Avery Brundage vowed to continue the Olympics with the legendary words, "The Games must go on." Nevertheless, as the Olympics suffered from increasing political pressure and uncertainty, economic aspects became the most important criteria.

'The sober Olympics' made their entrance. Despite the fact that Montreal had earned the title of organising the most sober Olympics ever in 1976, they turned into a financial fiasco. The organisation and the Olympics were plagued by boycotts and building scandals. After reaching this low point, the IOC distinguished itself by admitting that the Olympics were possibly too big. This led to the fact that Los Angeles was the only city to make a bid for hosting the 1984 Olympics. For the first time in history the organisation was in the hands of businessmen, with major sponsors entering the Olympics, never to leave again. The Los Angeles Olympics were an unprecedented economic success with huge consequences for the future of the Games. Strategically and economically, L.A. had put itself on the world map. As boycotts began to dominate the event, the political power and responsibility of the Olympics became evident. Iconographic architecture began to develop more strongly and form a visual language of its own that was no longer directly linked to the original ideology. The desirable image for a city was immediately translated into imposing buildings, an aspect that previously had been associated with the World Fairs. The Olympics functioned as an economic motor.

1972 Munich

Why Munich? **The Munich Olympics were intended to present a new, democratic and optimistic Germany to the world, as was evident from its official motto, 'The Happy Games'.**
Number of athletes: **7,134**
Number of represented sports: **195**
Number of represented nations: **121**
Number of medals: **gold 195, silver 195, bronze 210**
Olympic Medals

Olympic Logo

Munich1972
Number of main sponsors: **5**
Duration of Olympic event: **16 days**
Location of venues

Main stadium: **Olympiastadion**

Completion date: **1972**
Architects: **Günther Behnisch & Frei Otto**
Capacity: **80,000 seats**
Later use: the design of the stadium was considered revolutionary, with sweeping canopies of acrylic glass stabilised by metal cords used on such a large scale for the first time; until 2005 the stadium was home base for two football clubs, FC Bayern München and TSV 1860 München; it now only hosts special events such as the Air And Style Snowboard Event
Special factors:
- the Munich Olympics should present a new democratic and optimistic Germany to the world
- these Games were the largest yet, setting records in all categories, with 195 events and 7,173 athletes from 121 nations
- African nations threatened to withdraw all of their athletes if Rhodesia were not excluded
- Palestinian terrorists from the `Black September' group attacked the Olympic Village; they killed two Israelis and took nine members of the Israeli Olympic team hostage; the drama ended in carnage at the airport and the Games were stopped for 34 hours; IOC President Avery Brundage famously said, 'THE GAMES MUST GO ON!'

1976 Montreal

Why Montreal? **There was probably no special reason for the Games to be held in Montreal.**
Number of athletes: **6,084**
Number of represented sports: **198**
Number of represented nations: **92**
Number of medals: **gold 198, silver 199, bronze 216**
Olympic Medals

Olympic Logo

Montréal 1976
Number of main sponsors: **6**
Duration of Olympic event: **14 days**
Location of venues

Main stadium: **Olympic Stadium**

Completion date: **1976; the roof was finished in 1988**
Architect: **Roger Taillibert**
Capacity: **70,000 seats**
Later use: with a history of financial and structural problems, this stadium is a prime example of a white elephant; it is still used for sports and events
Special factors:
- the 1976 Olympic Games were marred by boycotts and drug allegations
- the Games were also a financial disaster for the province of Quebec; the enormous figure of $2 billion in expenditures placed them in debt for decades
- right before the Games were scheduled to open, 32 nations, most of them from black Africa, walked out when the IOC refused to ban New Zealand because its national rugby team was touring through racially segregated South Africa; the Games suffered greatly from this boycott; a lot of champions, especially in athletics, did not participate
- Taiwan also withdrew, after Communist China pressured its trading partner Canada to deny the Taiwanese the right to compete as the 'Republic of China'

1980 Moscow

Why Moscow? **Los Angeles was also a candidate for organising these Summer Olympics. Amid Cold-War tension the Games were awarded in turn to the USSR and the USA.**
Number of athletes: **5,179**
Number of represented sports: **203**
Number of represented nations: **80**
Number of medals: **gold 204, silver 204, bronze 223**

Olympic Medals

Olympic Logo

Number of main sponsors: **6**
Duration of Olympic event: **15 days**
Location of venues

Main stadium: **Luzhniki Stadium**

Completion date: **1980**
Architects: **I. A. Rozhin & Alexander Vasilyevich Vlasov**
Capacity: **85,000 seats**
Later use: **it is the biggest stadium in Russia and is still used for sports and events**
Special factors:
- the American president Jimmy Carter called for a boycott of the Games in Moscow because of the Russian invasion in Afghanistan; the boycott reduced the number of participating nations to 80, the lowest number since 1956
- the first Olympics to be held in a Communist country
- Aleksandr Dityatin earned medals in every men's gymnastics event, to become the only athlete ever to win eight medals in one Olympics
- 21% of the competitors were female - a higher percentage than at any previous Olympics

1984 Los Angeles

Why Los Angeles? **It was the only city bidding to host the 1984 Summer Olympics.**
Number of athletes: **6,829**
Number of represented sports: **221**
Number of represented nations: **140**
Number of medals: **gold 226, silver 219, bronze 243**

Olympic Medals

Olympic Logo

Number of main sponsors: **7**
Duration of Olympic event: **14 days**
Location of venues

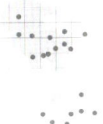

Main stadium: **Los Angeles Memorial Coliseum**

Completion date: **1932**
Architect: **John Parkinson**
Capacity: **76,000 seats**
Later use: **sports and events**
Special factors:
- for the first time, the organisation was in the hands of individuals (a consortium of business people) and not in the hands of the host city
- in reaction to America's boycott of the Olympics in Moscow, these Olympics were boycotted by a number of countries from the Eastern Bloc, including the Soviet Union, East Germany and Cuba
- large sponsors came into the picture, no longer to be displaced
- the games were largely an exercise in upgrading existing facilities, such as the Olympic Stadium of 1932, and the use of temporary structures
- the Coliseum was declared a National Historic Landmark on July 27, 1984, the day before the opening ceremony

1988 Seoul

Why Seoul? **It was a milestone in South Korea's development from dictatorship to democracy. South Korea was the second Asian nation to ever host the Olympic Games.**
Number of athletes: **8,391**
Number of represented sports: **237**
Number of represented nations: **159**
Number of medals: **gold 241, silver 234, bronze 264**

Olympic Medals

Olympic Slogan: **The world in Seoul, Seoul in the World**
Olympic Logo

Number of main sponsors: **8**
Duration of Olympic event: **15 days**
Location of venues

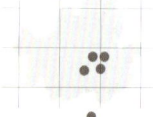

Main stadium: **Jamsil Olympic Stadium**

Completion date: **1988**
Architect: Kim Soo-geun
Capacity: **60,000 seats**
Later use: **the stadium is presently home to the K3 League football club Seoul United**
Special factors:
- **North Korea, still officially at war with South Korea, boycotted the Olympic Games, with Cuba, Ethiopia and Nicaragua joining the boycott**
- **student insurrections in South Korea were suppressed heavy-handedly by the police**
- **drug disqualification of sprinter Ben Johnson after his setting a world record on the 100m sprint**

BARCELONA	ATLANTA	SYDNEY	ATHENS
1992	1996	2000	2004

eneration | low cost | sustainable develop

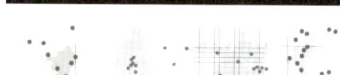

gnificant impacts on urban infrastructure

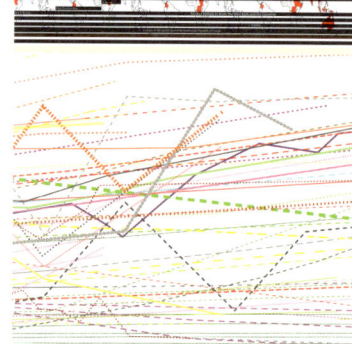

| 16 days | 17 days | 17 days | 17 days |

1992-2004: The Olympics are Commercialised

With the Cold War having left the Olympics in somewhat of a decline, 1989 meant the beginning of a new era of liberal democracy for many countries. The fall of the Iron Curtain allowed a regeneration of the Games as a public, commercial and entertainment success. In 1992, the Olympics took place in Barcelona. The trajectory of preparations had been carefully planned since the fall of Franco in 1981: the secret phase, we-are-the-Olympic-city-phase, rounding off phase, spin-off phase. Furthermore, the event was placed in a national context through co-celebrations: the World Fair in Seville and Madrid as Cultural Capital of Europe. Barcelona used the Olympics to improve the city on the level of urban planning: creation of the ring, the new metro line and renovation of the Olympic stadium. Barcelona also succeeded in putting itself on the map and becoming a major tourist city in Europe. Spin-off now seems to be even more important than the actual hosting of the Olympics. The Olympics have become an instrument of urban planning and commercialisation continues apace. Many major brands want to be associated with the Olympics. For example, Coca Cola became the official drink after the Olympics in L.A. and Swatch has made itself responsible for the timekeeping.

1992 Barcelona

Why Barcelona? **The 1992 Games – together with the Seville Expo and Madrid as Cultural Capital – were awarded to Spain as a token of recognition after its having ended the Franco dictatorship. Barcelona is also were IOC president Juan Antonio Samaranch was born.**
Number of athletes: **9,356**
Number of represented sports: **257**
Number of represented nations: **169**
Number of medals: **gold 260, silver 257, bronze 298**

Olympic Medals

Olympic Slogan: **Friends Forever**
Olympic Logo

Number of main sponsors: **8**
Duration of Olympic event: **16 day**s
Location of venues

Main stadium: **Estadi Olímpic Lluís Companys**

Completion date: **1927. Restored in 1989**
Architect: **Correa-Milà-Margarit-Buixadé & Vittorio Gregotti**
Capacity: **60,000 seats**
Later use: **the stadium has been the home of RCD Espanyol since 1998 and also served as the home of the Barcelona Dragons American Football team until 2003**
Special factors:
- fear of attacks by the Basque independence organisation ETA and Catalan nationalists
- there were no boycotts of the Barcelona Olympic Games, unlike the four previous Olympics
- with the exception of Afghanistan, this was the first time since the 1972 Munich Olympics that all of the IOC countries participated in the Games
- Apartheid in South Africa was abolished
- the Berlin Wall had fallen in 1989, West and East Germany had been reunited, Communism had collapsed in the Soviet Union
- Barcelona undertook an impressive urban transformation prior to the Olympic Games

1996 Atlanta

Why Atlanta? **The Atlanta Games were the first to be held without any governmental support or financing.**
Number of athletes: **10,318**
Number of represented sports: **271**
Number of represented nations: **197**
Number of medals: **gold 271, silver 273, bronze 298**

Olympic Medals

Olympic Slogan: **The Celebration of the Century**
Olympic Logo

Number of main sponsors: **8**
Duration of Olympic event: **17 days**
Location of venues

Main stadium: **Centennial Olympic Stadium**

Completion date: **1996**
Architect: **Arch. Heery International**
Capacity: **85,000 seats; after the Olympic Games, 45,000 seats**
Later use: **the stadium is the home of the Atlanta Braves baseball team**
Special factors:
- the Olympics were considered a success, thanks especially to the large presence of the Coca-Cola company, which is based in Atlanta
- in Centennial Olympic Park, in the middle of the city, a bomb exploded on 27 July, killing two persons and injuring 111
- in spite of heavy security measures, the hand of terrorism also struck in Atlanta, making it clear that the Olympics serve as a stage for other issues besides sports

2000 Sydney

Why Sydney? **There was probably no special reason for the Games to be held in Sydney.**
Number of athletes: **10,651**
Number of represented sports: **300**
Number of represented nations: **199**
Number of medals: **gold 298, silver 299, bronze 325**
Olympic Medals

Olympic Slogan: **Share the Spirit**
Olympic Logo

Number of main sponsors: **10**
Duration of Olympic event: **17 days**
Location of venues

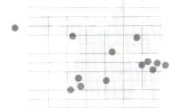

Main stadium: **Telstra Stadium**

Completion date: **1999**
Architect: **Bligh Lobb Sports Architects**
Capacity: **110,000 seats; after the Olympic Games, 80,000 seats**
Later use: **it is the largest ever built for the Olympics, as well as the largest stadium in Australia; it is still used for sports and events**
Special factors:
- IOC President Samaranch called the Olympics in Sydney "the greatest Games ever"
- Korea (South Korea) and the Democratic People's Republic of Korea (North Korea) marched together under the same flag
- Olympic projects were seen as a way of regenerating urban areas

2004 Athens

Why Athens? **The Games were awarded as compensation for not being chosen for the 1996 centennial hosting.**
Number of athletes: **10,651**
Number of represented sports: **300**
Number of represented nations: **201**
Number of medals: **gold 301, silver 301, bronze 327**
Olympic Medals

Olympic Slogan: **Welcome Home**

Number of main sponsors: **12**
Duration of Olympic event: **17 days**
Location of venues

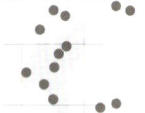

Main stadium: **Olympic stadium**

Completion date: **1979; renovated 2004**
Architect: **Santiago Calatrava**
Capacity: **72,000 seats; after the Games, 55,000 seats**
Later use: **the Olympic Stadium has been used at various times as a home base by the three major football clubs of Athens, Olympiacos Piraeus, Panathinaikos and AEK Athens**
Special factors:
- in 2004 the Olympic Games returned to Greece, home of both the ancient Olympics and the first modern Olympics
- by late March 2004, some Olympic projects were still behind schedule
- Athens constructed a new ring road, light-rail and tram connection just before the Olympic Games started
- after the attacks in New York and Madrid, security measures were even more strictly enforced
- for the first time, major broadcasters were allowed to put video coverage of the Olympics on the Internet

BEIJING
2008

The Olympics in 2008 and beyond?

Taking into consideration its own diminishing influence and the rising public animosity toward the scale of the Olympics, the IOC has set a number of higher goals for the next two Games to ensure that its ideology and authority remain intact. After a long period of putting the emphasis on economics, social issues are coming to the foreground. We see this in China, with the committee's peripheral conditions for the improvement of human rights, and in London, with the regeneration scenario for a socially weak area. How the goals are met is therefore location-specific, as 'global issues' are represented differently in each city.

2008 Beijing

Why Beijing? **The Chinese government has promoted the Games to highlight China's emergence on the world stage.**
Olympic Slogan: **One World, One Dream**

Olympic Logo

Number of main sponsors: **12**
Duration of Olympic event: **17 days**
Location of venues

Main stadium: **Beijing National Stadium**

Completion date: **2008**
Architect: **Herzog & de Meuron**
Capacity: **100,000 seats; there are plans to decrease the number of seats to 80,000 after the Olympic Games**
Special factors:
- **international criticism of the IOC for their choice of Beijing, because of China's dictatorial government, human rights violations, occupation of Tibet and threats to Taiwan; others praise the choice and its benefits for Beijing's 13 million inhabitants**

96 OLYMPIC FIRE — What Can We Learn From the Previous Olympics?

GLOBAL AND OLYMPIC TRENDS, 1896-2008

Length of
oil price $20   oil price $20   900 Giga barrels oi
                                                                                                                                                            0,5 p
                   15% desert   17% desert   20% desert   20% desert

                                                                  average travel time/distance/person/day 2hours
                                                                                              29 % urbanisation
                                                                                                  8 % infra
         inhabitants   average travel time/distance/person/day 66 km   70 km/h
         hosting city: 123.000 2.600.000 640.000 7.000.000 350.000   362.000 2.900.000 714.2000 1.240.000 4.300.000   8.200.000 370.000 1.600
                                                                     0,32 billion global ha   80%   7
                                                                                  $ 12.000.000
     duration Games 9 days 166 days 145 days 208 days 82 days   143 days 84 days 87 days 15 days 15 days   15 days 15 days 16 c
     participating countries24   24   12   22   29   44   46   46   42   49   59   69   72
            43 Olympic disciplines 109 Olympic disciplines   154 Olympic disciplines   129 Olympic disciplines 20 % facilities 13 % fa
            90 gold medals   103 gold medals   156 gold medals   156 gold medals   136 Olympic disciplines
            7 demonstration sports   9 demonstration sports   1 demonstration sport   3 demonstration sports 128 gold medals
            177 male Athletes   2141 male Athletes   2527 male Athletes   1204 male Athletes   2 demonstration sports
            22 male Athletes   43 female Athletes   64 female Athletes   290 female Athletes   3677 male Athle
                                                                                                                        385 female Athletes
                                 100 events   first tv broadcast of the Olympics
     380.000 visitors Olympic city 134.000 visitors   1 country broadcasting Olympic Games   2 countries broadcasti
                                         327.290 visitors   665.600 visitors   1.247.550 visitors Olympic city   1.247.290 visitors   1.500.

                                                                                                        3.325 miles driven per c
                   3000 annual hours per worker   2300 calories per da
                                                                                                  average life expectency North Americ
                                                                                                  average life expectency Europe
                                                                                                  average life expectency sub-Saharan

                                                                                                       4 billion people world p
                                                                                                       1.5 billion people ov
          15% European grey pressure
                                    4 children per woman   5 children per woman
                                                                                                      10 million people in warconfli
                                                                                                           -3
                                                                                                           7 BO

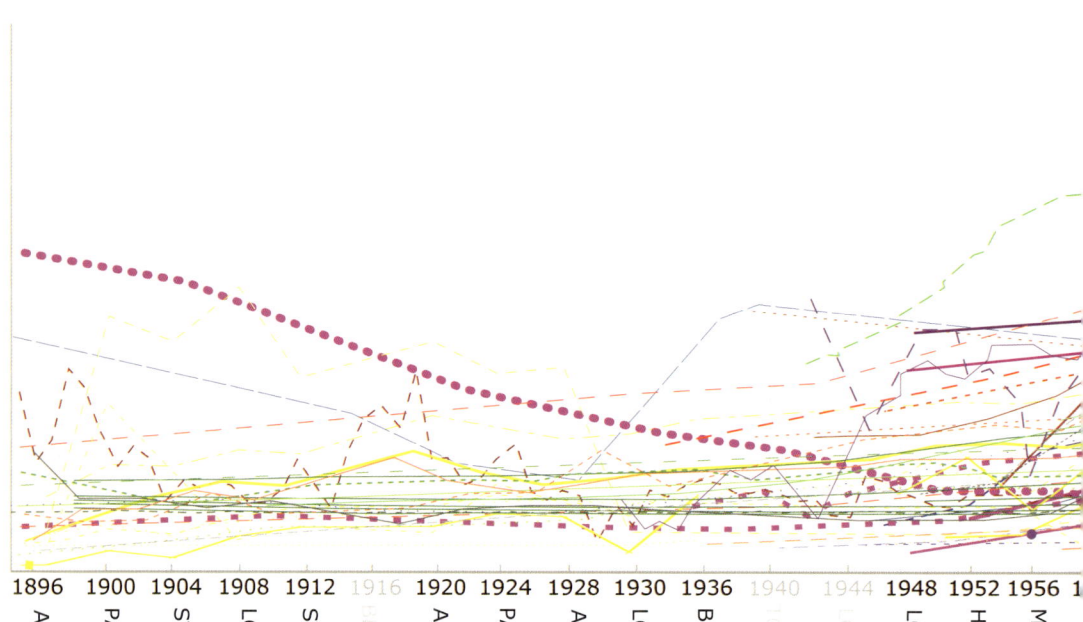

1896 1900 1904 1908 1912 1916 1920 1924 1928 1930 1936 1940 1944 1948 1952 1956

ATHENS PARIS ST. LOUIS LONDON STOCKHOLM BERLIN ANTWERP PARIS AMSTERDAM LOS ANGELES BERLIN TOKYO LONDON LONDON HELSINKI MELBOURNE

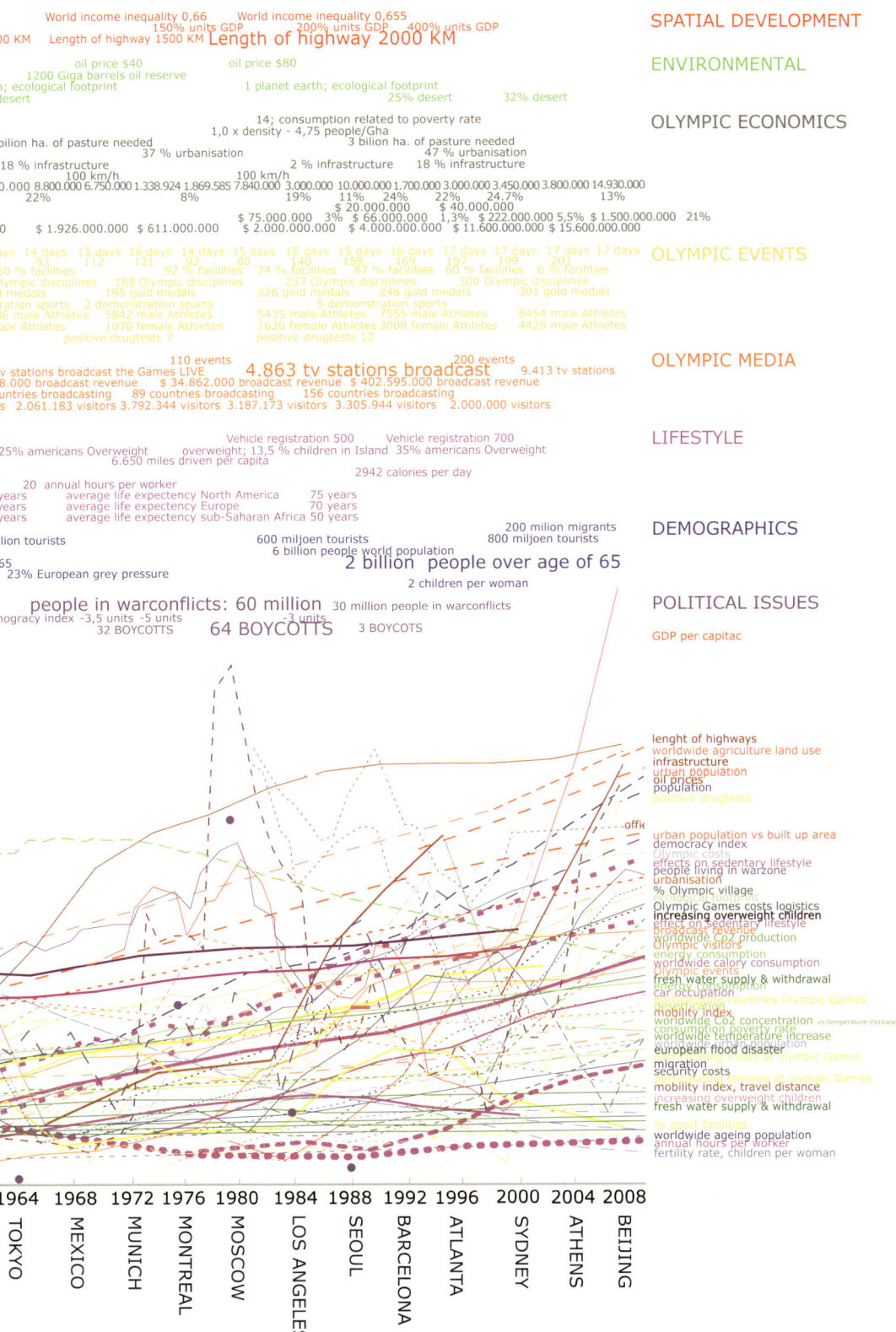

Political Trends, 1896-2008

However idealistically the Olympics may be presented, a darker period began in 1936, when the Olympic idea was entirely misused for Nazi propaganda. That success turned the Olympic arena into a political stage. To counteract this, the Olympic Committee focused more on sports and less on ideology. Since the bomb explosions in Atlanta, the fear of a terrorist attack by the ETA in Barcelona and September 11, security measures have greatly increased.

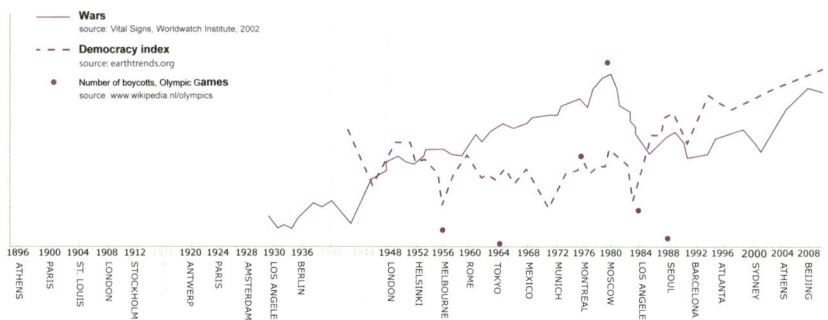

Olympic Economical Trends, 1896-2008

The Olympics are unthinkable without commercial support. Despite the idealistic viewpoint that commerce has no place in the Olympic arena, millions of people watch advertisements between sports broadcasts. It is hard to imagine that any government could entirely fund the Games. Therefore the Olympics are vulnerable to financial speculation and conflicts of interest that can veil the true core activities of the Olympics.

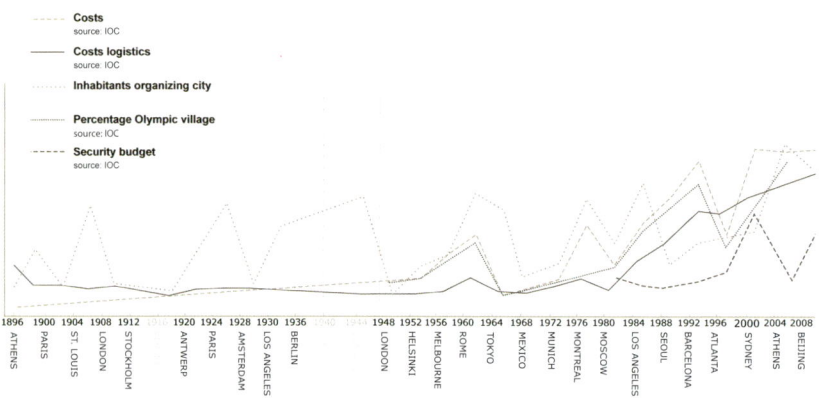

Olympic Events Trends, 1896-2008

Because of the IOC's organisational strategy and fixed policy, the increasing emancipation of women and a greater number of Olympic demonstration sports since the 1928 Olympics in Amsterdam, the Olympics have become more popular and have turned into a high-profile spectacle.

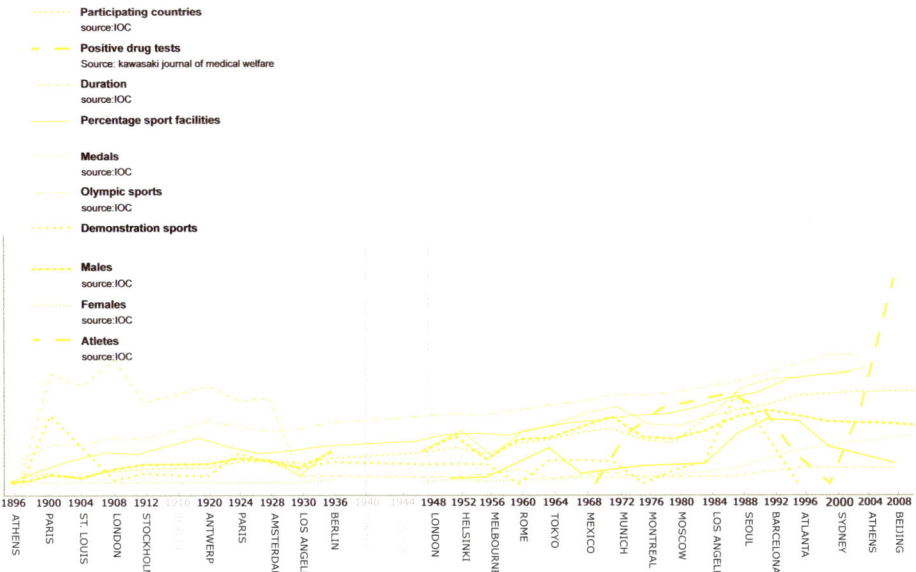

Olympic Media Trends, 1896-2008

Since the advent of the media age during the Berlin Olympics, the Olympics have grown significantly. The number of bids rapidly increased as budgets grew larger and national representation became more important. The growth stopped after the Olympics in Tokyo. Budgets and organisations became so large that the popularity of hosting the Olympics reached its lowest point. The IOC decided that the next Olympics would be run on a more sober budget. However, media attention and national representation were in such contradiction to this tighter budget that in Montreal it almost led to the city's bankruptcy.

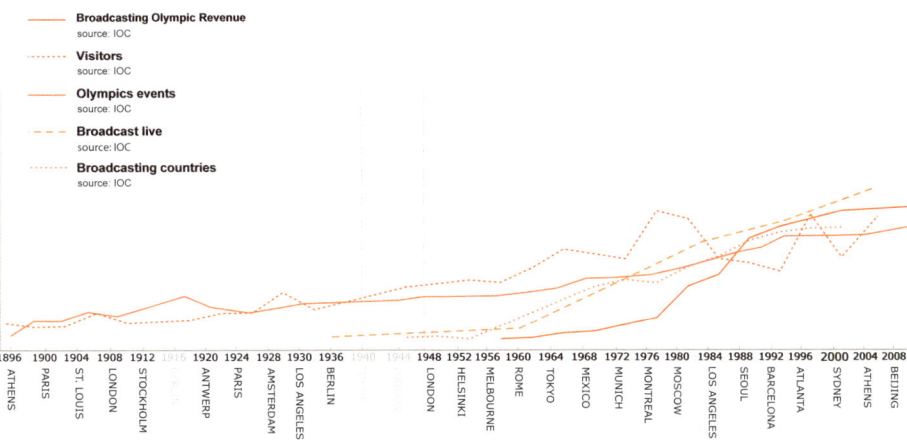

Environmental Trends, 1896-2008

The Brundtland Report of 1987 put forward the need to employ sustainable development in order to protect natural resources and create a higher quality of life for future generations. The relationship between sports and the environment has been high on the IOC's list of priorities since the Centennial Olympic Congress in Paris in 1994. In the history of the Olympic Games, Sydney was the turning point in the successful implementation of sustainable development strategies by using environment-friendly technologies.

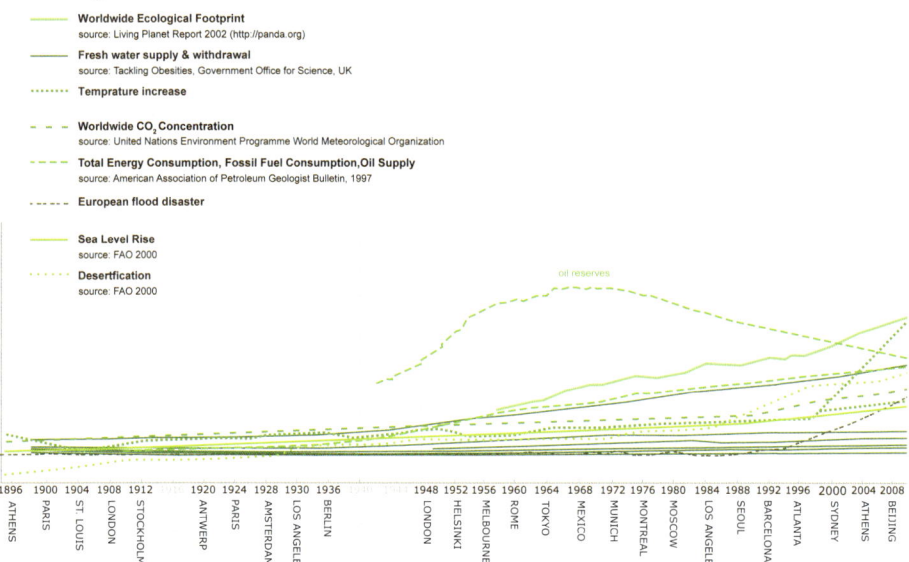

Lifestyle Trends, 1896-2008

Changes in lifestyles as well as higher consumption rates of foods that are rich in fat are contributing considerably to overweight worldwide. Since 1980, the growth rate of obesity has accelerated markedly and it is increasingly becoming a public health concern. Population and consumption data reveal that socio-economic and cultural factors such as a reduction of physical activity, technological change and more passive entertainment are affecting the spread of obesity throughout the world.

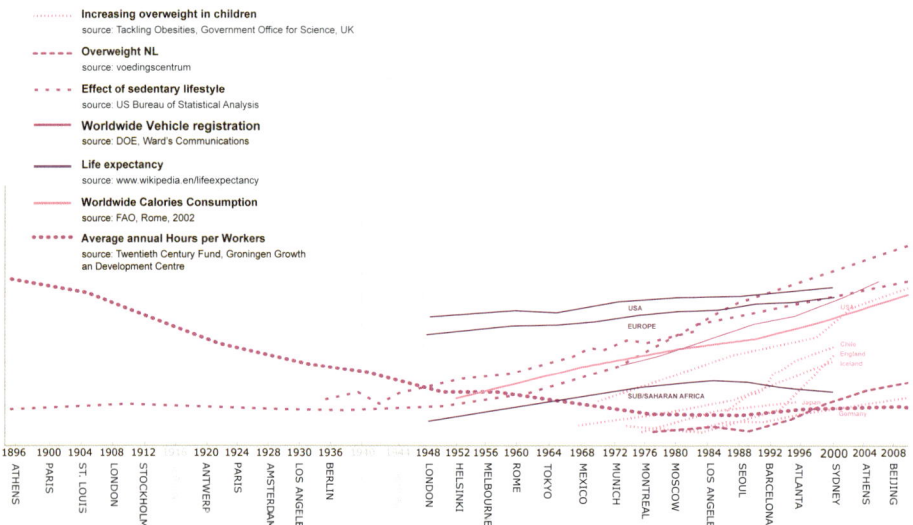

Demographic Trends, 1896-2008

For the first time in history, more than half of the world's population is living in cities, and that number is still rising. At the same time, international migration is higher than ever before. Because of this migration, the population in contemporary cities is a mix of different cultures and backgrounds. Whilst total income is growing in the cities, income inequality is also becoming larger. The age gap between the developed countries that are dealing with an ageing population and the underdeveloped countries whose population remains young has widened.

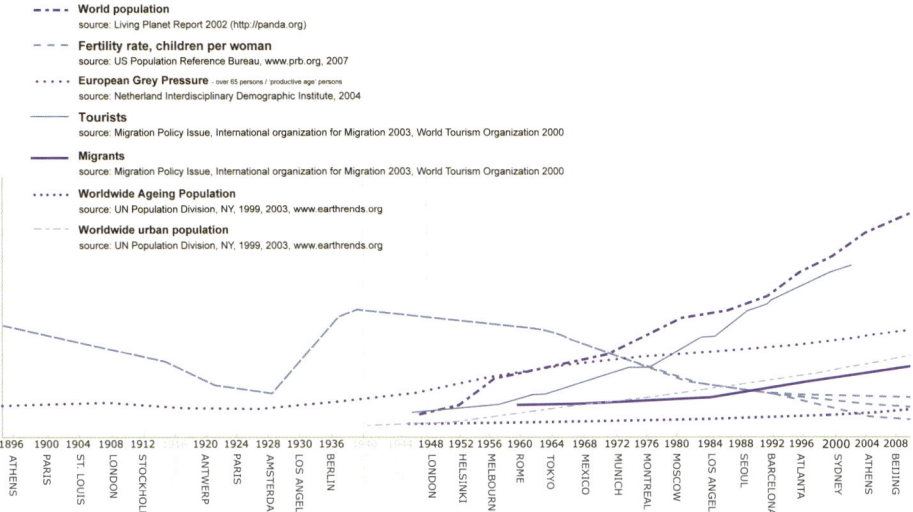

Spatial Development Trends, 1896-2008

Increasing mobility reduces the trade barrier, enabling poor regions to become more competitive. On the other hand transportation also has negative impacts such as pollution, collisions and congestion. That's why Olympic cities like Athens and Sydney have developed sustainable 'mobility strategies'.

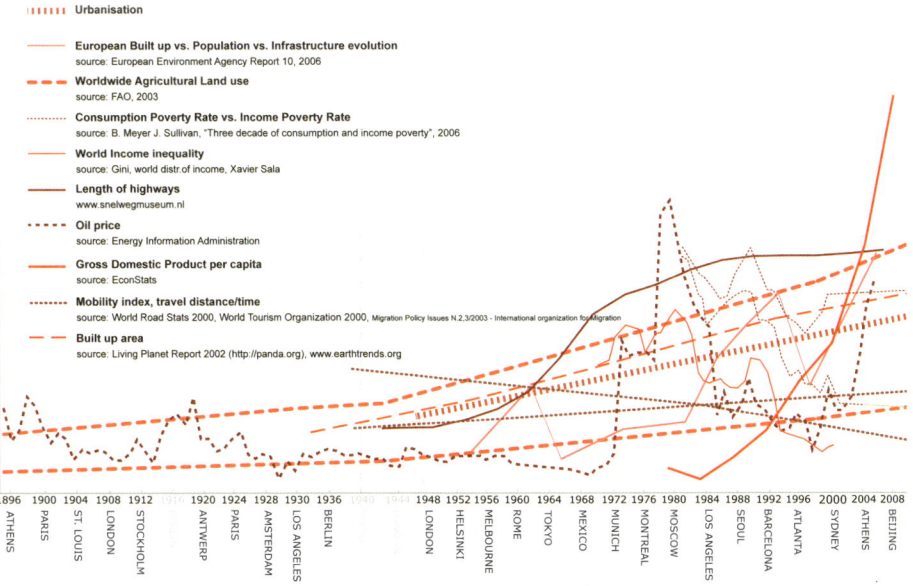

'We have space and we need more urbanisation. What more can you ask for?'

John Bos interviewed by Mieke Dings

John Bos is a member of the Provincial Executive for the PvdA [Dutch Labour Party - MD] in Flevoland. He concerns himself with the portfolios of welfare and care, youth policy, education, water, living and sports.

Involvement with Olympic Games 2028: Immediately after the 2004 Games in Athens, when Erica Terpstra [at the time already president of NOC*NSF - MD] and Prince Willem-Alexander spoke out in favour of having the Games in the Netherlands, we endorsed the idea and said that part of it might very well take place in Flevoland. This idea is now being further developed and of course we follow the NOC*NSF's lead in this.

Playing an Olympic sport? Jogging and fitness are not yet Olympic events and calling my jogging 'running' would be promoting it to something it is not. I also ski.

Most impressive Olympic Games: Sydney. I was really touched by the Australians' involvement and enthusiasm. That really gave the event flavour and of course it goes with their culture, in which sports and health play an important role.

Memorable sports moment: I have two: the volleyball finals we won in Atlanta (1996) and Ellen van Langen's winning a gold medal in Barcelona (1992).

You mentioned Sydney as the most impressive Games so far, especially because of the energy they radiated. Are these Games an inspiration for your ideal Games in 2028?
Absolutely. I can already feel how the idea of the Games is creating a bond in our country, focusing our energy and attention on issues where we need each other and where we can strengthen each other; it is not about where we differ. My ideal Games contribute to a feeling of being Dutch. Barcelona is an inspiration and example as well, because there we have seen what an enormous international boost the Games can give if you manage to cleverly combine the Games and the development of your country.

And you see a central role for Flevoland in this?
Certainly. One of the most important points in our favour is that we have the space for large-scale facilities. Also, the southern part of Flevoland still largely needs to be developed, if only because the city of Almere will grow from 180,000 to 350,000 inhabitants by 2030. Those people will need housing and facilities as well. Combining those two issues is killing two birds with one stone, and at the same time it answers the criticism that the Games only cost money.

Which Olympic facilities would be possible in Flevoland? For the bid by Amsterdam, at the time, you researched the possibility of an Olympic Village.
Indeed, and of course the possibility is always there, providing it is done in such a way that we can use the Village for regular housing purposes afterwards. We also have room for various stadiums of a size of which there are hardly any in the Netherlands, but which we do need to play our part on the international scene. The Field Hockey Association, for instance, has for some time now been contemplating a new stadium which will put us on the map. Flevoland has room for this. Finally, we have enough water to hold rowing and sailing events.

Surely the public at large will not come to Flevoland for a bit of sports?
Millions of people already live within a 30 km radius around Almere and another 200,000 inhabitants will follow. I'm certain they will want to use these stadiums. Almere's field hockey club is already looking for more space. If we can combine the stadiums with facilities such as after-school care and leisure, we can reach a large public. Naturally, we will have to invest in their accessibility.

Are the people of Flevoland keen on this at all?
The Games are generating energy, especially among the younger people who

are into sports and exercise. We therefore absolutely want to make a link to sports in general. And then we are not just talking about gyms and fitness centres – the days when everyone was simply playing volleyball in the gym are gone – but also skate centres in the neighbourhoods and other sports that attract young people. They not only promote health, but social cohesion as well. We find that parents still feel it's important for their children to join sports clubs where they can make friends and interact. The business community is also happy with these efforts to promote Flevoland in a wider sense. Companies are already hiring top athletes for clinics and training programmes.

Does the green polder landscape offer the athletes any extra benefits?
It often does seem to matter what a swimming pool or stadium looks like – in Sydney, Inge de Bruyn said that the large pool with all the stands and spectators was inspiring – but whether the view matters, I couldn't say. I do find that participants in the UPC Holland Triathlon enormously enjoy cycling and running in the polder. I therefore see it as a challenge to do as much justice as we can to the vastness of the polders and the water in and around the facilities, and maybe during the Games too.

So we can expect to see a spacious green Olympic Village in the polder?
If we want to make it really, really green and also realise 60,000 houses for those 200,000 people I mentioned earlier, then we will need a lot more space than we have in just Flevoland alone. We have to be realistic. The beauty of Flevoland is that there is green and water everywhere. We want to keep it that way and even actively facilitate it. Almere is close to the Oostvaardersplassen [a nature reserve – MD] but it is and will remain a real city.

Aren't the Games the ultimate chance for Flevoland to put itself on the world map as a healthy, recreational region, including a green and experimental Olympic Village?
I totally agree with that. In the Village itself we can do all sorts of experiments, for instance building on or near the water. Such housing will also draw the attention of the international world of architecture, as is happening now with Adri Duyvesteijn's [Almere's alderman for Spatial Planning – MD] winning the Rotterdam-Maaskant Award [for persons who have made an important contribution to architecture/landscape – MD]. However, we must keep in mind that such houses are not for everyone.

So you will welcome architects and city planners with bright ideas?
Yes, always, but we also follow NOC*NSF's lead. One of the first stages of the Olympic Plan is to create a climate of sports-mindedness and that's what we are concentrating on now. These early stages are especially attractive and crucial to Flevoland because they provide the leads that fit in with developments within Flevoland. The Games are the icing on the cake.

Which specific plans to promote sports-mindedness are you working on now?
We are showing that we think sports and health are important in many ways. We stimulate sports-mindedness by initiating small projects, supporting communities, getting organisations to exchange ideas, hooking up athletes with companies, etc. We also want to demonstrate that we are capable of organising these types of events. It's all still in the very early stage, but we've made a start. This summer we will have the World Championship long-distance triathlon and there is the Top Sports Hall in Almere, which hosts many events such as the Dutch Open Badminton and various activities by the Dutch Handball Association. And of course we have the 5 km ice track FlevoOnice, with all sorts of summer activities coming up. We have also published a wonderful magazine, Sportive Flevoland, which details everything we have to offer in the area of sports and all our plans for the future.

How old will you be in 2028 and where will you be watching the Olympic Games then?
I will be over 60 by then and I'll be on the Oostvaarders dike, watching one of the Olympic events right there.

Can you think of a sports slogan to make the country rally behind the idea of hosting the Games in Flevoland?
It would be wonderful to revive the grandeur and uniqueness of Cornelis Lely's 'grand plan for the Zuiderzee' [Lely was the engineer who proposed closing off the Zuiderzee from the North Sea and draining parts of it – MD] and to apply this spirit to a new project that is also unique.

'Create enough grass plots and sports clubs in neighbourhoods'

Jet Bussemaker interviewed by Mieke Dings

Jet Bussemaker is State Secretary of Public Health, Welfare and Sports (VWS). Before this she has held various positions at the University of Amsterdam and was a Member of Parliament for the PvdA [Dutch Labour Party – MD].

Involvement with Olympic Games 2028: I am very closely involved because VWS, together with Economic Affairs and the cities of Amsterdam and Rotterdam, is contributing to the costs of the Olympic Plan 2028. So I am also a member of the council for the Olympic Plan. Within the Ministry of VWS we have appointed Rob de Vries, the former director of the Sports Division, as programme manager for the Olympic plan. So, in fact we are at the very heart of things.

Playing an Olympic sport? Yes, I play tennis and I used to do a lot of cycling.

Most impressive Olympic Games: Pfff… Well, when I see images of the Games in Amsterdam in 1928 I must say I am deeply impressed. Partly because I then think how wonderful it would be to have the Games here again 100 years later. My house is not very far from the old Olympic Stadium and each time I walk by I can picture how it must have been at the time and how it will be in 2028.

Memorable sport moment: There are so many, and by mentioning names now I'm afraid of not doing justice to so many others. Of course there have been achievements that make you sit on the edge of your seat, such as the swimmer Pieter van den Hoogeband's gold medal in Athens (2004) and Ellen van Langen's winning a gold medal on the 800 metres in Barcelona (1992). And of course Anky van Grunsven's equestrian achievements. But I wouldn't want to short-change other athletes, of course.

What do you hope to achieve with the Games?
I hope that the games will be one big sports festival, with lots of different people and a diversity of sports groups. I also hope that the Games will not only inspire the top athletes but also encourage all those other people to engage in exercise. The key question in the Olympic Plan, therefore, is how we can make a sporting nation of the Netherlands.

How do you create a sports climate?
We will encourage sports and exercise in every conceivable way. Together with the sports federations and the NOC*NSF we are going to create an innovative offer for citizens who are not active in sports, like the elderly or young people around 16, 17 years of age. There is also the recently launched National Action Plan for Sports and Exercise that uses unorthodox methods to get people to start exercising in their neighbourhood or home and we will address young people in the right way, for instance by setting up projects together with schools. But there are many other ways as well. In Groningen, some people got together and then knocked on everyone's door in the neighbourhood to ask who would like to go for a walk every now and then. So now they have a walking club. And in Amsterdam there are a number of Islamic women who previously could go out only if accompanied by their husbands, and who now have formed an informal running club together.

Top athletes play an important role in inspiring the general population. For the National Action Plan, I have appointed several athletes as ambassadors, including field hockey player Minke Booij and table tennis player Trinko Keen. And a lot of football players from the Football Foundation are involved in the project 'Scoring for Health'. They educate children and parents about exercise and proper food – and with success: after all, the effect is much bigger if Edgar Davids comes to your school than if I do.

Sports unite, you said earlier. The Games, however, often seem to divide us.
One of the goals of the Games, obviously, is to unite the whole world. It is true

that they do not always succeed in this. Our goal within VWS is to use the preparations for the Olympic Games to at least unite the people here, especially the people who are not yet active in sports. Sports encourage people to meet; they enhance integration. It is no coincident that sports clubs often have the function of a village square. The same may be true on a global level, even if it is a process of trial and error.

You just mentioned the running club of Islamic women. That doesn't sound like sport is enhancing integration.
True, it is still an Islamic club. But I think it's sufficient that these women at least get some exercise and go out together. I see such clubs as a temporary phenomenon, a transitional phase on the road to more integrated clubs.
In 2005, Teheran hosted the first Islamic Women's Games, and 1600 women from 40 countries participated. It's easy to say we disapprove of such Games but I think they are a step in the right direction. Emancipation always precedes integration. I expect the Dutch delegation in 2028 to form an accurate representation of our society.

Do you regard the 'burkini' as a tool for integration through sports?
Frankly, I find all this fuss about the burkini rather tedious. When I answered questions in Parliament I compared the burkini with the new Speedo swimsuit, which is just as closed and covering. I only judge swim clothing by criteria of hygiene and decency, and the burkini passes that test with flying colours. As far as I'm concerned the burkini is a tool to get those women to swim, to exercise.

You said earlier that sports may contribute to a safer environment. In what way?
Sports can be an outlet for the urge to move, a way to deal with aggression and to learn how to deal with other people. If there are no sports facilities, young people will find other outlets. I think sports can be a very positive contribution, not only as an outlet but also as a way of learning how to interact, of learning that you can have differences of opinion but still play together. I am working with Bert Koenders [the Minister for Development Cooperation - MD] on a programme called Sports and Development Cooperation which, among other things, concerns itself with sports in conflict areas. In such areas, sports are used to encourage contact between groups that used to be enemies. And we also use sports as part of treatments in youth welfare work. We currently have 50 pilot projects where sports clubs and youth care organisations are working together, and there you see how juveniles who are totally unmanageable when they see a psychologist or psychiatrist, are completely revived on the sports field. Playing, the element of meeting others, is very important.

What still needs to be done for our nation to be truly sporting in 2028?
In 2016 we already have to be a true sporting nation, with more people exercising. And of course we have to make sure that the infrastructure and facilities are ready. It is too early now to already make definite plans, but we should take all of this into account in existing plans and have 'no regrets' options.
And let's not forget that it is not just about buildings. We need them of course, but they will be meaningless unless large parts of the population support the Olympic Plan. So we should first make sure that there are sufficient sports facilities in the communities: grass plots, Cruyff Courts, Krajicek Playgrounds. There must be an attractive offering of sports. This means that urban planners have to plan sufficient sports facilities in the neighbourhoods and that civil servants must make sure that these facilities are evenly distributed across the city.

How old will you be in 2028?
Not too old to still be involved: 67.

Where would you prefer to watch the games then?
Everywhere. I'll make sure to go and take a look in every stadium. And most certainly in the beautiful Olympic Stadium that I pass by so often now.

Can you think of any sports quote or slogan to make our nation a more sporting one?
You have to shoot in order to score; a quote from Cruyff.

WHAT C
WE EXP
THE FUT

CAN
ECT IN
URE?

Global and Olympic Trends, 2008-2028

108 OLYMPIC FIRE   What Can We Expect in the Future?

inequality 0,655   World income inequality 0,635
% units GDP   400% units GDP   SPATIAL DEVELOPMENT
ghway 2000 KM   3000 ton freshwater
                              oil price $60   150 (CO2) ppm (temp.)% 200 (CO2) ppm   ENVIRONMENTAL
                    European flood disasters 65 units   European flood disasters 200 units
h; ecological footprint   2 planet earth; ecological footprint
          25% desert   32% desert   42% desert
ption related to poverty rate   OLYMPIC ECONOMICS
 people/Gha
         3 billion ha. of pasture needed   1,2 billion global ha
infrastructure   47 % urbanisation   60 % urbanisation
              18 % infrastructure   120 km
000 10.000.000 1.700.000 3.000.000 3.450.000 3.800.000 14.930.000
       11%   24%   22%   24,7%   13%
     $ 20.000.000 $ 40.000.000
   3% $ 66.000.000   1,3% $ 222.000.000 5,5% $ 1.500.000.000 21% $ 800.000.000 8,2%
000 $ 4.000.000.000 $ 11.600.000.000 $ 15.600.000.000
ys 15 days   16 days   17 days   17 days   17 days   OLYMPIC EVENTS
es   1599   269   197   201
       87 % facilities 60 % facilities 6 % facilities
ympic disciplines   300 Olympic disciplines
edals   246 gold medals   301 gold medals
5 demonstration sports
Athletes 7555 male Athletes   6454 male Athletes
le Athletes 3008 female Athletes   4428 male Athletes
gtests 12
                   200 events   OLYMPIC MEDIA
stations broadcast   9.413 tv stations broadcast the Games LIVE
     $ 402.595.000 broadcast revenue $ 1.494.028.000 broadcast revenue
5 countries broadcasting   220 countries broadcasting Olympic Games
    3.305.944 visitors   2.000.000 visitors   3.150.000 visitors
         Vehicle registration 700   Vehicle registration 800   LIFESTYLE
ren in Island 35% americans Overweight   overweight; 40 % American children
       2942 calories per day   3700 calories per day
           10.000 miles driven per capita
         average life expectency North America   80 years
         average life expectency Europe   75 years
         average life expectency sub-Saharan   DEMOGRAPHICS
n tourists   200 million migrants
people world population 800 miljoen tourists   8 billion people world
   2 billion people over age of 65   +3 units temporary index
                                12% world population over age of 65
               2 children per woman   30% European grey pressure
                                                                 POLITICAL ISSUES
     30 million people in warconflicts
     3 BOYCOTS
                                                    GDP per capitac
                                                    population
                                                    urban population
                                                    urbanisation
                                                    worldwide Co2 production
                                                    lenght of highways
                                                    democracy index
                                                    worldwide agriculture land use
                                                    infrastructure
                                                    oil prices
                                                    urban population vs built up area
                                                    effects on sedentary lifestyle
                                                    official poverty rate income
                                                    increasing overweight children
                                                    Olympic Games costs logistics
                                                    ecological footprint
                                                    european flood disaster
                                                    effect on sedentary lifestyle
                                                    people living in warzone
                                                    % Olympic village
                                                    worldwide calory consumption
                                                    broadcast revenue
                                                    fresh water supply & withdrawal
                                                    Olympic visitors
                                                    desertification
                                                    energy consumption
                                                    Olympic events
                                                    car occupation
                                                    mobility index
                                                    worldwide Co2 concentration vs temperature increase
                                                    energy consumption
                                                    consumption poverty rate
                                                    worldwide temperature increase
                                                    worldwide urban population
                                                    increasing overweight children
                                                    migration
                                                    security costs
                                                    participating females at olympic Games
                                                    fresh water supply & withdrawal
                                                    mobility index, travel distance
                                                    worldwide ageing population
                                                    annual hours per worker
                                                    fertility rate, children per woman

1988 1992 1996 2000 2004 2008 2012 2016 2020 2024 2028

SEOUL BARCELONA ATLANTA SYDNEY ATHENS BEIJING LONDON

Tangible Legacy

Through the years, the Olympics have proven they are unparalleled in their ability to put a city on the map in terms of architecture, municipal development, city marketing, sports infrastructure, economy and tourism. In brief, the Olympics are guaranteed to leave a visible legacy, apart from all the intentions of sport itself. In some cases, this means that a city is left with white elephants. In more successful cases, something of lasting quality is added to the city, not so much in terms of imposing buildings, but infrastructure, public spaces, public transport, renovation and repair.

Intangible Legacy

The main aim of the IOC is to embed and organise certain values within a specific cultural context. The IOC promotes the development of a vision in which the emphasis is placed on intercultural bonds through sports, the equality of men and women, an aversion to exclusion, collective production, voluntary work, developing a healthy sports culture, developing know-how and promoting the message of peace. It is precisely these explicit yet intangible goals that finally ensure the power of the Olympics. This has been the major constant feature of the Olympics and reason for its ongoing strength throughout its approximately one hundred-year history.

The Olympic Movement

The ambition to again place the ideals of the Olympics at the top of the agenda was formalised at the International Symposium on Legacy of the Olympic Games, 1984-2000 on 14 and 16 November 2002. The IOC stated that "The possible long-term effects, the benefits for the community and the possible contribution of each bid to the community of the Olympic Movement should be considered as key aspects." It therefore is important that an effort be made to implement 'global issues' in 'local contexts', so that the Olympics again have a clear role in society.

A New Legacy

Everything points to an increasing realisation of the power of the Olympics, starting from the innocent beginnings of the Games as a fraternising peaceful event, to a period in which the propaganda power of the Olympics became clear, to symbolism that surpasses the primary meaning and values of the Games and the entry of mass media and commerce. Due to their worldwide visibility the Olympics have become politically sensitive, a target for both boycotts and terrorism. This has major implications for the urban configuration of the Olympic site, where the major emphasis is on security and control. With all of these priorities taking precedence over sport itself, the original objectives of the IOC have become increasingly less relevant. Since the Olympics have risen from a strong ideology, each bid starts with the pronouncement of an ideal, an ideology. In 1896 this was 'brotherhood', in 1976 'frugality', in 2008 it is the commitment to improve human rights and in 2012 it will be aimed at 'sustainability', This ideology is then concretely represented in logos, images, campaigns, city branding, medals, architecture, urban planning, stamps etc. Although originally money did not seem to play a role in the hosting of the Olympics, the economic aspect became more and more dominant after the Los Angeles Olympics in 1984. In some cases, economic growth even determined the ideology, exemplified in the economic power of the IOC itself. As a tool for creating a healthier city, economy or population, the Olympic Games have changed considerably. Originally they were focused on short-term results, such as fraternisation between the athletes, while nowadays the emphasis lies on long-term results that exceed the Olympics themselves.

Political Trends, 1988-2028

The gap between a zone of peace and a zone of turmoil will increase due to polarization causing income divergence.

- **Wars**
  source: Vital Signs, Worldwatch Institute, 2002
- **Democracy index**
  source: earthtrends.org
- **Number of boycotts, Olympic Games**
  source: www.wikipedia.nl/olympics

Olympic Economic Trends, 1988-2028

The long-term beneficial effects of decisions regarding investment, trade, corporate relocation, government spending, convention sites and the location of major sporting events will likely be among the most enduring legacies of the Games.

- **Costs**
  source: IOC
- **Costs logistics**
  source: IOC
- **Inhabitants organizing city**
- **Percentage Olympic village**
  source: IOC
- **Security budget**
  source: IOC

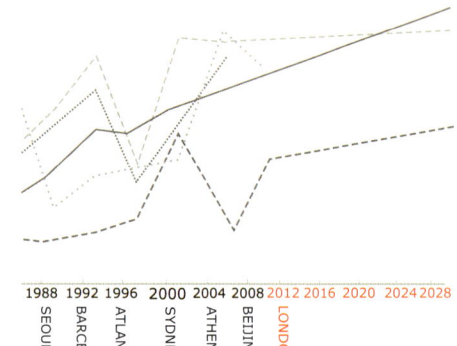

Olympic Events Trends, 1988-2028

High sports achievements are considered to be a confirmation of a more or less fundamental belief in progress in western culture, not only in sports but also in science, technology and economy.

- **Participating countries**
  source: IOC
- **Positive drug tests**
  Source: kawasaki journal of medical welfare
- **Duration**
  source: IOC
- **Percentage sport facilities**
- **Medals**
  source: IOC
- **Olympic sports**
  source: IOC
- **Demonstration sports**
- **Males**
  source: IOC
- **Females**
  source: IOC
- **Atletes**
  source: IOC

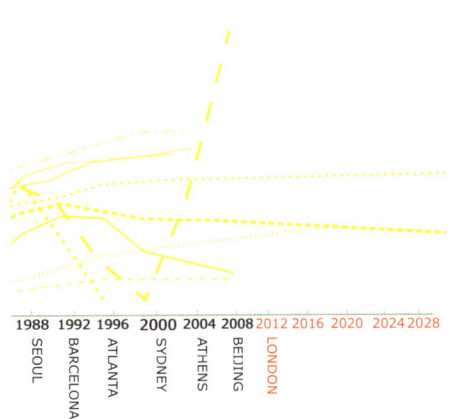

Olympic Media Trends, 1988-2028

The impact of media coverage in hosting cities could positively affect foreign direct investment, conventions, businesses' location and tourism.

- **Broadcasting Olympic Revenue**
  source: IOC
- **Visitors**
  source: IOC
- **Olympics events**
  source: IOC
- **Broadcast live**
  source: IOC
- **Broadcasting countries**
  source: IOC

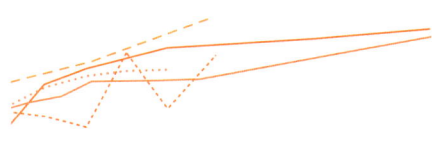

Environmental Trends, 1988-2028

Global urban warming has important implications for human comfort, health and well-being. Natural systems will be destabilized, creating risks to human health in some developing countries such as crowding, food scarcity, poverty, and local environmental problems.

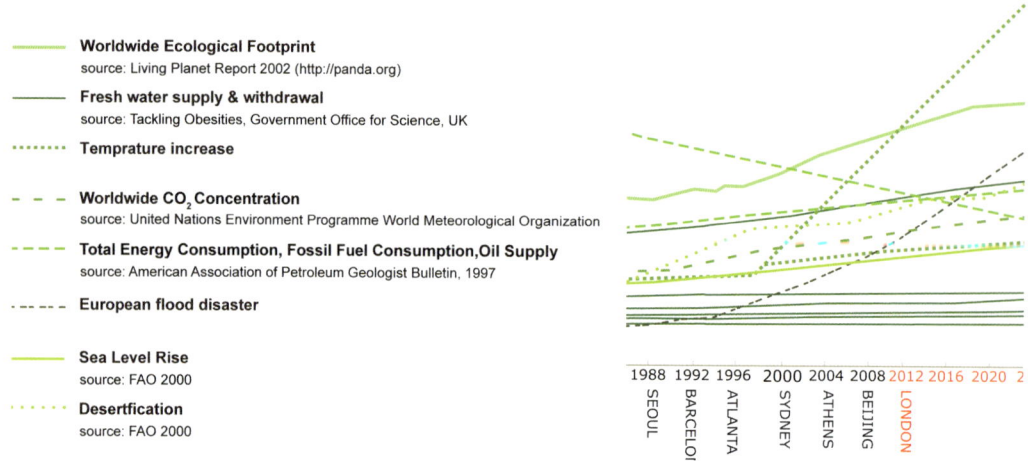

- Worldwide Ecological Footprint
  source: Living Planet Report 2002 (http://panda.org)
- Fresh water supply & withdrawal
  source: Tackling Obesities, Government Office for Science, UK
- Temprature increase
- Worldwide CO_2 Concentration
  source: United Nations Environment Programme World Meteorological Organization
- Total Energy Consumption, Fossil Fuel Consumption, Oil Supply
  source: American Association of Petroleum Geologist Bulletin, 1997
- European flood disaster
- Sea Level Rise
  source: FAO 2000
- Desertfication
  source: FAO 2000

Lifestyle Trends, 1988-2028

In contemporary societies people rely more and more on the automobile for transportation. This reliance contributes to a sedentary lifestyle, an obesity epidemic, and poor health. Obesity and associated chronic diseases are the greatest public health problem in most countries in the world.

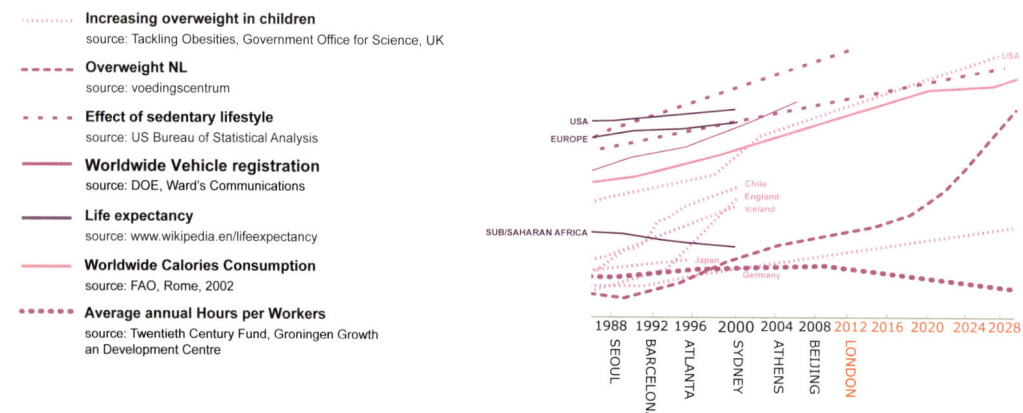

- Increasing overweight in children
  source: Tackling Obesities, Government Office for Science, UK
- Overweight NL
  source: voedingscentrum
- Effect of sedentary lifestyle
  source: US Bureau of Statistical Analysis
- Worldwide Vehicle registration
  source: DOE, Ward's Communications
- Life expectancy
  source: www.wikipedia.en/lifeexpectancy
- Worldwide Calories Consumption
  source: FAO, Rome, 2002
- Average annual Hours per Workers
  source: Twentieth Century Fund, Groningen Growth an Development Centre

What Can We Expect in the Future?   OLYMPIC FIRE   115

Demographic Trends, 1988-2028

A large and ever-increasing fraction of the world's population is living in cities, and the disproportionate share of resources used by these urban residents, cities and their inhabitants are key drivers of global environmental change.

- - - - **World population**
source: Living Planet Report 2002 (http://panda.org)

- - - **Fertility rate, children per woman**
source: US Population Reference Bureau, www.prb.org, 2007

· · · · · **European Grey Pressure** - over 65 persons / 'productive age' persons
source: Netherland Interdisciplinary Demographic Institute, 2004

——— **Tourists**
source: Migration Policy Issue, International organization for Migration 2003, World Tourism Organization 2000

——— **Migrants**
source: Migration Policy Issue, International organization for Migration 2003, World Tourism Organization 2000

· · · · · · **Worldwide Ageing Population**
source: UN Population Division, NY, 1999, 2003, www.earthrends.org

- - - - **Worldwide urban population**
source: UN Population Division, NY, 1999, 2003, www.earthrends.org

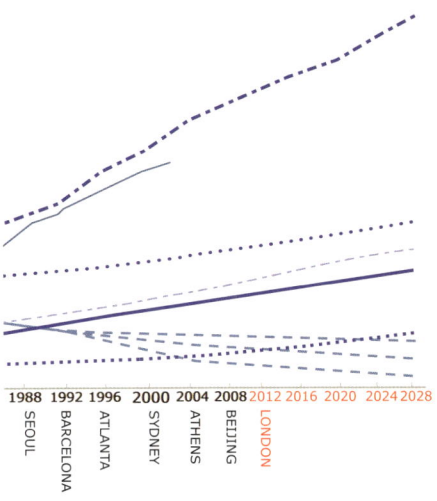

1988 1992 1996 2000 2004 2008 2012 2016 2020 2024 2028
SEOUL BARCELONA ATLANTA SYDNEY ATHENS BEIJING LONDON

Spatial Development Trends, 1988-2028

On all continents, a relative decline in average urban growth rates has been observed for the last 20 or 30 years, compared to those of the preceding decades.

ııııııı	**Urbanisation**		
———	**European Built up vs. Population vs. Infrastructure evolution** source: European Environment Agency Report 10, 2006		
— — —	**Worldwide Agricultural Land use** source: FAO, 2003		
· · · · · ·	**Consumption Poverty Rate vs. Income Poverty Rate** source: B. Meyer J. Sullivan, "Three decade of consumption and income poverty", 2006		
———	**World Income inequality** source: Gini, world distr.of income, Xavier Sala		
———	**Length of highways** www.snelwegmuseum.nl		
- - - -	**Oil price** source: Energy Information Administration		
———	**Gross Domestic Product per capita** source: EconStats		
· · · · · · ·	**Mobility index, travel distance/time** source: World Road Stats 2000, World Tourism Organization 2000, Migration Policy Issues N.2,3/2003 - International organization for Migration		
— —	**Built up area** source: Living Planet Report 2002 (http://panda.org), www.earthrends.org		

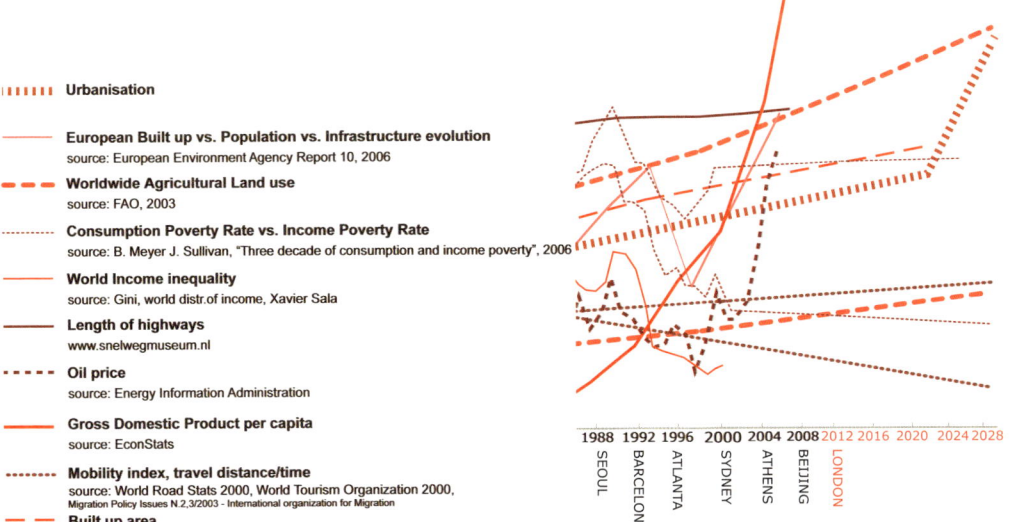

1988 1992 1996 2000 2004 2008 2012 2016 2020 2024 2028
SEOUL BARCELONA ATLANTA SYDNEY ATHENS BEIJING LONDON

'The Olympic Games as a Motor for Urban Renewal'

Kees Christiaanse interviewed by Harry den Hartog

Kees Christiaanse is a partner in the architectural firm KCAP Architects & Planners and a professor of architecture and urban development at the ETH in Zurich. Since 2007 he also teaches as a visiting professor in the Cities Programme of the London School of Economics.

Involvement in the Olympic Games 2028: KCAP Architects & Planners is currently working with Allies & Morrison Architects and EDAW on an Olympic Legacy Masterplan for the redevelopment of the Lea Valley area in East London after the Games are finished in 2012.

Plays the Olympic sport: I sail and ski, but not at the Olympic level!

Memorable sports moment: Nothing really comes to mind. Oh, yeah: Ard and Keessie [the Dutch skaters Ard Schenk and Kees Verkerk who won several Olympic medals in the 60s and 70s - HdH].

What's the essence of your plan for redeveloping Lea Valley?
The Olympic Games are being planned for an underdeveloped part of the city which is in urgent need of revision and revitalisation. The context is a combination of old districts, industrial wastelands and the neglected valley of the river Lea. The area offers a unique opportunity to give East London a valuable position in the metropolitan area again. The presence of the Olympic Games, which only last a few weeks, is being seized as an opportunity for one of the largest urban renewal operations in Europe. The tremendous intensification and the investment that goes with it will be used as a catalyser for long-term upgrading. Part of the infrastructure for the Games will lead a new life as facilities for the new city district. What is especially important is the network function of public spaces as a matrix for urban development.

What can the Netherlands learn from London?
The strategy has to be well-thought out in advance. An event like this is an opportunity you only get once. London's idea of using the Games as a motor for urban renewal is not new. Barcelona also did it, in 1992. It worked very well there; public space in particular profited hugely. But it was a disaster with the World Fairs in New York (1964) and Montreal (1967). And the investments in the Olympic Games in Athens (2004) also came to nothing, leaving tremendous wastelands in their wake.

That was a lost opportunity...
Not only a lost opportunity, but also very bad for the entire urban area! They are still facing years of dealing with areas and buildings that require enormous amounts of money for upkeep or demolition. By using a large event to revitalise a district, you kill two birds with one stone.

What can the Games be used for in the Netherlands?
In the Netherlands we should take advantage of the Games to above all strengthen certain parts of the Randstad as a polycentric urban agglomeration in Western Holland and connect them better to each other, for instance by improving public transport. Outside the Randstad, very few problems come into play. It's quiet there; the relationship between built-up and undeveloped land is reasonable and there are no great logistic problems.

Apart from Barcelona, are there lessons to be learned from other large events?
The Games in Los Angeles (1984) were a success, but did not contribute much added value to the city afterwards. Cities like Amsterdam and Berlin still have Olympic stadiums that function well. But, to my knowledge, the only event that had real urban allure was the one that took place in Barcelona. This has also been true of several World Fairs recently. In Lisbon, it looks like an attractive new city district is actually being created. What will happen in Seville is still relatively uncertain.

Where will the Olympic fire soon be burning?
It's better to spread the Games over several cities, but near a transportation corridor. Here in the Netherlands we should bring Almere into the picture, for example, and see whether it's possible to have something take place on the coast near the Hook of Holland. Strategic steps can also be taken for urban renewal zones, like the area around the Kuip stadium in Rotterdam.

What can the Games offer the Netherlands?
First of all, it is a very interesting occurrence, because it brings in a tremendous amount of money and puts an area on the map. It's an international branding factor for the Netherlands. It initiates all sorts of secondary economic and cultural activities.

Is the Netherlands ready for it?
Very few other countries, with perhaps the exception of Singapore and Switzerland, are so well-organised and have such harmonious relations between business and government as the Netherlands. Our problem is the lack of generous donors. But if the business world can be mobilised, there's a very good chance that we will win the bid for the Olympic Games. If the Greeks can do it, so can we.

In the race for 2012, KCAP/ASTOC also designed an Olympic Village for Leipzig...
There was an internal competition going on in Germany for the nomination, with plans for the Games to be concentrated in one location. They didn't get it. Germany would have been better off following the same strategy used during the European football championships, in other words dividing the action over several stadiums in different cities and then having the players fly back and forth by plane. The Netherlands is much smaller, so transportation between stadiums is not a problem and can be done by helicopter, for example. In Leipzig the plan also focused on the revitalisation of a small, formerly industrial harbour area. After the Games, Leipzig would have had a new city district there.

What will be left of the Olympic feeling in Lea Valley after the Games?
The Olympic Stadium will be scaled back after the games. Some 20,000 of the originally 80,000 seats will be left over, situated in a recessed pit. The swimming pool designed by Zaha Hadid will also be kept, as well as a few other buildings. We are trying to integrate them into the district. The park along the River Lea is the most vitally important aspect, however.

Do you see any problems in terms of organising the Olympic Games?
No. Of course there's always the risk of sabotage or terrorism. And that danger is even greater because of fools like Wilders [a right-wing politician known for his anti-Islamic opinions - HdH].

Finally, how old will you be in 2028 and where would you like to be when you are watching the Games?
By then I will – hopefully – be 75 and probably I will be sitting as usual in the Kuip, in the KCAP's Skybox.

Could you give us a motto for the Dutch Games 2028?
Randstad as Olympic Ring City.

'Amsterdam has a name of tolerance to live up to'

Job Cohen and Carolien Gehrels in a dual interview by Mieke Dings

Job Cohen (JC) is Mayor of Amsterdam and a member of the PvdA [Dutch Labour Party – MD]. He was formerly State Secretary of Justice and Rector of Maastricht University.

Carolien Gehrels (CG) is Amsterdam city councillor for the PvdA and responsible for the Sport and Culture portfolio, among other things. Previously she was managing director of Berenschot Communicatie, where she helped design the city marketing of Amsterdam.

Involvement in the Olympic Games 2028:
JC: It all started at the Games in Athens (2004), where I had been invited as mayor of an Olympic city, and where the question of whether we shouldn't do it another time was being bandied about. Then the NOC*NSF invited me and several other people to the Winter Games in Turin to think about the idea further. There I very enthusiastically stated that the Games could inject tremendous vitality into the Netherlands. After that, the NOC*NSF started taking the idea seriously. Ivo Opstelten and I immediately agreed that there shouldn't be any discussion about where the Games would take place. We think it was more important to make 2028 a real option for the Netherlands.
CG: In May of 2006, a few months after the Games in Turin, I became city councillor for Sport and Culture – a kind of Olympic councillor, in fact. The combination of these two broad spheres of action – which was not inspired by the plans for the Games, by the way – makes it possible to connect all sorts of things like the economy, health, environmental planning, innovation and accessibility. Such connections offer many opportunities for our city as well as opportunities for hosting the Olympic Games.

Plays an Olympic sport:
JC: No, not anymore. I used to play field hockey and tennis, and also non-Olympic sports.
CG: At one time I was a fanatic korfball player; that was an Olympic sport only once, in 1928. Nowadays I bike and walk.

Most impressive Olympic Games and memorable sports moment:
CG: I thought the opening ceremony in Los Angeles 1984 was so beautiful, with 84 grand pianos being played at the same time. And it was absolutely fantastic that our DJ Tiësto could open the Games in Athens – especially because he is such big hero amongst young people.
JC: This is a very complicated question, because there are so many of them. On the tragic side, I remember Munich 1972. On the cheerful side, I can still vividly recall how Anton Geesink became judo champion in Japan, and how our volleyball players in Atlanta performed so magnificently. What I also found extremely exceptional were the Games in Sydney, where a good friend of mine was chef d'equipe, so I was able to experience them from close up. And of course that's also where we won the most medals in our Olympic history.

What do your ideal Olympic Games 2028 look like?
CG: They take place in the Netherlands, in the Randstad [the urban agglomeration of Western of Holland – MD]. Ideally, we will utilise everything we have in terms of infrastructure, sports accommodations, hotels and roads and we will also use the Games to develop the country with an eye to the future. We should think of the Randstad in the broad sense, or even beyond that. Eindhoven already has made great name for itself with swimming, of course, and Theo Bos has put Alkmaar on the map with bicycling. We must make this a joint effort; it's not only about the accommodations, but also the clubs, the volunteers, the recreational sports. An event like this forces you to make decisions. I think Barcelona (1992) is the best example; the Games were hosted there with the idea that it would be good for the Catalonians, who traditionally have a hard time agreeing with one another, to have a common goal. I think a common goal like that would be good for the Dutch too. It creates a communal feeling of opening the windows to the

world and to the future.

JC: The magnitude of the Games is such that they could never be held in Amsterdam alone. The entire country has to be involved. The Games can jump up accessibility, as happened in Athens with a new metro line from the airport to the city. The Games are a goal on the horizon for improving very many aspects of our society. And not just: "It's something to think about" or "We'll set up a committee to deal with it." A great deal of administrative power will be necessary in order to produce a lasting legacy.

What kind of opportunities can the Games present to Amsterdam?

CG: Lots of them. We can do something with the Olympic Village within the scope of the 'double city' Almere – Amsterdam. If we simultaneously tackle the infrastructure, we'll make a lot of the residents in those cities happy. Besides that, I see the Games as a chance to upgrade existing accommodations as much as possible. Right now we are already working on the Wagenerstadion in the Amsterdamse Bos – the Wembley Stadium for field hockey. We want to expand the capacity of the Amsterdam Arena to 75,000 people or more. We are already preparing the old Olympic Stadium for larger events by building a warm-up track for the athletes. That will make this stadium – one of the oldest Olympic stadiums still in good repair – a triple-A location. This stadium marks the beginning of a sports axis that cuts across the Zuidas district, currently undergoing development, and ends at the Wagnerstadion. We are already intensifying this axis, also for all of the businesspeople who will soon be working in the Zuidas district and wanting to hit a ball at lunchtime or play field hockey after work. So a lot of new facilities are going to be built there.

JC: In the near future we will be able to accommodate various sports here. Besides field hockey, football, and track and field events, there will also be tennis, equestrian sports in the Amsterdamse Bos and various indoor sports such as basketball and volleyball. We can pick out a fantastic spot for the Olympic Village, but it could be outside Amsterdam as well. That can give a strong boost to both accessibility and tourism.

What are the must-see spots for the athletes and the public?

CG: The Amsterdamse Bos, the Olympic stadium, the canals, the Museumplein, the Dam, but also the intersection of the sports axis and the Zuidas. The guests will be visiting many of these places of their own accord. They will want to stay here a while longer, sleep in beautiful hotels, make a boat tour of the canals, walk around the Pijp, the Baarsjes or the Rivieren districts; they will want to enjoy everyday life – and culture is one the most important elements in this.

How can we combine sports and culture even more?

CG: We can develop innovative formulas in order to show sports and the splendour of Amsterdam to the public and to the world. We have to think creatively about this. For instance, one of my dreams – if we succeed in getting the prologue of the Giro d'Italia here in 2010 – is to have the runners take off from the stage in the Concertgebouw while the orchestra plays from the balcony. Once they arrive at the Museumplein they turn a corner and end up in the Olympic Stadium. For me, that's the ultimate connection between sports and culture. With the Olympic Games we will bring in world-class cultural events to add lustre to the celebrations. But fashion and product development can also bring innovation to the world of sports while getting a boost from the Games themselves. We have enough to offer in this area: soon we will have Experimenta Design here; we already have Droog Design, Marcel Wanders and so forth. Of course, Eindhoven is also very strong in this department and that's why we should work together in this.

What issues will Amsterdam put on the map by having the Games here?

JC: I think that sustainability and tolerance would be great issues to put on the map with the Olympic Games. Amsterdam is traditionally a city with a tremendous influx of people from totally different cultures and we have a name of tolerance to live up to. The Games are a good reason to bring tolerance back in the spotlight again.

Does tolerance really go together with the polarising effect that the Games also usually have?

JC: Well, I think that the more often political problems are associated with sports, the more important it is to plead for tolerance. Naturally it will always be a celebration of athletes, where that fine maxim "participating is more important than winning" does not altogether apply, but nevertheless it does attest to tolerance and, ultimately, willingness to recognise the achievements of the best. In that sense, tolerance amongst athletes is reflected in society. In general, sports promote social cohesion because they require discipline and create responsibilities. On the whole, these characteristics contribute to better social relations. That's why it is also so important to invest not only in top sports but also recreational sports, which can profit from this.

CG: We can use the Olympic Games and many other events to develop talent and make and strengthen connections with the clubs, so that the top and the base nurture and inspire each other. I see an opportunity for basketball, for example. When you bicycle through Amsterdam, you see more and more kids playing basketball. It's a sport that's in vogue, partly because America has a top-class team that appeals to the imagination. Just recently the MyGuide club was formed in Amsterdam. The Games can be a great long-term objective for developing that club, building a good hall where kids can train a couple of times a week and in that way not only spreading the sport, but also cultivating talent.

The plans for holding the Games in Amsterdam in 1992 didn't work out. Why do we suddenly have a chance of bringing the Olympic Games here now? What have we learned from 1992?

CG: This time we are going at it much more thoroughly and starting much earlier. Back then it was just an idea and people took it from there. Now it is a movement initiated by the NOC*NSF and we are starting at the base, which is to say, getting our sports climate in order. We are doing feasibility studies and research on spatial possibilities; we have to prove that we are a land of sports in 2016, yet the decision will only be made in 2021. So we have much more time and opportunity to make people enthusiastic. And from my own experience I can testify that when you become aware of everything that the Games can bring about, you automatically start believing in them.
My fellow councilman Lodewijk Asscher's recent visit to Stockholm is a good example. He went to a completely sustainable ecological district, which was only there because Stockholm had made a bid for the Games in 2004. In other words, simply making a bid can bring about improvements such as this. 2028 is close enough to know that we have to start now and far enough away to be able to prepare our plans well.

JC: At that time I lived in Maastricht, so I can't speak about the failure of 1992 from my own experience. That failure did make it clear, however, that the Games must be more than simply a celebration of sport. The entire country must stand behind them and that means greater profit must be gained than from those few weeks of activity alone.

How will Amsterdam show it is ready for the Games over the next few years?

JC: The Sport Plan recently presented by Carolien Gehrels thoroughly examines the connection between general and top sports. To be able to host the Games, we above all must prove that we have a good sports climate and are capable of organising events. Amsterdam has applied to the NOC*NSF as a candidate for one of the top sports and education centres, and that means that we have to meet strict requirements, in particular that eight federations must be willing to organise programmes for top sports in Amsterdam. What's more, we are working hard on having the Giro start in Amsterdam in 2010 and we would like to play a main role in the World Cup Football in 2018. We don't yet have any plans ready for Amsterdam for the Olympic Games. Naturally we are always thinking about the development of the country and the Amsterdam region, and the Olympic Games fit in perfectly with this. They can even speed up such plans. The underground infrastructure in the Zuidas will have to be ready by then and the entire Axis must be in a much further stage of development. But I don't think it would be wise to make our own Olympic plans at an early stage like this.

How old will you be in 2028 and where would you like to watch the Olympic Games?

CG: 60. And naturally I will be in Amsterdam in the Olympic Stadium.
JC: 81. Me too. I'll hobble over there on my cane.

Have you got a sports quote or motto to warm up the people of Amsterdam for the Olympic Games in 2028?

CG: The top inspires the base and the base nourishes the top. This way I've included all Amsterdammers.
JC: The Olympic Games bring vitality.

WHY THE NETHERLANDS?

OLYMPIC FIRE 123

THE NETHERLANDS IS TOLERANT AND OPEN!

According to the United Nations' Human Development Index (HDI), the Netherlands ranks among the top ten of 150 nations in terms of high quality of life. This score is determined by measuring education, life expectancy, living standards and income.
The Netherlands, holding 7th place for democratic development, is also a highly developed country in terms of its political institutions, political liberties, electoral system, civil rights and freedom of press. For transparency versus corruption, the Netherlands is the 8th least corrupt nation in the world. The Netherlands also ranks 7th in accepting new citizens per capita.

Why the Netherlands? **OLYMPIC FIRE** 125

HDI (human development index)

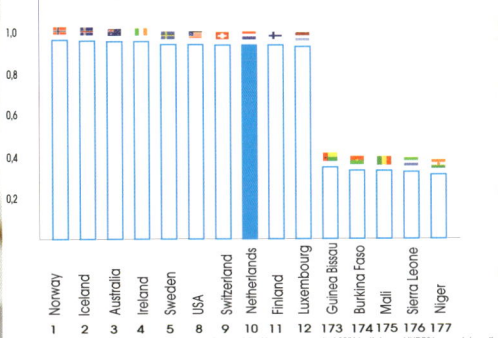

democracy ranking

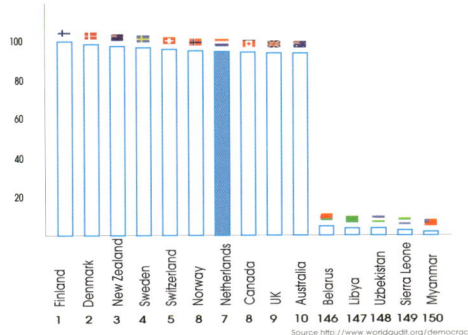

transparency ranking

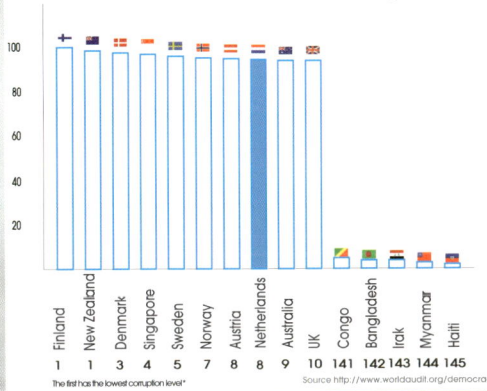

immigration, new citizen per capita x1000

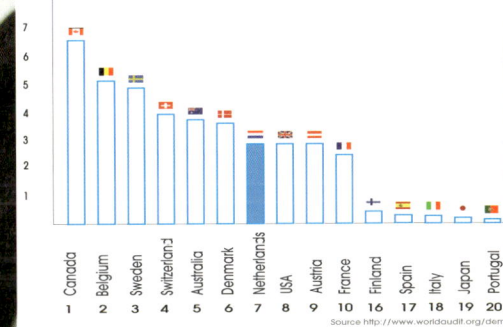

national pride

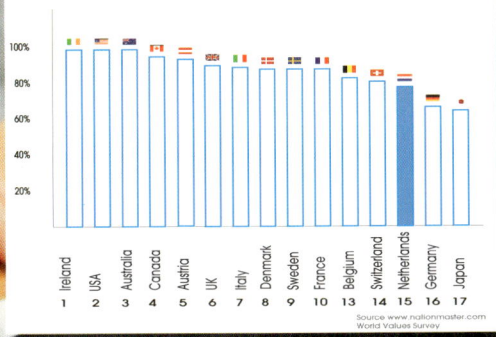

THE NETHERLANDS IS WEALTHY AND GENEROUS!

Even though the Netherlands is a small country in terms of physical area, it has the 16th largest economy in the world and its GDP capita holds 10th place. The Netherlands is one of the world's wealthiest nations.

The prevailing opinion used to be that Dutch society was stingy; however, the Netherlands is one of the most generous nations in the world, giving more than 4 billion dollars a year in economic aid, and ranking in the 6th place. It holds 8th place in the world for taxation as percentage of GDP. Compare this to the economies of the United States and Germany, which are respectively 20 times and 4 times larger than the Dutch economy: they respectively contribute only 3 billion and 2 billion more.

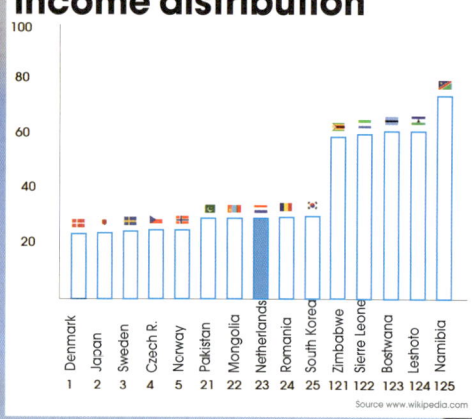

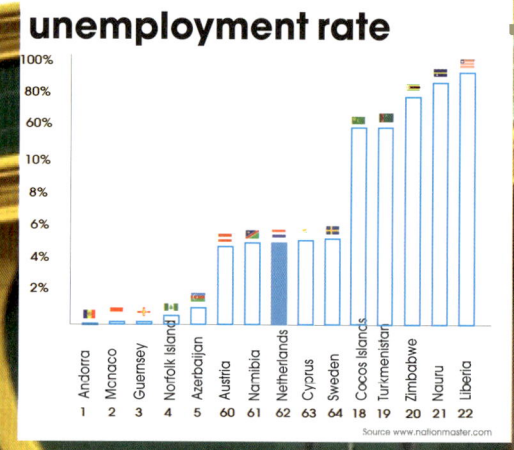

Why the Netherlands? **OLYMPIC FIRE**

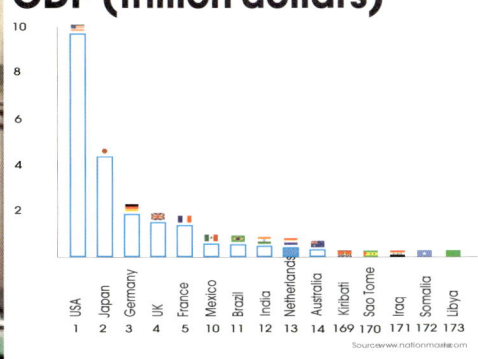

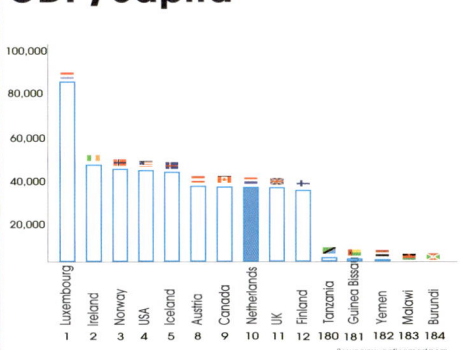

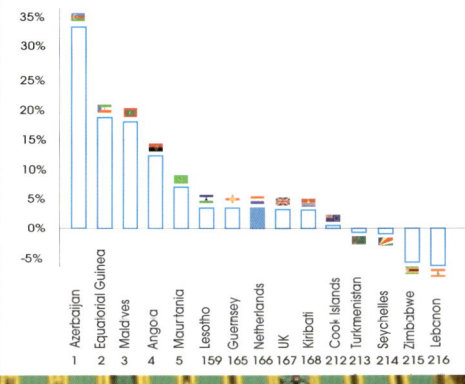

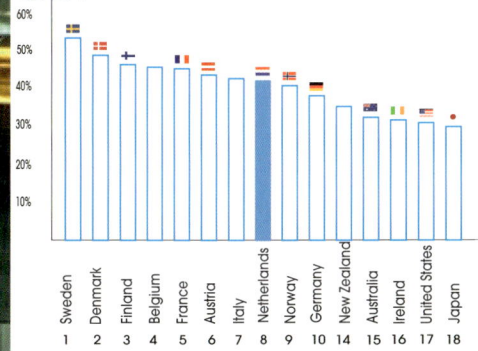

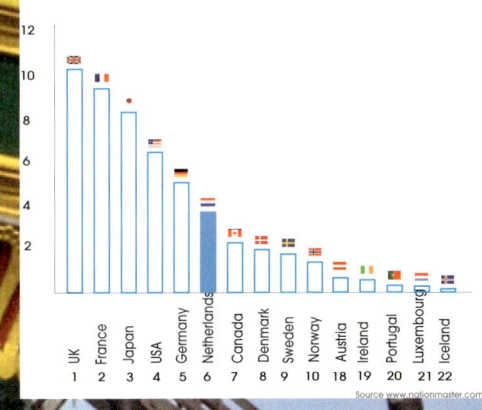

THE NETHERLANDS IS OVERWEIGHT AND NEEDS TO DO MORE SPORTS!

One of the biggest concerns of our society nowadays is obesity, due to the sedentary lifestyle and surplus food production in developed countries. According to the Body Mass Index, more than 40% of Dutch people are overweight. In other European countries, however, the problem of overweight is even worse. Dutch people are in 5th place amongst Europeans for time doing sports, but in Finland and Sweden people spend 60% more time doing sports than the Dutch do.

THE NETHERLANDS HAS LOTS OF INFRASTRUCTURE BUT IS CAUGHT IN A TRAFFIC JAM!

The Netherlands is a well-connected country in terms of infrastructure. Even though it is a small country, it is a world hub with the 4th busiest airport in Europe and the 12th busiest in the world. Rotterdam is the largest port in Europe and third largest in the world in terms of cargo.

The Netherlands has the densest network of roads in Europe, the busiest railway lines and the largest network of closely connected waterways.

Even with its extensive public transport systems, the country has a strong dependency on private automobiles. The Dutch railway system is the most highly congested in Europe and the third in terms of overall use. What is the alternative for reducing the country's dependency on cars in the future?

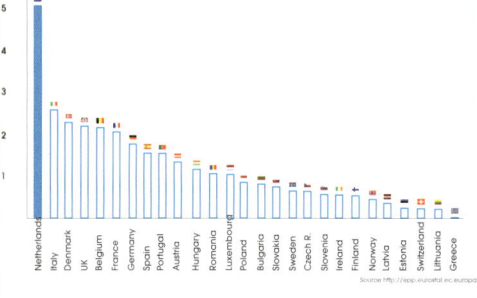

railway network utilisation (million passenger/km year)

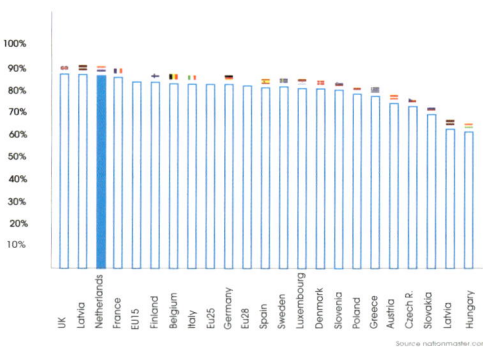

% passenger/km by cars in Europe

Why the Netherlands? **OLYMPIC FIRE** 131

biggest ports by cargo (million ton/year)

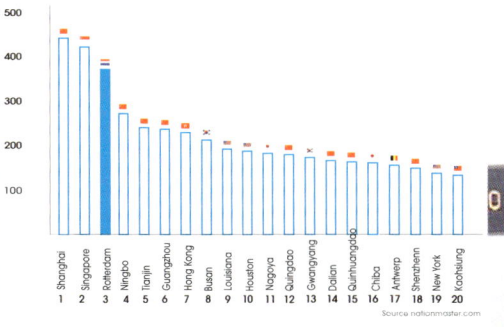

biggest airports by passengers (million/year)

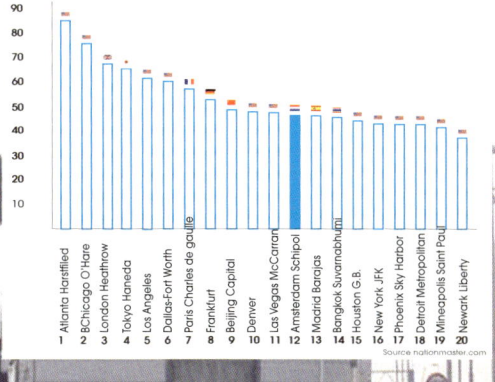

motorway density (km/1000km²)

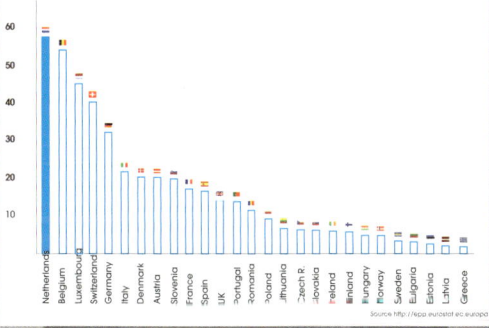

waterway density (km/1000km²)

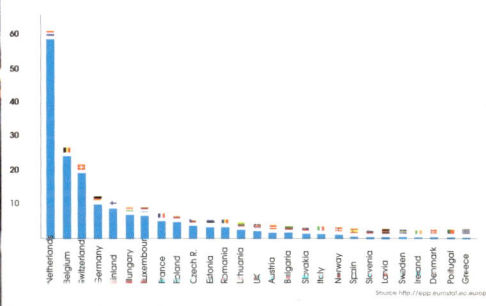

% passenger/km by busses in Europe

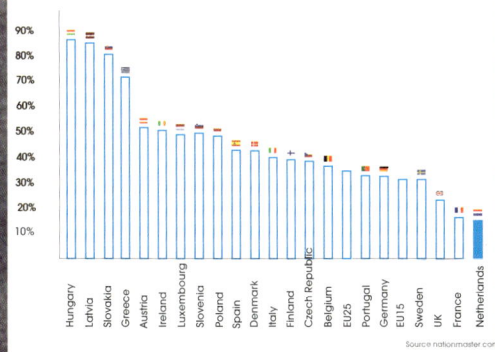

% passenger/km by rail in Europe

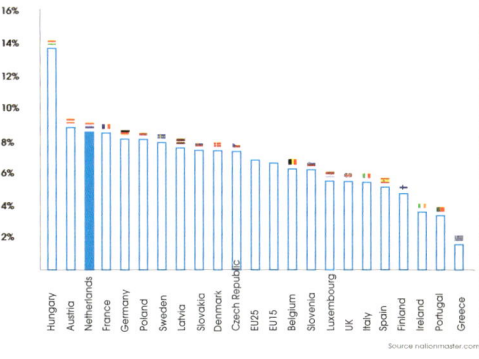

THE NETHERLANDS IS CONSCIENTIOUS AND PROTECTS ITS ENVIRONMENT!

After Belgium, the Netherlands is the country with the highest anthropogenic impact. Its population density is very high. Despite ranking second, after Denmark, in the generation of waste per capita, ranking amongst the top 20 for CO_2 emissions per capita, being 6th for the presence of NO_2 in the air, and one of the countries with the least acreage of protected land per capita, the Netherlands is number 1 in controlling pollution as a percentage of GDP.

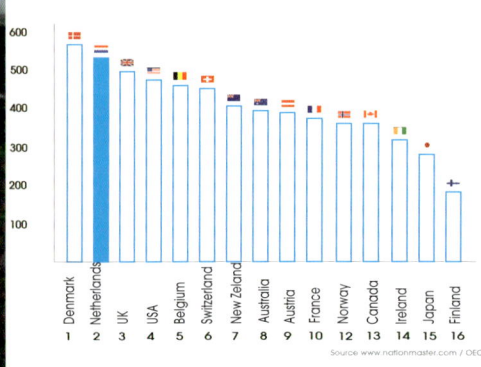

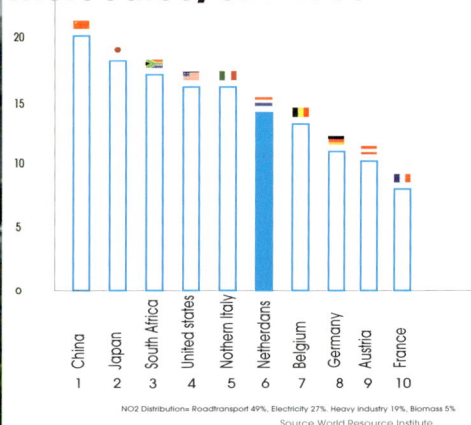

Why the Netherlands? **OLYMPIC FIRE**

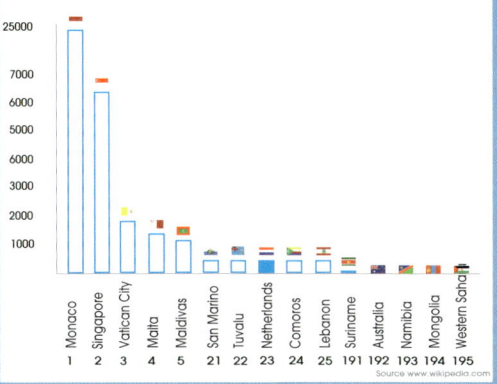

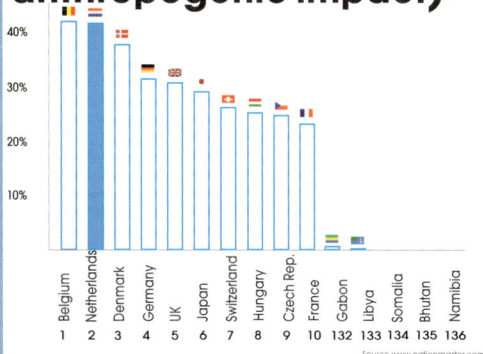

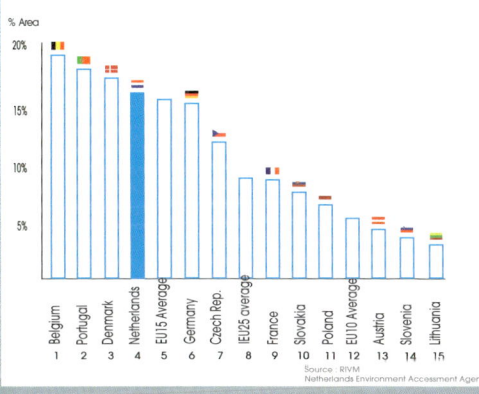

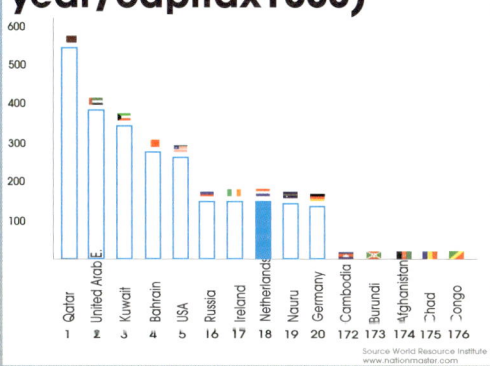

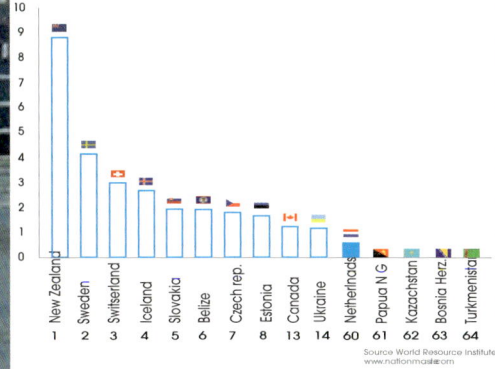

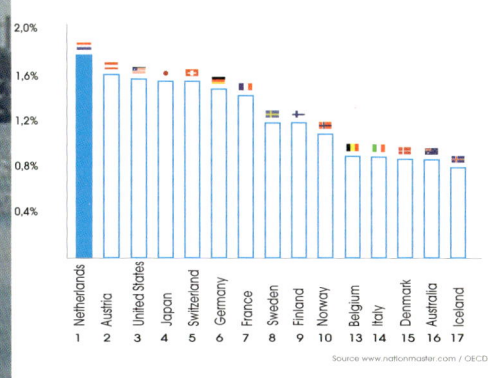

THE NETHERLANDS IS TOTALLY WIRED!

In term of mass media, the Netherlands is a well-connected country. In Europe it ranks as the number 1 country for cable television subscriptions and 3rd for Internet accessibility.

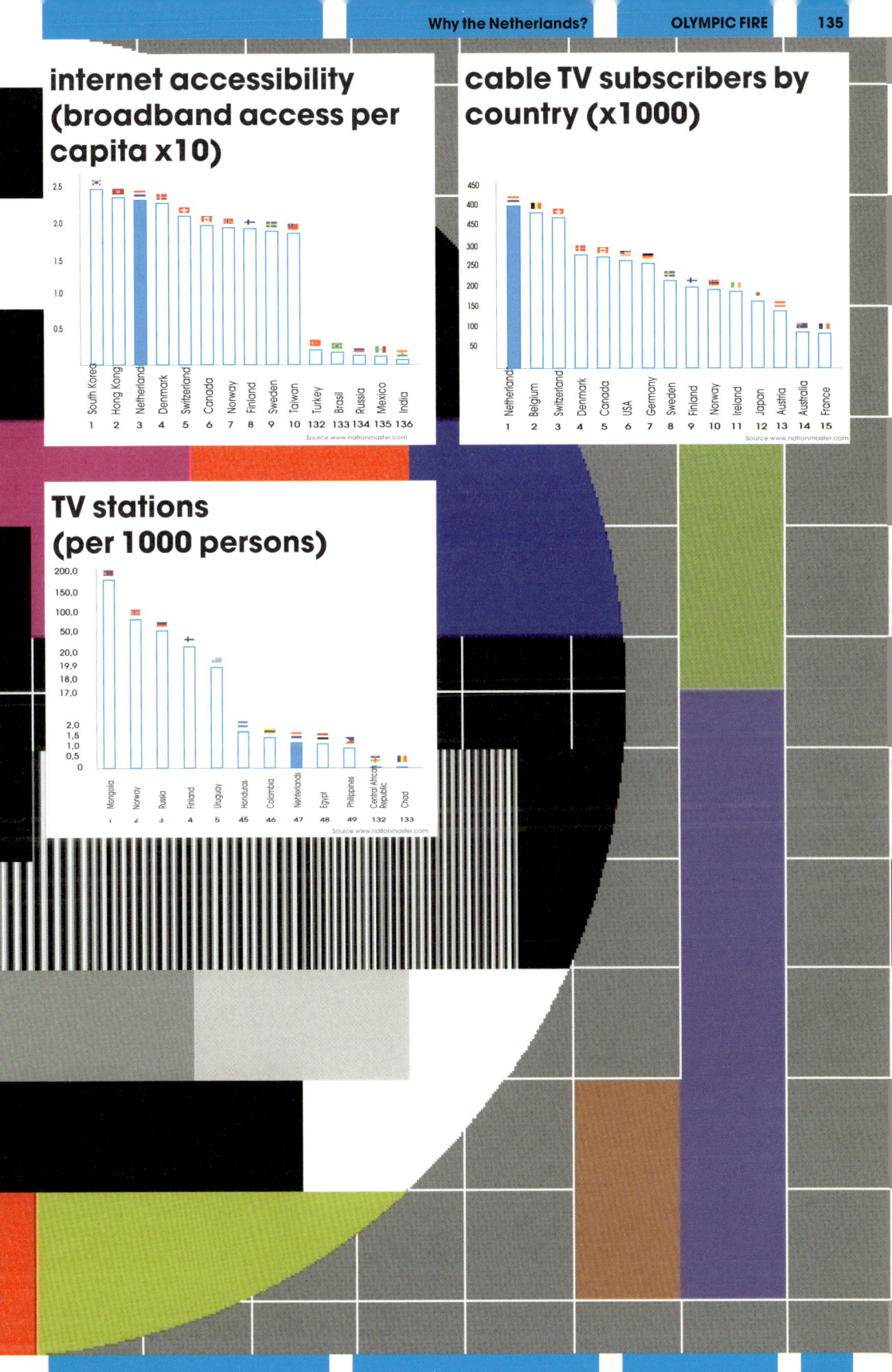

Future bids?

The Olympics have become a global phenomenon. Although athletes from all over the world participate in them, historically most of the Games have been held in Europe, the United States and Australia. In the future, we can expect a more equal distribution across the world. Once financial and political issues are overcome, it's a matter of showing that you can do it. There is a good chance that the Games will be held in Africa – most likely South Africa, if it proves capable of organizing the World Cup in 2010. The emerging economic importance of Arab, South American and Southeast Asian countries will also have an impact on the selection of host cities. It is quite probable that each continent will take turns organizing the games in the near future.

So, why the NL? Why in 2028?

How can the Netherlands compete in this context? What kind of example can we offer to the world? Why and when would the NL be chosen?

In 2012, the Games are going to be held in Europe; if the continental rotation system is followed, 2016 might go to South America, 2020 to Africa, and 2024 to an Arab country. This would give Europe another chance in 2028, and seeing as the 1928 Games were held in Amsterdam, the centennial anniversary of those Games would give the Netherlands a unique selling point.

NL has a well-established, wealthy economy, has an ageing population with long life expectancy, and is densely populated, highly educated, intercultural, innovative, organized, open, and democratic, and has good infrastructure. Yet Dutch society is also suffering from environmental pressures, social segregation, climate change, obesity and bureaucracy. One could argue that the current state of the NL is the future of the world! The population of the world is still growing, there is a global economy and our natural resources are under pressure: what are we going to do?

The Netherlands has become highly successful in dealing with spatial planning. Being forced to adapt to nature necessitates technical know-how, pragmatism, radical thinking and a belief in your own abilities, but also social cohesion, transparency and openness.

The Netherlands can organize large-scale events, and of course we also have our long history of water management and landfill legacy, but why would the world want the Netherlands to organize the Olympic Games? What can we offer that they could learn? What kind of Olympic proposal besides a technical bid would attract worldwide attention? Could the dream of a sports-minded and healthy society, in combination with reinvigorated, radical spatial planning, become the deciding factor?

On the other hand, what would the Netherlands gain? How could we benefit from organizing the Olympic Games? Can a three-week event account for such large-scale investments?

It can, if we organise the Olympics in a way that has a national impact but international resonance: combining the Olympic programme with the issues of migration and mobility by establishing a sustainable relation with water, for instance, or dealing with urban density and sprawl in a sensible way.

'Games in the heart of Europe, powered by energy from the new Falling Lake'

Rudolf Das interviewed by Mieke Dings

Rudolf Das is a visual futurologist. For many years he has managed a firm for technical illustrations, together with his identical twin brother Robbert Das. They still illustrate and publish together on a regular basis. Their most recent book is Toekomstflitsen (Flashes of the Future) (Tirion Publishers, 2004).

Involvement with Olympic Games 2028: No. I have in the past made some sketches for possibilities in Rotterdam, which at the time was considering competing with Amsterdam for the 1992 bid. I sketched a few stadiums, pointed out where the swimming pool complex might be built and how the city could involve Ahoy [a sports/convention centre in Rotterdam - MD]. But that was all. I have also, when the Olympic site in Munich was under construction, made a number of survey drawings of the entire site. At the time everybody was really taken aback by the roof construction that Frei Otto had designed for the stadium.
Practicing an Olympic sport: I play tennis.
Most impressive Olympic Games: That's not very difficult to answer. The Games in Munich in 1972 with the drama of the Israeli athletes.
Memorable sports moment: The first thing that comes to mind - being a terribly old person of course - is that Fanny Blankers-Koen won just about anything there was to win in London in 1948.

What will the world look like in 2028?
That's not so far ahead, a mere twenty years. I don't think that anything will have changed essentially then. My greatest hope is that we will be able to control the coal disaster looming on the horizon. In the next few years China and India will build almost 900 power plants fuelled by coal. They will want to build them very fast and they will not install the purification systems we have here in the West. Besides, they will transport all the coal over land, which will lead to even more carbon dioxide emissions. The pollution will be enormous.
There is hope though, in the development of new nuclear energy. The new reactors will not be cooled by water but by liquid sodium. They can use any type of waste for fuel. This new nuclear energy will not only solve our waste problem, it will also be much more terrorist proof, because the fuel (contaminated plutonium and uranium 239) cannot be used to make bombs. It also is much more energy-efficient. China, India and Japan have already ordered the first reactors.
If by then we make hybrid or electric cars mandatory, we will have solved the biggest problem.

And what will the Olympic Games look like then?
The Games should be a major event that unites people because they all watch the same thing at the same time, and television will enhance this effect. Few people realize the impact of such a mega sports event. Athletes and the audience can communicate with each other because they all literally and figuratively speak the same language. This year, in Beijing, there will be no way to prevent thousands of human contacts between Chinese people and visitors. And all the people watching the games on TV at home will have a better understanding of the country as well. That's why I think we should not overemphasize political issues now, but should wait a little until mutual contacts have generated more space and understanding.

Should we cherish the Olympic spirit?
Most certainly. After all, it is the spirit that brings together people from all over the world. The only thing I don't like very much is this continuous tussle about who gets to organize the Games where. About ten years ago I made some drawings for a permanent site for the Games in Greece, where they could be held every four years with global financial support. That has been a serious option for a while. But then the Americans were also bidding and commercial interests

offered so much money that the international sports federations couldn't refuse. All countries, in the end, see the Games as an opportunity to make money.
Actually, it would be a good thing to give a continent like Africa – threatened by poverty to be reduced to some sort of nature reserve only visited by holidaymakers but long since deserted by the Africans themselves – an enormous boost by organizing the Games there. But then, Africa has no money, except for the South, maybe. If only a few of those rather heavy-set types over there who have gathered enough money and put it all in their own pockets would make a generous gesture…

What will the Olympic Games 2028 be like in the Netherlands?
I'm not so sure we should emphasize the Netherlands too much. I favour working with the Benelux, Germany perhaps, and France. After all, these are the countries that have propagated the idea of European collaboration, an idea that fits in seamlessly with the Olympic spirit. Call this area the 'Heart of Europe' or something like that. This will offer more opportunities to raise funds and find locations for all the sports events and facilities.

Why not go out onto the water?
We could of course dike in the Markermeer [the southern part of the former Zuiderzee not yet reclaimed as land – MD] and hold the games there. We might as well build the second airport there that we seem to need so desperately in addition to Schiphol.

Which spatial issues could be boosted by the Games?
If we keep growing at this pace, we will have 20 million people in 20 years' time. In that case we should stop developing 'Vinex' locations [new large-scale urban developments – MD] and opt for ground-saving measures. I can see us living in so-called 'hill buildings', where houses and gardens are not stacked vertically but at an angle of 45 degrees. These could be built in densities of 70 houses per hectare, whereas the average Vinex development offers not even half that number. At the bottom we can first build the Olympic facilities, then put all the cars on top of that, so we can use the space between the buildings for green, water and a couple of main roads.
The roads should also change considerably. In twenty years' time we will have the first automated lanes. On the main highways we can then drive automatically if we want to. The other day I made a test drive at the Ministry of Transport. We had eight cars lined up and we had to let go of the steering wheel because the road was controlling us by means of infrared induction. At one point they brought the front car to an abrupt halt, and because of the radar distance-guarding system the other cars also immediately stopped. A very efficient system. Let's take humans out of the equation on the main roads; they can take a nap or read the paper.

Will these high-tech novelties also influence the Games themselves?
Yes, we can see that even now. Time measuring equipment has become so sophisticated that the length of the swimmers' nails can make a difference. You notice how swimmers like Inge de Bruyn grow their nails so they can touch the finish a split second sooner. And now there is this new swimsuit that has more buoyancy, so you can go even faster. Other tools will be perfected as well, such as drugs. And of course the increasingly clever training methods that have become so complex that no one but the experts still understand them.
I personally believe that the Olympic Games should be careful not to get carried away by all these high-tech fireworks and try to stay as close to sports as possible. The primitive aspect of sports is precisely what will be its appeal in tomorrow's technical world. We very much like to see 'normal' people. Maybe the Games ought to be split up: one with drugs and one without, just like the Tour de France, which probably will be organizing two separates events long before that.
In the future, viewers will have access to much more information about the condition of the athletes: what is their heart rate? How much did they eat? How much did they drink? Etc. This information, which is now the exclusive domain of coaches, will strengthen the competitive element.

What can we expect in the area of sustainability?
By that time we must of course be able to generate emission-free energy. Besides new nuclear power plants we could make much better use of windmills. The windmills we are currently using have not yet matured. In fact, they are even worse

than the windmills our ancestors built 450 years ago. A miller could slow down his mill by reefing in the sails, while our modern windmills have to be taken out of operation at force 7 or higher – the very point at which there occurs a quadratic increase of energy production – because the poles they stand on start to vibrate too much. No wonder, when you put such heavy generators in them! They should have been placed on the ground. In this way green energy is of course much too expensive. By placing a small propeller at the back, turning in the opposite direction of the front propeller, the problem would partly be solved.

I propose to also create a huge reservoir before the coast of Zeeuws-Vlaanderen [the most south-western province – MD] for windless days. This reservoir, about the size of Texel [one of the islands in the north; 600 km2 / 230 mile2 – MD] will be surrounded by a ring-shaped dike with turbines and pumps on one side. When winds are really strong, you use the green wind energy to pump the seawater out until the water level inside the dike is 40 to 50 meters lower. Then, on days with very little wind, you let the water back in (driving the turbines), and in this way you generate a lot of energy for very little money. This idea for a so-called 'Falling Lake' is now being studied by the Innovation Platform, and the big energy companies are all very enthusiastic.

This lake would also be a great place to hold the rowing event. By the way, can't all these athletes generate their own energy?
Well, running seems to generate energy. Suits and shoes are currently being developed that generate electricity while you run. But of course the amounts are very small.

In what kind of buildings will we be watching the Games?
In a marvellous stadium surrounded by clusters of other buildings to house all those other sports. May be we could have a village in the shape of the Olympic rings with a huge horn in the middle.

A regular stadium, then?
Yes, I think that works best. We can all be watching it on television, but we would rather experience the cheering crowds. The swimming championships the other day were a great success precisely because there was a crowd. At least, that's what the swimmers themselves said. One huge super stadium for all sports would not be a good idea; it is too chaotic. Besides, people often come specifically to watch one sport.

And where in the heart of Europe will this Olympic Stadium arise?
It will have to be on a large site that has a lot of space and lies at some sort of transportation crossroads. I don't know where that is, either. In twenty years' time traffic will be even more congested than it is now. The train will have become an obsolete invention, having lost out to automatic buses and automated lanes.

Do you think that the heart of Europe has a chance for the 2028 bid?
I don't hold much hope for it. In the end it is the political powers that be that will decide these things, and if we take a global view and look at all the continents, we see that Western Europe has had its turn quite often already. And if the games do take place in Europe, then perhaps in Greece, in the form of a permanent site.

How old will you be in 2028 and where will you be watching the Olympic Games then?
I won't be alive anymore. No, I would be 99 years old and I'm not going to make that. But if I do, I will be watching everything from my easy chair. I wouldn't be able to do much more anyway. I should count myself lucky if I can still hold open my eyelids with matchsticks by then.

Can you think of a sports motto to prepare us for the coming of the Games?
Not a sports motto, but "Up, Sammy, look up, Sammy" [a phrase from a well-known Dutch song – MD]. You can interpret that symbolically, but it also literally refers to korfball players who have to aim high in order to score points and by doing so might even qualify it to become an official Olympic event.

WHAT IS CURRENT STATE OF NL SPORT FACILIT

'Why would I care what a hall looks like?'

Anton Geesink interviewed by Mieke Dings

Involvement with Olympic Games 2028: I am an honorary member of the recommending committee, which is a representative and ceremonial function. However, when the nomination takes place in 2020 I probably won't be a member any more because then I will be approaching 90.

Still practicing an Olympic sport?: No, all my time is devoted to my work as an IOC representative in the Netherlands, which is a lot of work. I do a little walking and that's about it. I haven't practiced judo for ages.

Most impressive Olympic Games: That's an easy one. They are and always will be the Games in Tokyo where I won a gold medal myself. The fact that I won it in Japan, the homeland of judo, made it even better.

Memorable sports moment: I don't remember all the names, but I think all sportspeople are super. Anyone with an Olympic title – myself excluded – is super. Like those Russian heavyweights, or Greco-Roman wrestlers: marvellous.

As an athlete, did you see anything of the cities where the Games took place?
No, hardly anything at all. During the games I was mostly on the mat or at other locations in the Olympic Village. Because you have everything there: an athletics track, a restaurant. There is no need to leave the Village.

You must have seen something of the surroundings from within the Village?
No. Those Villages were always situated at the edge of town, just outside the zone with the nice buildings. You had nothing to do with the surroundings or with the atmosphere outside the Village. My match in Tokyo was on the very last day of the Games, anyway.

And in the training period before that?
Well, I did know Japan before, of course. I had been coming there regularly since 1956. I found it a beautiful country with wonderful people, and still find it so. Prior to the Games I would train in an area some 600 kilometres south of Tokyo. The university was in rural surroundings, so that was a bonus. I would train a lot there in the woods, in the water, and so on.

Did you feel that your surroundings influenced your achievements?
No, I never thought about it like that and I've never consciously sought out places either. I would also train in the mountains in Austria or France and in the woods near Utrecht, and in large cities as well. It didn't make much difference to me.

Where in the Netherlands would you situate the Games?
I have no idea. We are talking about 2028, which is two or three generations beyond my time. If I were good at speculating I would be working on the stock exchange.

What must still be done in order to be ready for 2028?
There's not much work still to be done in terms of sports-mindedness, because nowadays some 30 to 35 percent of the population is engaged in organised sports. Which is an awful lot. We will have to build more facilities though, as there aren't enough of those yet.

Do you have any tips for the architects? You have competed in several halls after all.
Well, the judo hall in Tokyo was one of the best I've ever seen. But of course that is also because I won a gold medal there. It was a nice, big hall.

What did it look like?
Like I said: nice and big. What more can I say? Why would I care what a hall looks like? I went there to win my judo match, not to look at the hall.

How old will you be in 2028 and where will you be watching the Olympic Games then?
I will be 94 then and I'll be watching them at home.

Can you think of a sports quote or slogan to make the country rally behind the idea of hosting the Olympic Games 2028?
There is no need for that at all. It is such a well-known event. There will be plenty of people who will come to enjoy the games.

'No reason to get excited'

Jaap van Ginneken interviewed by Mieke Dings

Jaap van Ginneken is an author and researcher in the fields of mass psychology, communication and culture. As a university lecturer he is associated with various educational institutions. He recently published Handbook for the World Citizen. Intercultural Communication, an Introduction (Boom Educational Publishers, 2008).

Involvement with the Olympic Games 2028: None.
Olympic sport: I sometimes play ping-pong just for fun and every now and then I walk up a mountain. I used to play field hockey and tennis.
Most impressive Olympic Games: "The upcoming Games in Beijing, because I was in Tiananmen Square on 8 August 2007 at 08:08:08 p.m. for the kick-off. Or, rather, I was in the crowd, which was kept at great distance from the proceedings, so I only saw what actually happened later on CNN. It was a weird experience.
Memorable sports moment: The Black Power salute by two Afro-American athletes at the Olympic Games in Mexico (1968) made quite an impression on me.

How does a large-scale sports event like the Olympic Games affect the masses?
For all countries, the Olympic Games are in the first place an exercise in national pride. Every country identifies with its own athletes and feels that their achievements also reflect on ordinary citizens. If the Netherlands wins many medals, the Dutch immediately feel a lot better. Research shows that in countries that have just won an important match, the next day the stock market index goes up. The guys on the floor are still high on testosterone and become overconfident.

And what happens when a country loses?
Then you see a short, massive national depression. The effect is less with the Olympic Games because there are so many different sports, so there are always other matches to win. With the Football World Cup or European Cup it is different, and then we often see dismal scenes, like when Clarence Seedorf missed a penalty in the European Cup quarterfinal against France. The entire country immediately said he was too arrogant to begin with.

How does this nationalism relate to the Olympic ideal of fraternisation?
The Olympic ideal has been corrupted in many respects. The Olympic Games should contribute to international understanding, but they often do not. One of the reasons is that they create a wave of benign nationalism, and another is that there is always some kind of boycott going on. Besides, the question is whether it is wise to have a depoliticised domain in international collaboration. Does this enhance dialogue? By the way, we were lucky that the Netherlands wasn't boycotted in 1928 because of our colonial history; it could have happened, with good reason. So let us not forget to search our own conscience every now and again. If Geert Wilders is prime minister in 2028, we can count on a boycott by the Arabic world. So much for fraternisation through the Olympic Games.

What effect can the Olympic Games in 2028 have on the Netherlands?
I doubt whether the Netherlands should want to host the Games at all. We do have to realise that Amsterdam is about the size of an average French, English or German provincial town. The Netherlands is really a city state; it is the Randstad with a bit of grass around it. Both Amsterdam and Rotterdam constantly bite off more than they can chew by thinking they are world cities. If the Netherlands wishes to organise the Games, then these two cities will have to do it together, anyway. Actually, I would propose to do it in collaboration with the Ruhr region.

Why the Ruhr region?
Because it is a large, rich region with many facilities and it is very close by. I'm just saying that it strikes me as odd that we do consider collaborating with Belgium but that the thought of collaborating with Germany doesn't even enter our heads. Whereas the Games could actually benefit from this type of existing network in a united Europe. After all, the games leave behind a lot of empty packaging and put a lot of

pressure on infrastructure and public administration. Already having both in place beforehand would be handy.

The Olympic Games 2028 as humble pie?
That wouldn't be such a bad thing. Of course we have our strong points; we are good at logistics and services, partly because we have always been very oriented towards the three major language and cultural areas around us. At the same time we overestimate this 'internationality' by thinking that we can just join in with the game of the big boys. This overestimation of ourselves is characteristic of our identity. We always think we don't have an identity, but we definitely do. And it is a very irritating one: besides this overestimation of ourselves, there's our attitude of "no reason to get excited." This is often regarded as rudeness by people abroad. The advantage of this attitude is that we are not easily driven crazy, but it also means that here the Olympic Games will never inspire as much bonding here as we now see in China. Where the Chinese see the Olympic Games as a springboard to the world at large, we tend too often to think we are the centre of the world. Actually the Games are nicest in countries that are not so very rich yet, because there they can really make a difference. We will just be building all these stadiums that maybe later will be useless.

Besides the stadiums, can you think of any other structures that intensify massive sports experiences?
Stadiums are of course wonderful inventions because they choreograph the experience of mass participation and enthusiasm. The seats are arranged in such a way that everyone can follow the action while at the same time see each other's reactions, which has a feedback effect. With electronics you can imagine even more effective formats, such as stadiums with huge screens that show all of the events simultaneously, or interactive Games where the crowd joins in via Wii, or democratically decides whether the ball is played over the right or left wing.

Is there any danger in the mass nature of the Games?
One of the characteristics of crowd behaviour is that it is erratic, and therefore susceptible to sudden changes. This is why riot control is so very difficult.

Finally: how old will you be in 2028?
Either dead or 85, but then I will have to do more exercises!

And what would be your favourite spot to watch the Olympic Games?
Where I'm sitting right now, the most beautiful spot in the world, in a park on the Côte d'Azur.

Can you think of a sports quote or slogan to make the country rally behind the idea of hosting the Olympic Games 2028?
Johan Cruijff immediately comes to mind: "Every advantage has its disadvantage and every disadvantage has its advantage".

WHAT IS OLYMPIC PROGRAMME & SCHEDULE?

WHAT IS THE SCHEDULE & PROGRAMME?

SPORTS VENUES AND VOLUME

SPORTS CATEGORIES			TOTAL VOLUME (m³)	TOTAL AREA (m²)
SPORTS		DISCIPLINES		
Aquatics		Diving	46728.00	3245.00
		Swimming	170986.32	13410.96
		Synchronized swimming	165003.26	10083.84
		Water polo women	143717.26	8348.24
		Water polo men	146931.12	9621.36
TOTAL AQUATICS			**673365.97**	**44709.40**
Archery			59704.13	9766.08
TOTAL ARCHERY			**59704.13**	**9766.08**
Athletics	track	Running		
		Running x 4		
		Running hurdles		
	field	Discus		
		Hammer		
		High jump		
		Javelin		
		Long jump		
		Pole vault		
		Shot put		
		Triple jump		
	road	Marathon		
		Running steeplechase		
		Walk		
	combined	Decathlon		
		Heptathlon		
All athletics			1632869.36	105756.57
TOTAL ATHLETICS			**1632869.36**	**105756.57**
Badminton			44436.38	4778.08
TOTAL BADMINTON			**44436.38**	**4778.08**
Baseball			1241201.92	82557.87
			202291.64	20642.00
TOTAL BASEBALL			**1443493.56**	**103199.88**
Basketball			167700.85	9957.24
TOTAL BASKETBALL			**167700.85**	**9957.24**
Boxing			74955.55	6211.17
TOTAL BOXING			**74955.55**	**6211.17**
Canoe / kayak		Flat water	1826565.60	333132.00
		Slalom	81046.40	10664.00
TOTAL CANOE/ KAYAK			**1907612.00**	**343796.00**
Cycling		Road	468000.00	156000.00
		Track	110338.92	11700.84
		Mountain	144000.00	36000.00
		BMX	132291.94	10499.36
TOTAL CYCLING			**854630.86**	**214200.20**
Equestrian		Dressage	414023.14	18532.32
		Jumping		
		Eventing	409512.00	50322.00
			633220.00	158305.00
TOTAL EQUESTRIAN			**1456755.14**	**227159.32**
Fencing			32630.40	6600.00
			29331.07	2715.84
TOTAL FENCING			**61961.47**	**9315.84**
Football			4348997.50	228631.04
TOTAL FOOTBALL			**4348997.50**	**228631.04**
Gymnastics	Artistic	Men's arena		
		Women's arena	375000.00	37376.00
	Rhythmic		52605.50	5535.36
	Trampoline		85702.46	8570.25
TOTAL GYMNASTICS			**513307.96**	**51481.61**
Handball			103771.49	11555.04
			27918.05	3404.64
TOTAL HANDBALL			**131689.54**	**14959.68**
Hockey			241202.80	32712.80
			55085.51	8884.76
TOTAL HOCKEY			**296288.31**	**41597.56**
Judo			71281.54	8351.36
TOTAL JUDO			**71281.54**	**8351.36**

What is the Olympic Programme & Schedule? **OLYMPIC FIRE** **165**

Olympic Games Volume (2008)
28 sports
38 disciplines
302 events

74 Main venues (excl. sailing)
14 warming up venues
96 training venues

SPORTS CATEGORIES			
SPORTS	DISCIPLINES	TOTAL VOLUME (m³)	TOTAL AREA (m²)
Modern pentathlon	Fencing	36271.87	4650.24
	Shooting	36362.98	3189.74
	Riding Running		
	Running	22500.00	7500.00
	Swimming	38168.06	3975.84
TOTAL MODERN PENTATHLON		133302.92	19315.82
Rowing		3316732.80	522696.00
TOTAL ROWING		3316732.80	522696.00
Sailing (excluded from total)		0.00	0.00
TOTAL SAILING		0.00	0.00
Shooting		4280000.00	535000.00
TOTAL SHOOTING		4280000.00	535000.00
Softball		243366.28	19886.99
TOTAL SOFTBALL		243366.28	19886.99
Table tennis		45657.94	7275.76
TOTAL TABLE TENNIS		45657.94	7275.76
Taekwondo		35848.35	4858.24
TOTAL TAEKONDO		35848.35	4858.24
Tennis		134236.36	9863.27
		31909.87	2900.90
		42771.55	3888.32
		50107.29	4555.21
TOTAL TENNIS		259025.07	21207.70
Triathlon	Swimming	4400260.00	579700.00
	Cycling	600000.00	200000.00
	Running	300000.00	100000.00
TOTAL TRIATHLON		5300260.00	879700.00
Volleyball	Volleyball	189577.25	13244.64
		67600.00	5200.00
		28224.00	3136.00
	Beach Volleyball	119184.00	10464.00
		96203.71	11732.16
TOTAL VOLLEYBALL		500788.96	43776.80
Weightlifting		62868.00	6956.00
TOTAL WEIGHTLIFTING		62868.00	6956.00
Wrestling		76704.67	8280.64
TOTAL WRESTLING		76704.67	8280.64
TOTAL PROGRAMME IOC		**27,993,605.10**	**3,492,824.97**

OLYMPIC VILLAGE			
ADITIONAL FACILITIES		TOTAL VOLUME (m3)	TOTAL FOOTPRINT (m2)
Olympic Village	Olympic Family accomodation	260000.00	9285.71	1000
	International area including retail, visitors welcome center, Olympic museum	2042873.06	5604.59	
	Residential Area including retail, recreation, polyclinic etc.			
	Sevices/Training facilities			
	Recreation/Leisure			
	Community facilities	6048000.00	50921.14	17000 A
Media Center		462000.00	16500.00	
		208000.00	10400.00	
		75000.00	5000.00	1
TOTAL OLYMPIC VILLAGE		**9,095,873.06**	**97,711.44**	
TOTAL		**37,089,478.16**	**3,590,536.42**	

166 OLYMPIC FIRE   What is the Olympic Programme & Schedule?

VOLUME OF MAIN VENUES

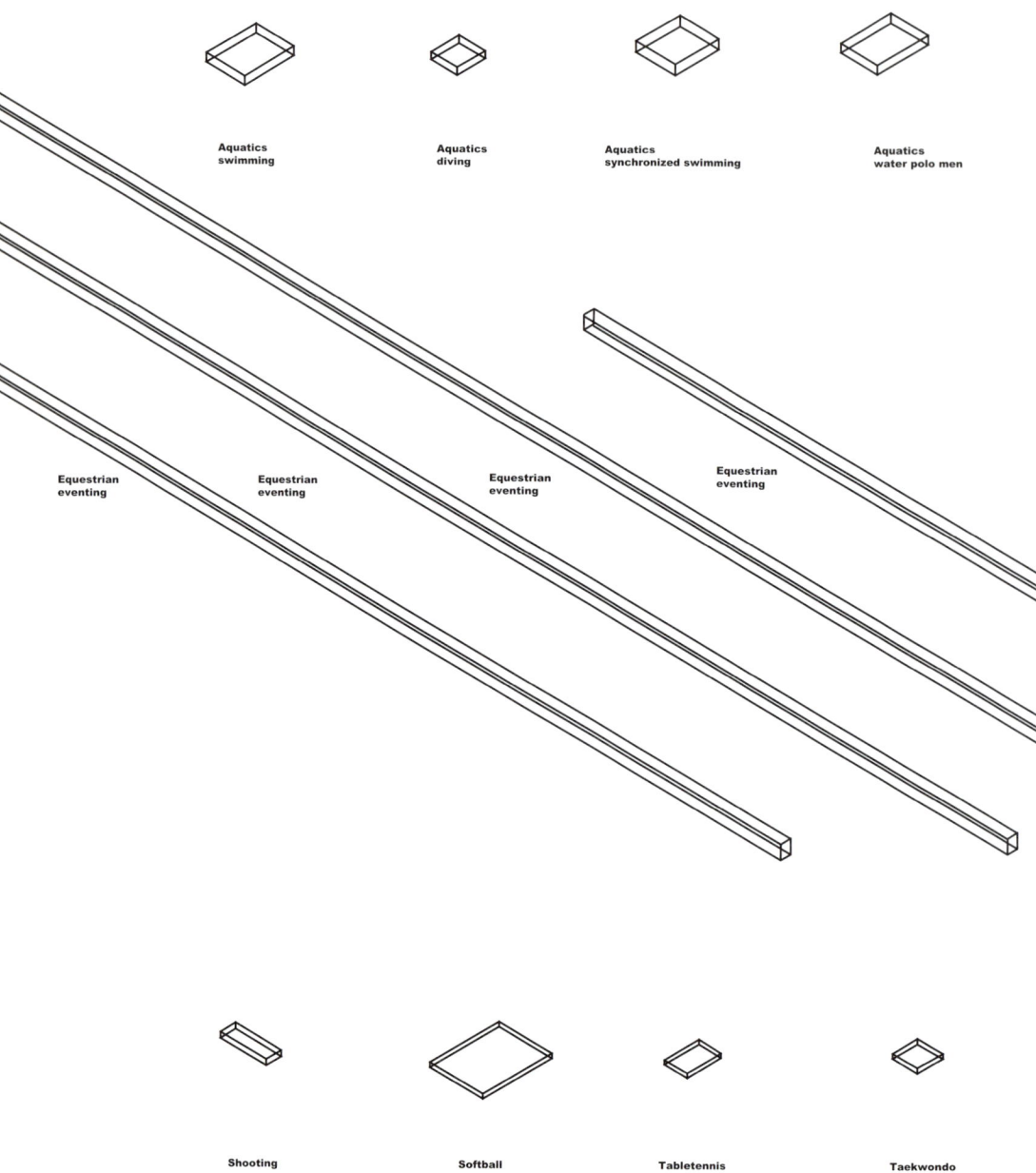

What is the Olympic Programme & Schedule? OLYMPIC FIRE 167

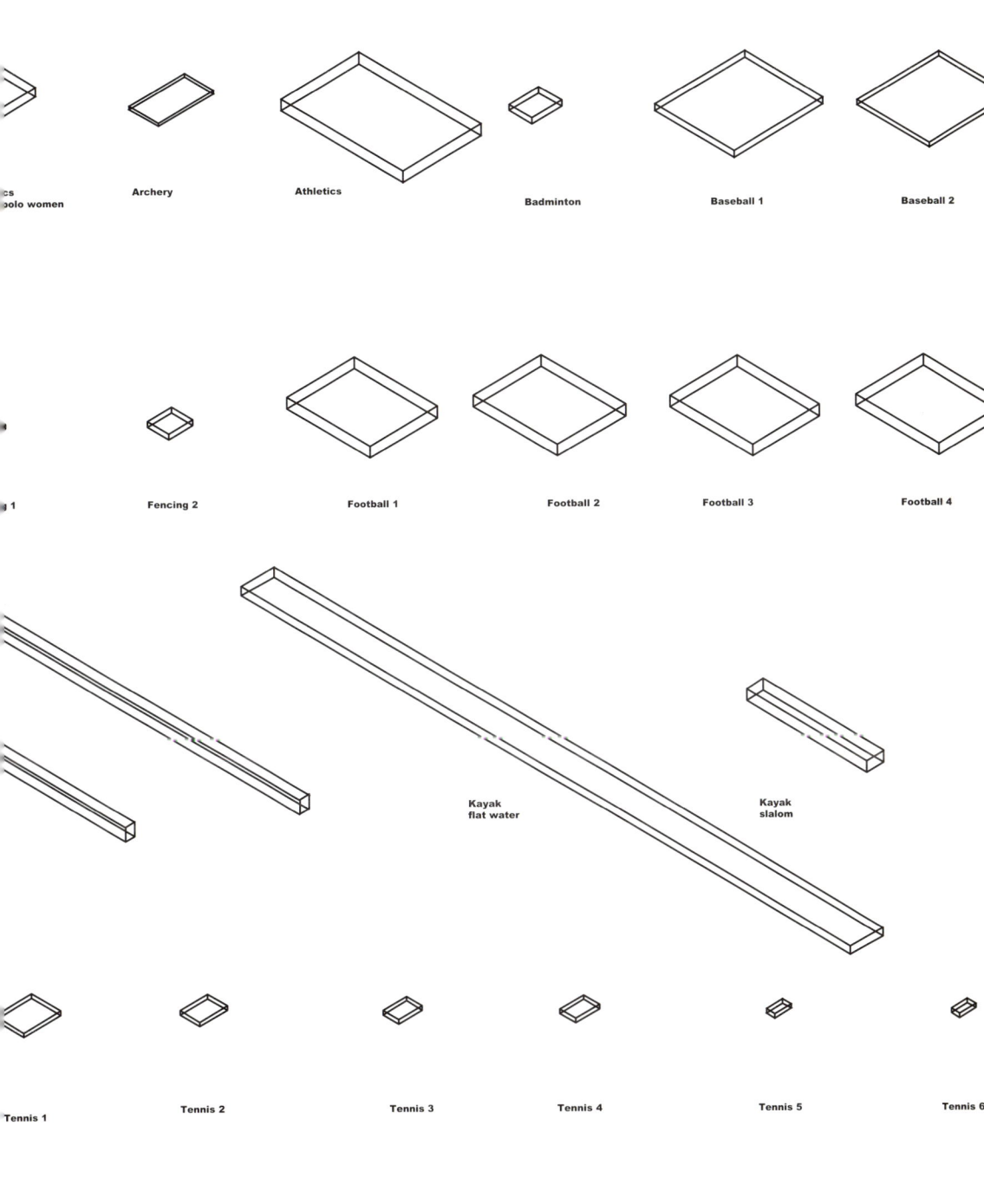

VOLUME OF MAIN VENUES

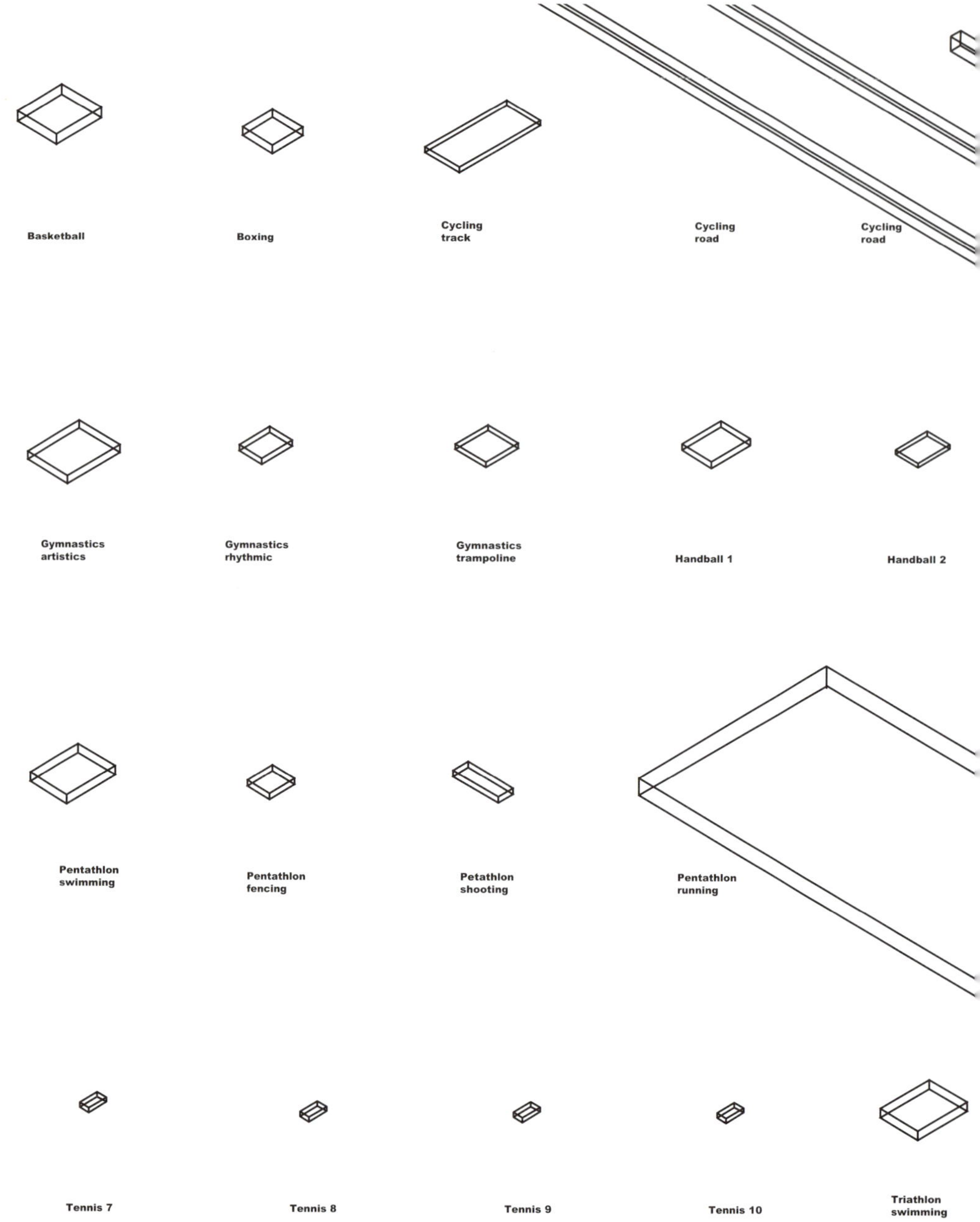

Basketball	Boxing	Cycling track	Cycling road	Cycling road

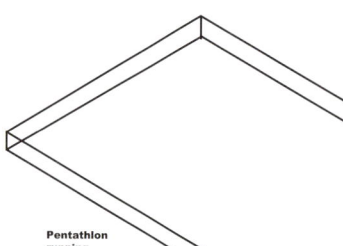

Gymnastics artistics	Gymnastics rhythmic	Gymnastics trampoline	Handball 1	Handball 2

Pentathlon swimming	Pentathlon fencing	Petathlon shooting	Pentathlon running

Tennis 7	Tennis 8	Tennis 9	Tennis 10	Triathlon swimming

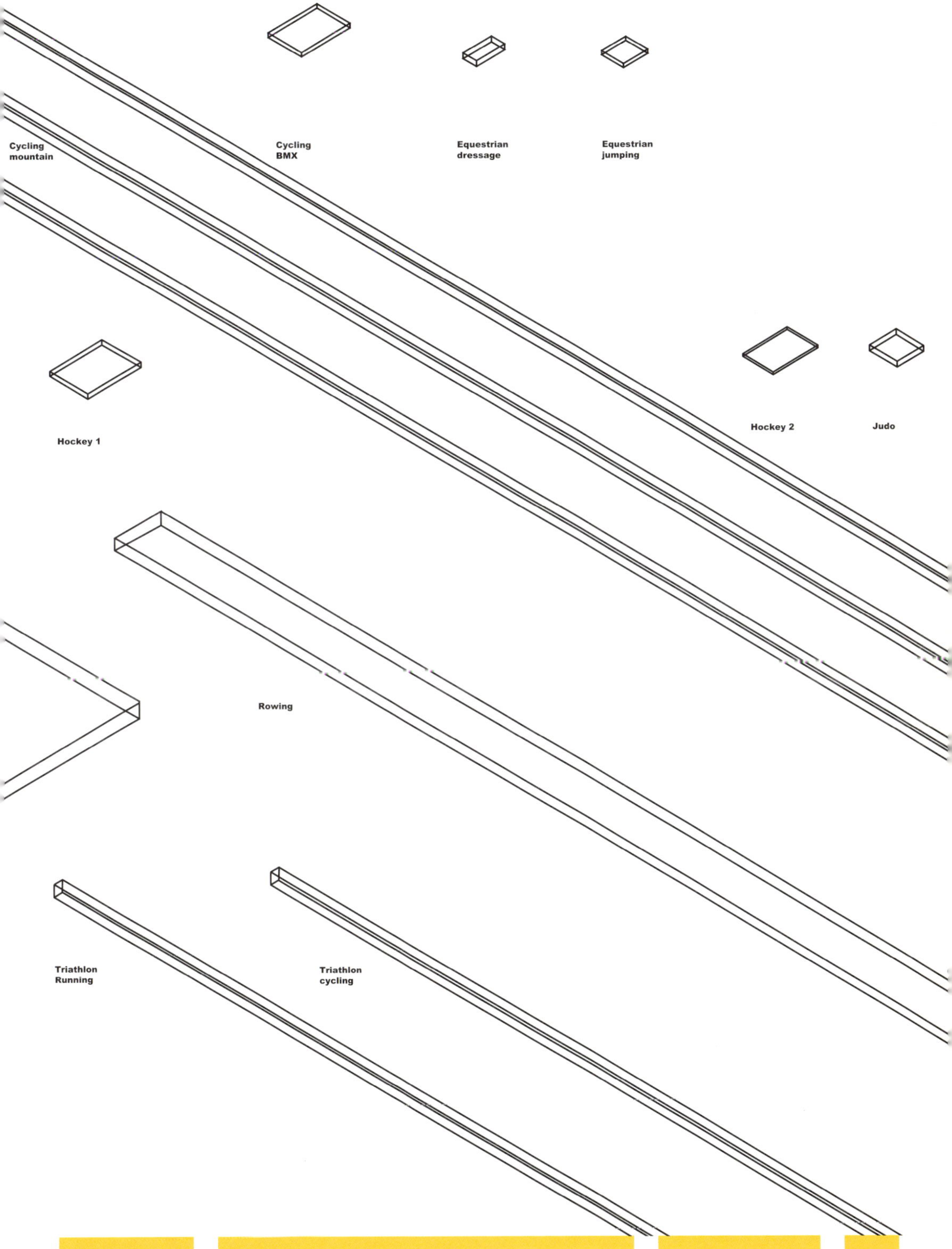

What is the Olympic Programme & Schedule? **OLYMPIC FIRE**

Cycling mountain

Cycling BMX

Equestrian dressage

Equestrian jumping

Hockey 1

Hockey 2

Judo

Rowing

Triathlon Running

Triathlon cycling

170 OLYMPIC FIRE — What is the Olympic Programme & Schedule?

VOLUME OF WARMING UP & TRAINING VENUES

Volleyball 1

Volleyball 2

Volleyball 3

Beach Volleyball 1

Beach Volleyball 2

Aquatics swimming

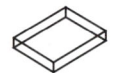
Aquatics swimming

Aquatics swimming

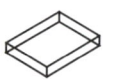
Aquatics swimming

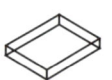
Aquatics swimming

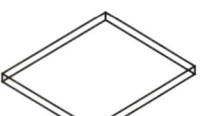
Baseball

Baseball

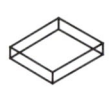
Basketball

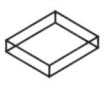
Basketball

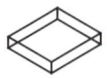
Basketball

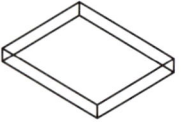
Football

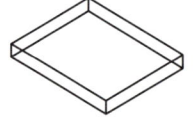
Football

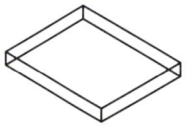
Football

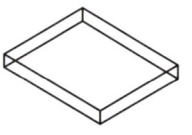
Football

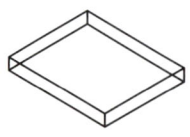
Football

Gymnastics artistics

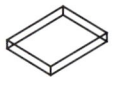
Gymnastics artistics

Gymnastics artistics

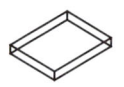
Gymnastics artistics

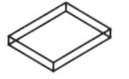
Gymnastics artistics

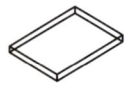
Hockey

Judo

Judo

Kayak slalom

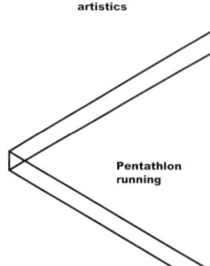
Pentathlon running

Volleyball

Volleyball

Beach Volleyball

Beach Volleyball

What is the Olympic Programme & Schedule? OLYMPIC FIRE 171

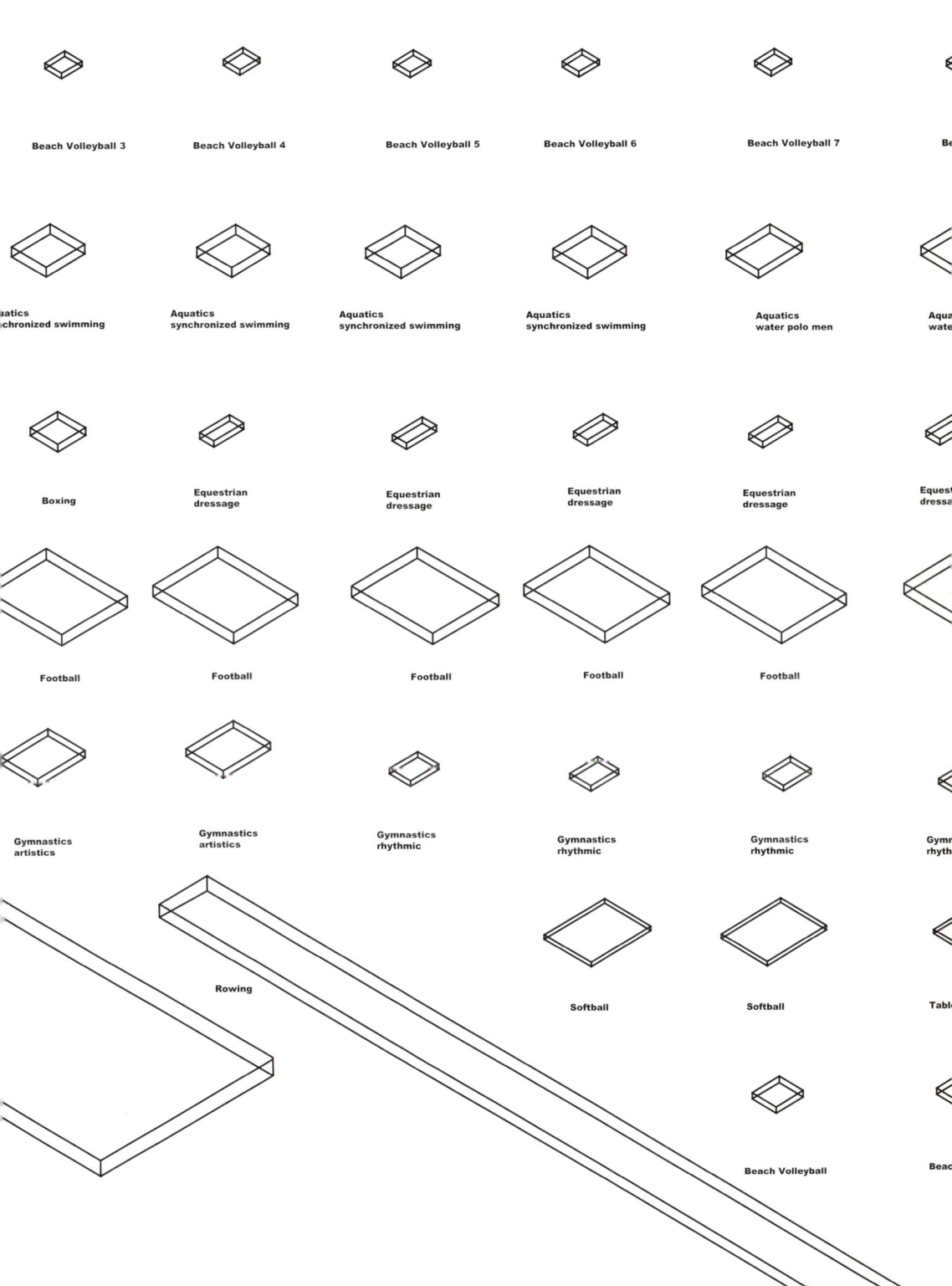

172 OLYMPIC FIRE — What is the Olympic Programme & Schedule?

VOLUME OF WARMING UP & TRAINING VENUES

Beach Volleyball 8   Weightlifting   Wrestling

Aquatics water polo women   Aquatics water polo men   Aquatics water polo women   Archery   Athletics

Equestrian dressage   Equestrian jumping   Equestrian jumping   Equestrian jumping   Equestrian jumping

Football   Football   Football   Football   Football

Gymnastics rhythmic   Gymnastics rhythmic   Gymnastics rhythmic   Gymnastics trampoline   Gymnastics trampoline

Tabletennis   Tabletennis   Taekwondo   Tennis   Triathlon swimming

Beach Volleyball

Weightlifting

Wrestling

Wrestling

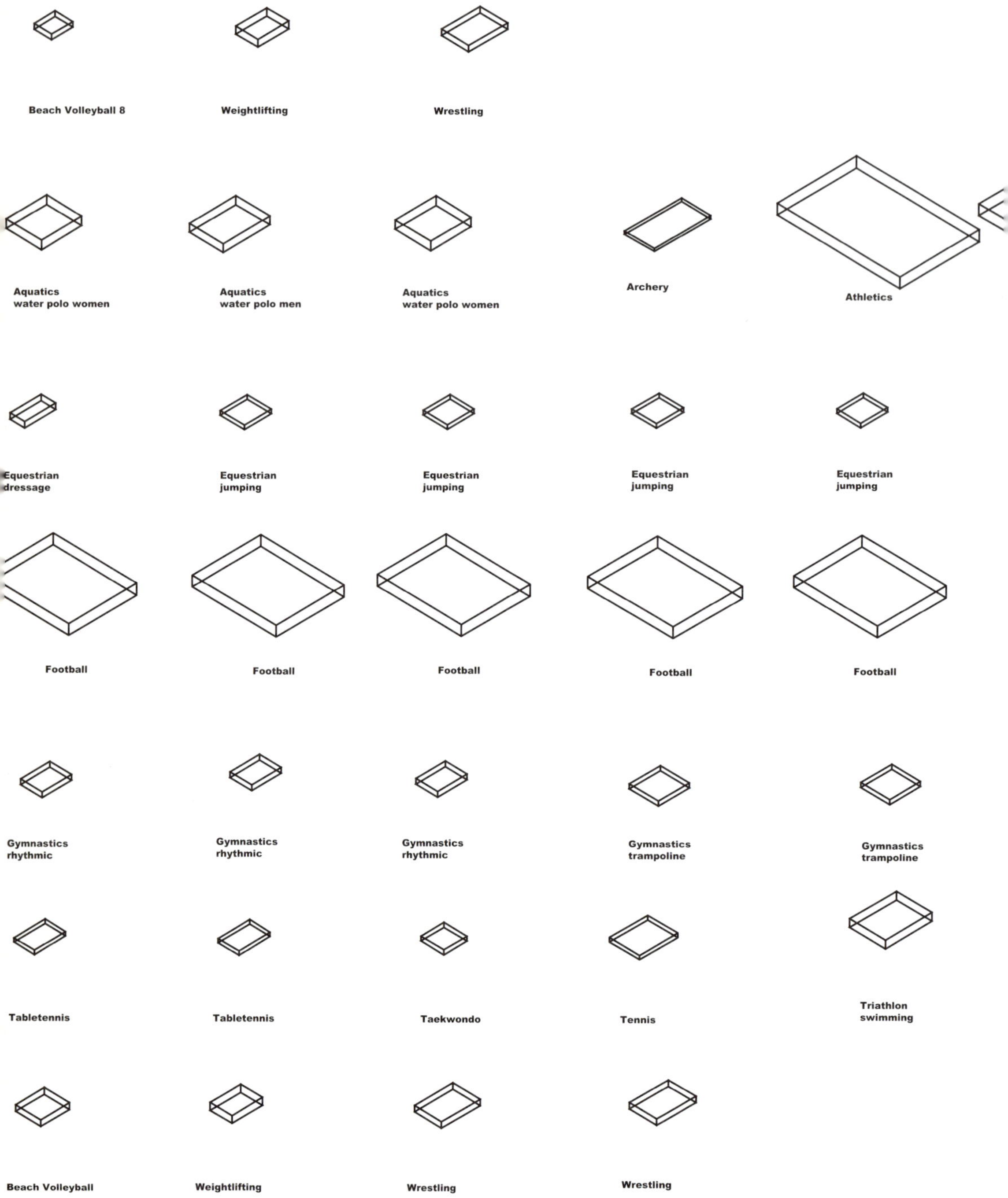

Venues, Warming up & Training venues 27,993,605 m³

What is the Olympic Programme & Schedule? **OLYMPIC FIRE** 173

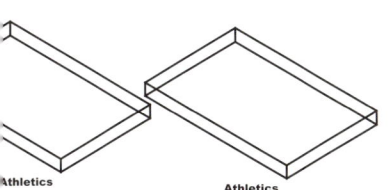  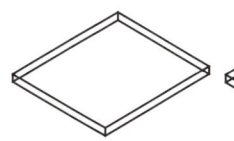 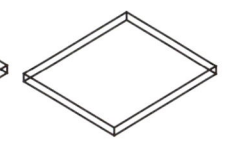

Athletics   Athletics   Badminton   Baseball   Baseball

Equestrian jumping   Equestrian jumping   Equestrian jumping   Equestrian jumping   Fencing   Football

Gymnastics artistics   Gymnastics artistics   Gymnastics artistics   Gymnastics artistics   Gymnastics artistics   Gymnastics artistics

  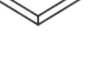

Handball   Handball   Handball   Handball   Hockey   Hockey

Volleyball   Volleyball   Volleyball   Volleyball   Volleyball   Volleyball

VOLUME OF THE OLYMPIC VILLAGE AND MEDIA CENTRE

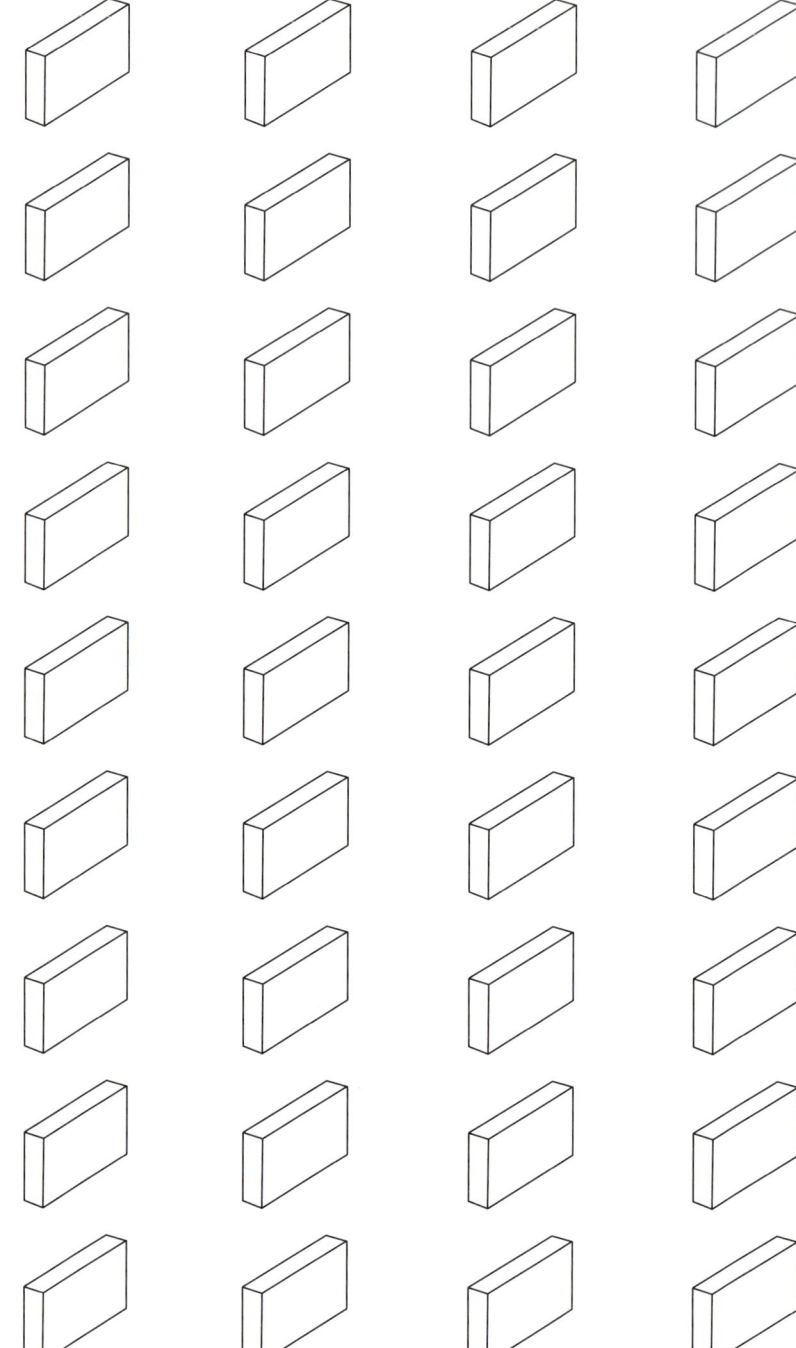

Media Center 283,000 m³ & Olympic Village & Facilities 8,812,000 m³

What is the Olympic Programme & Schedule? **OLYMPIC FIRE**

TOTAL OLYMPIC VOLUME

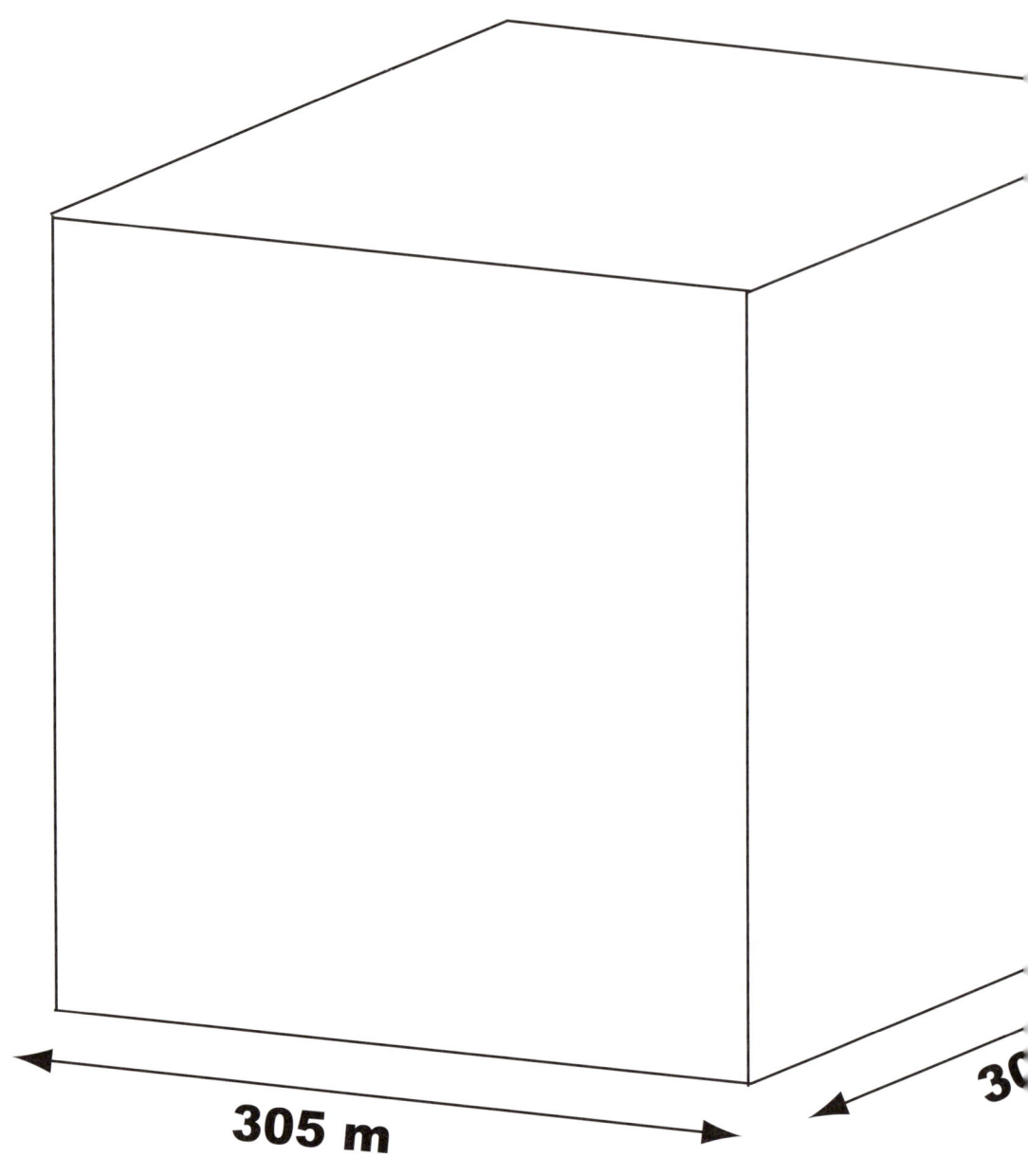

3,4 million m²
28,5 million m³
(without sailing and public hotels)

OLYMPIC FIRE

305 m

m

OCCUPANCY RATE OF MAIN VENUES
DURING THE 17 DAYS OF THE GAMES

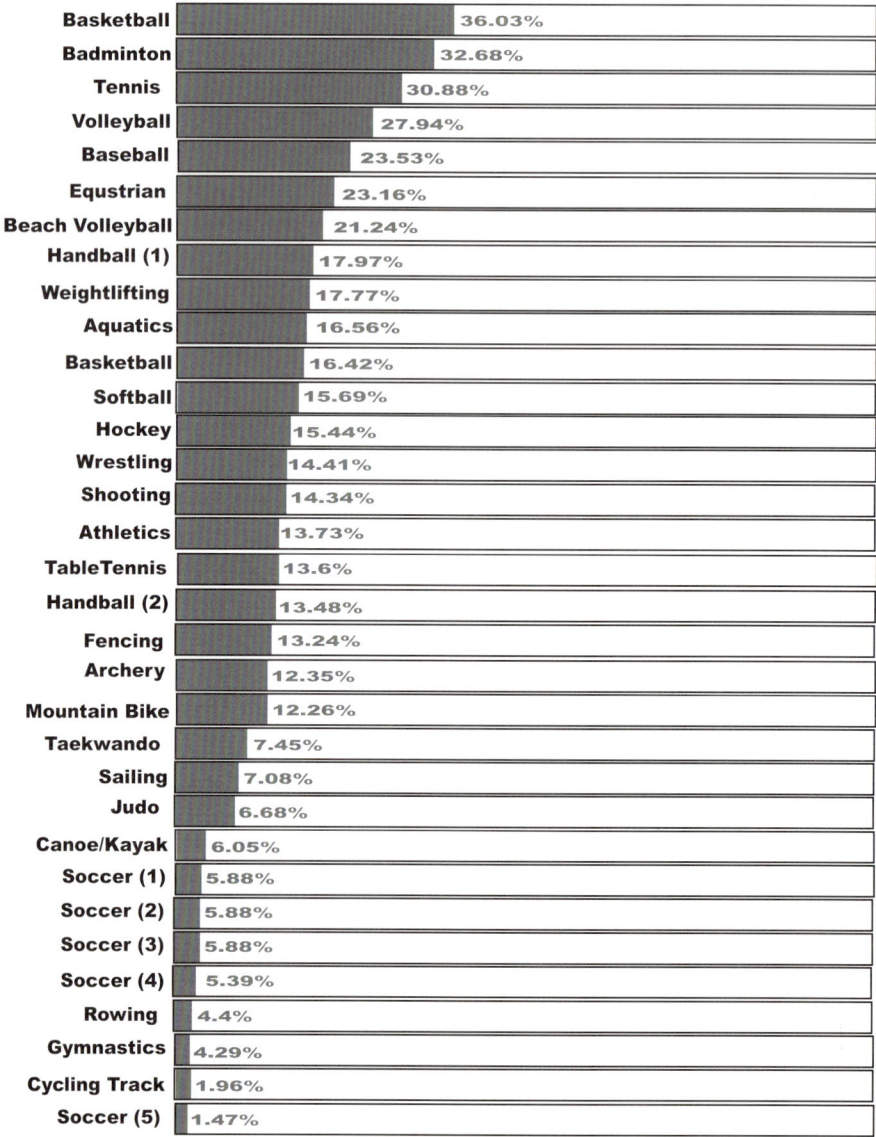

Sport	Occupancy Rate
Basketball	36.03%
Badminton	32.68%
Tennis	30.88%
Volleyball	27.94%
Baseball	23.53%
Equstrian	23.16%
Beach Volleyball	21.24%
Handball (1)	17.97%
Weightlifting	17.77%
Aquatics	16.56%
Basketball	16.42%
Softball	15.69%
Hockey	15.44%
Wrestling	14.41%
Shooting	14.34%
Athletics	13.73%
TableTennis	13.6%
Handball (2)	13.48%
Fencing	13.24%
Archery	12.35%
Mountain Bike	12.26%
Taekwando	7.45%
Sailing	7.08%
Judo	6.68%
Canoe/Kayak	6.05%
Soccer (1)	5.88%
Soccer (2)	5.88%
Soccer (3)	5.88%
Soccer (4)	5.39%
Rowing	4.4%
Gymnastics	4.29%
Cycling Track	1.96%
Soccer (5)	1.47%

each venue

Occupancy rate per sport over 17 day's

AVERAGE OCCUPANCY RATE OF MAIN VENUES DURING THE 17 DAYS OF THE GAMES

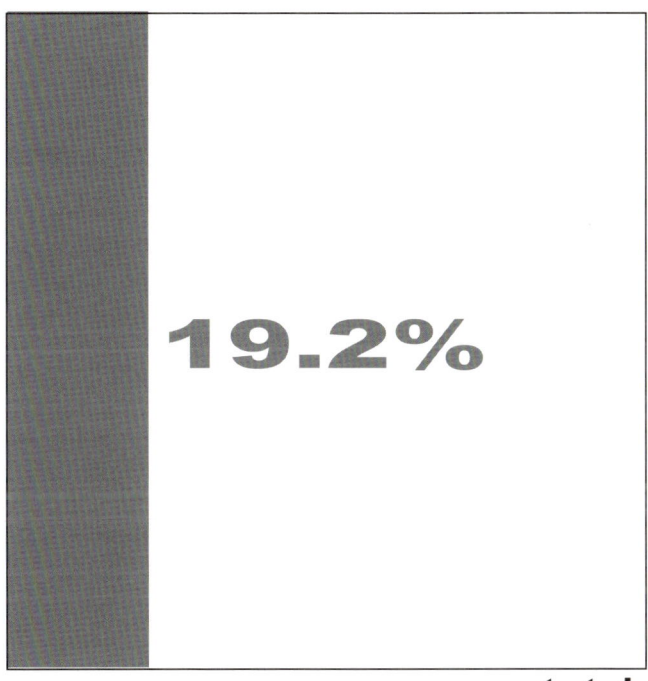

total

Average overall occupancy rate over 17 day's

| 180 | OLYMPIC FIRE | What is the Olympic Programme & Schedule? |

ONE VENUE GAMES

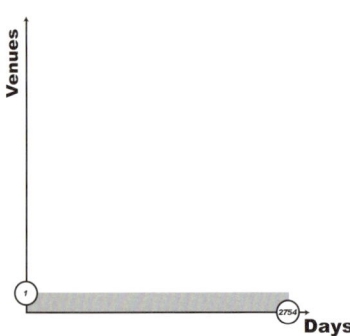

2,754 days = 1 venue = 1,017,845 m³

ONE YEAR GAMES

365 days = 8 venues = 3,775,262 m³

ONE MONTH GAMES

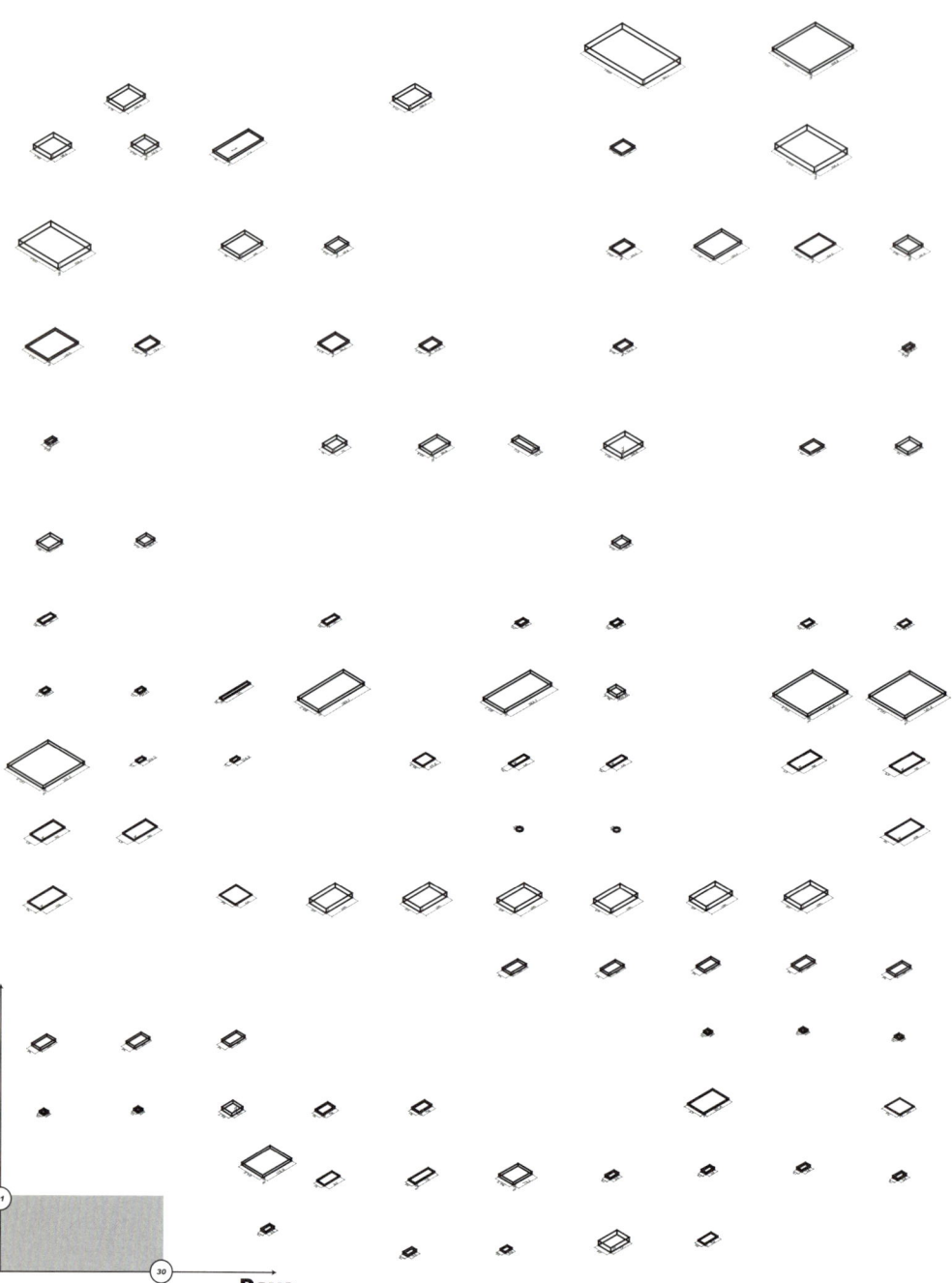

31 DAYS = 91 venues = 51,437,760 m³

ONE WEEK GAMES

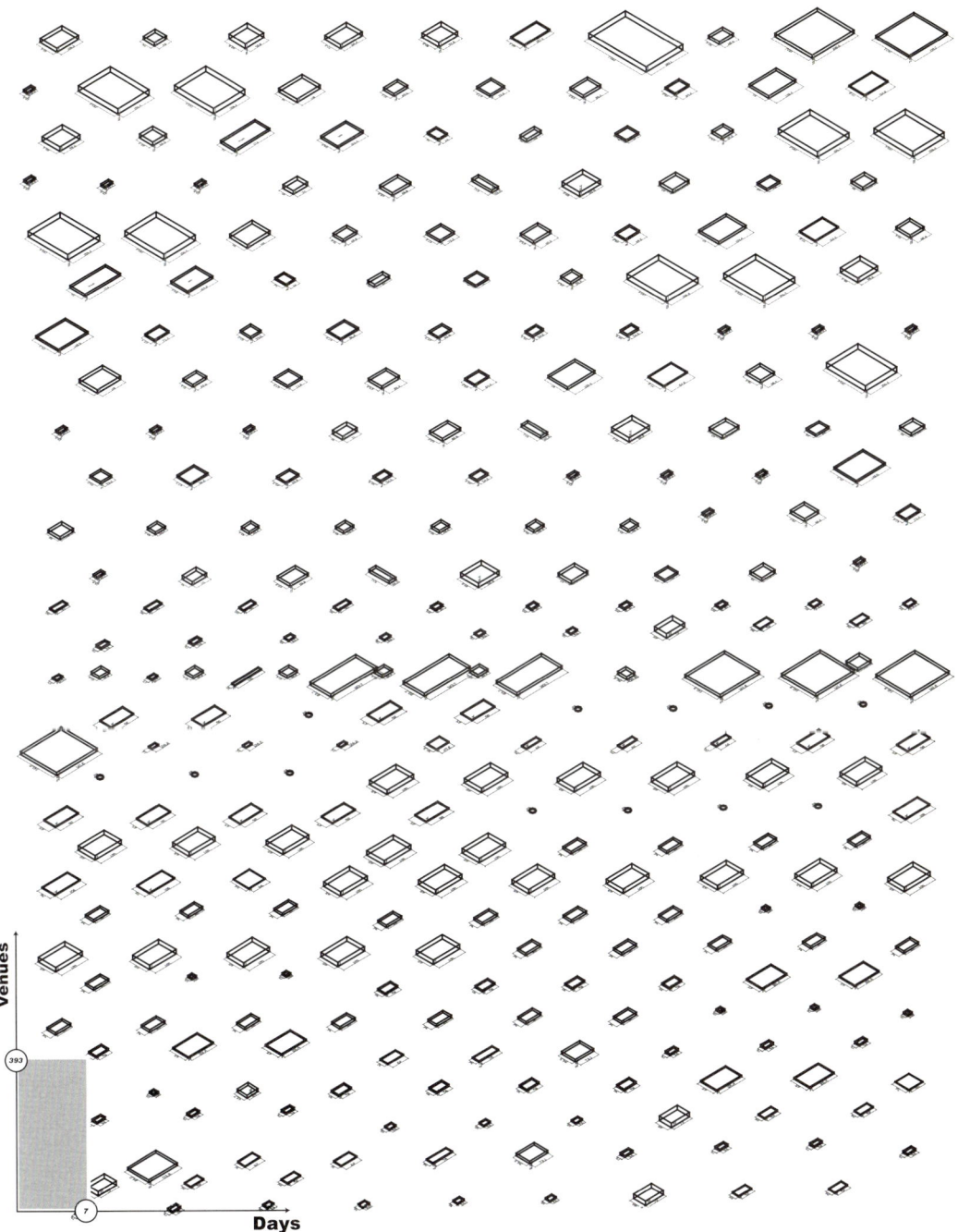

7 DAYS = 393 venues = 196,939,928 m³

ONE DAY GAMES

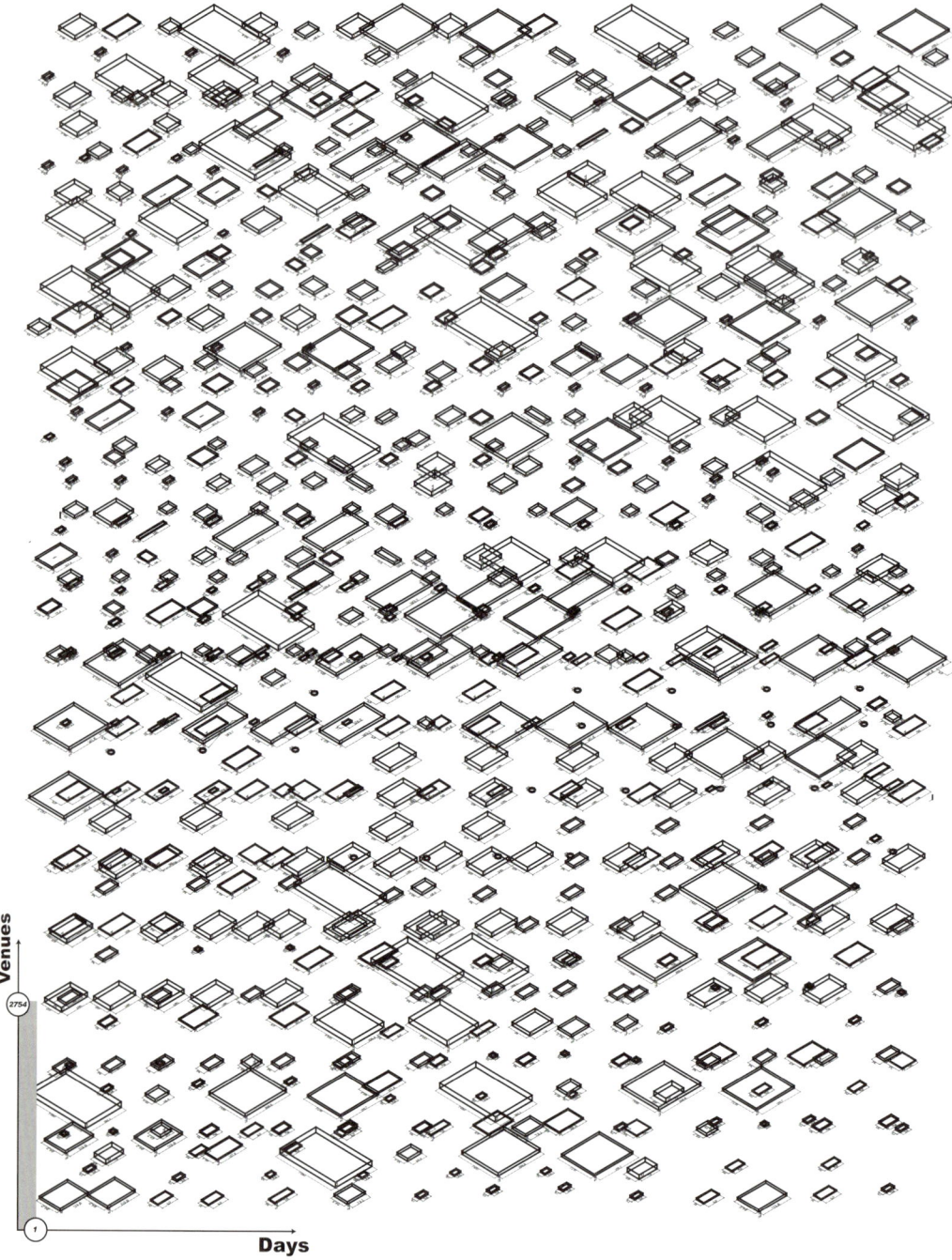

24 HOURS = 2,754 venues = 402,918,488 m³

SAME MOMENT GAMES

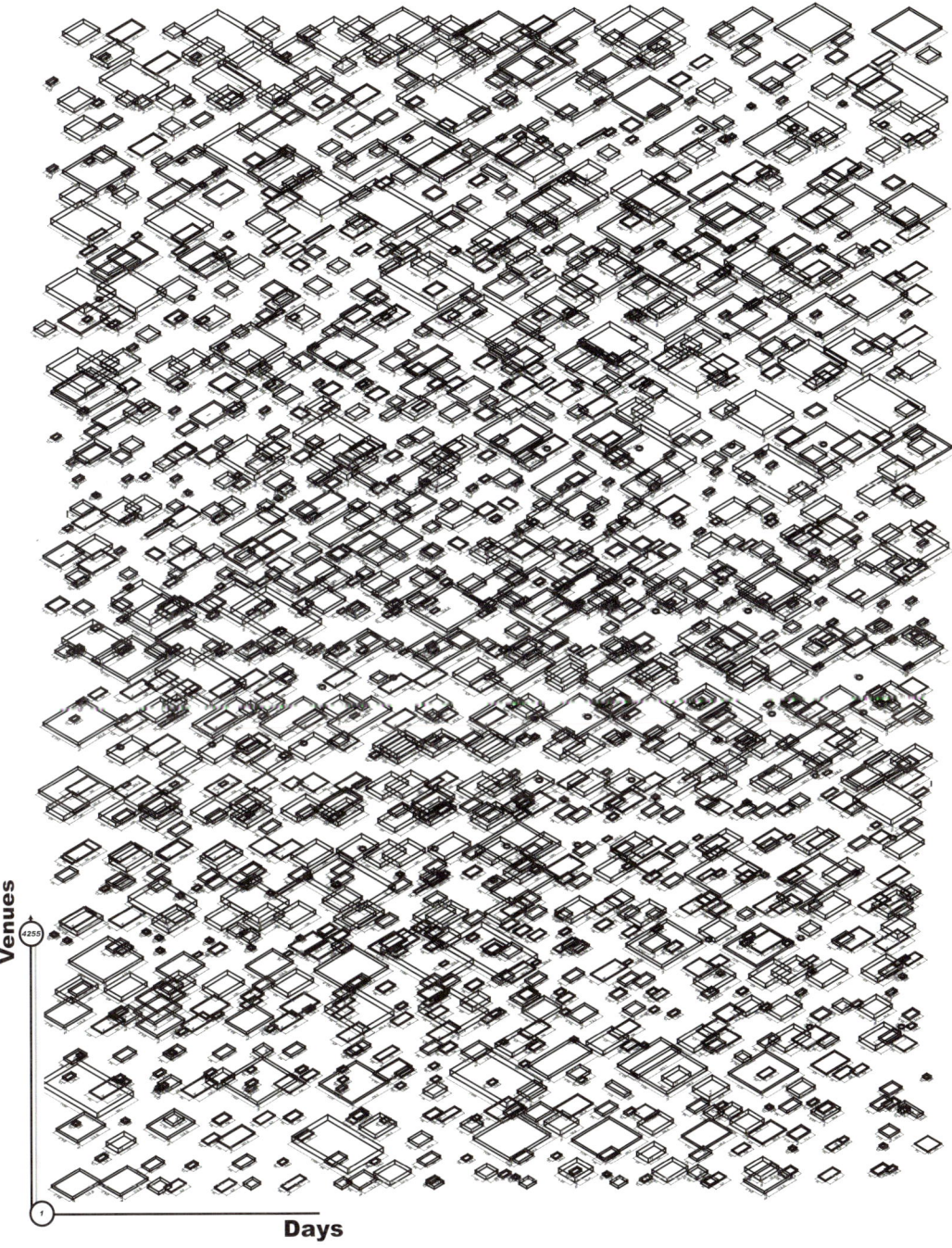

4,255 venues = 1,812,366,466 m³

PLAYING WITH THE OLYMPIC VOLUME

Coastal Skyline

Rotterdam Waterfront

Amsterdam Crosses

Schiphol Airport Pyramid

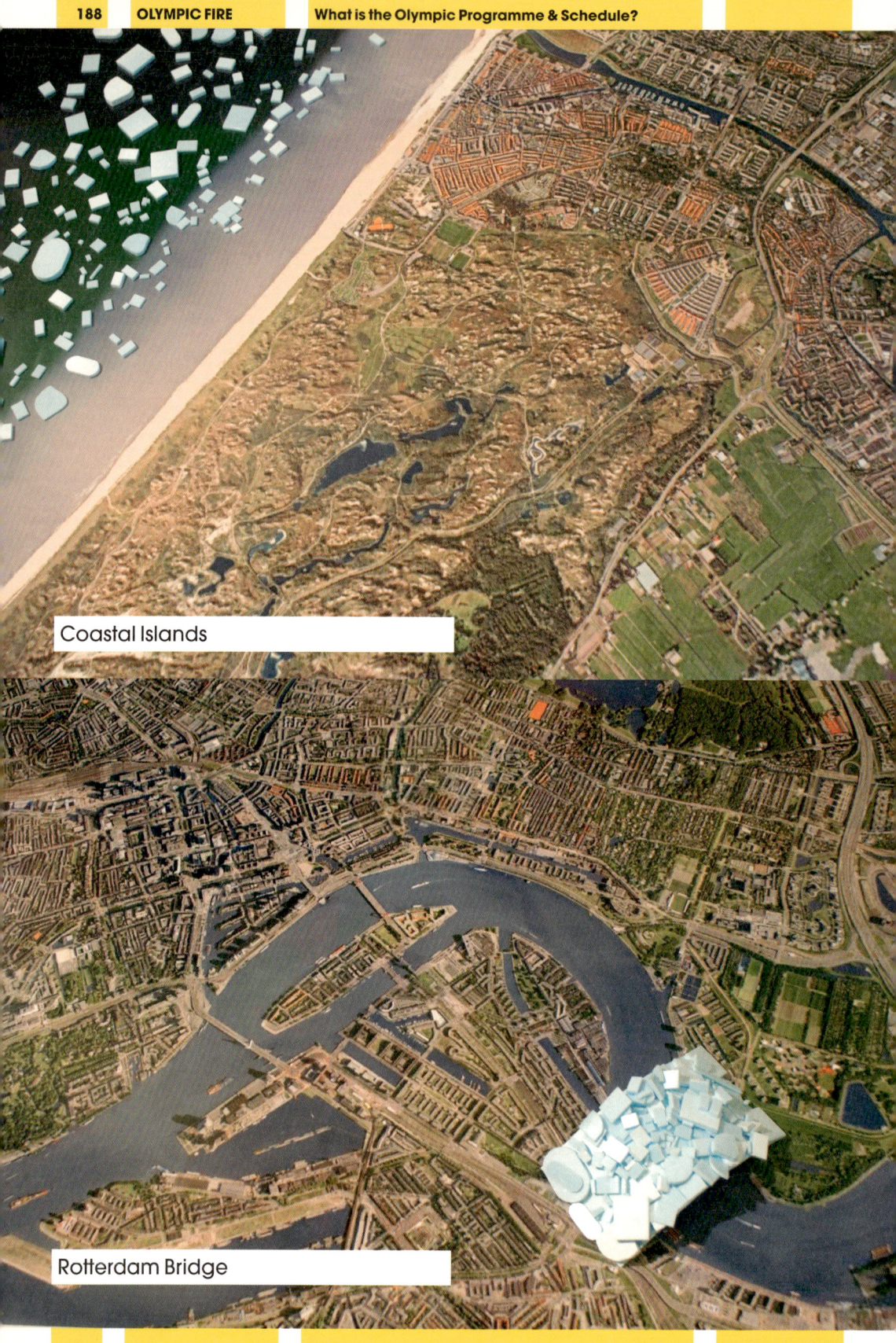

Coastal Islands

Rotterdam Bridge

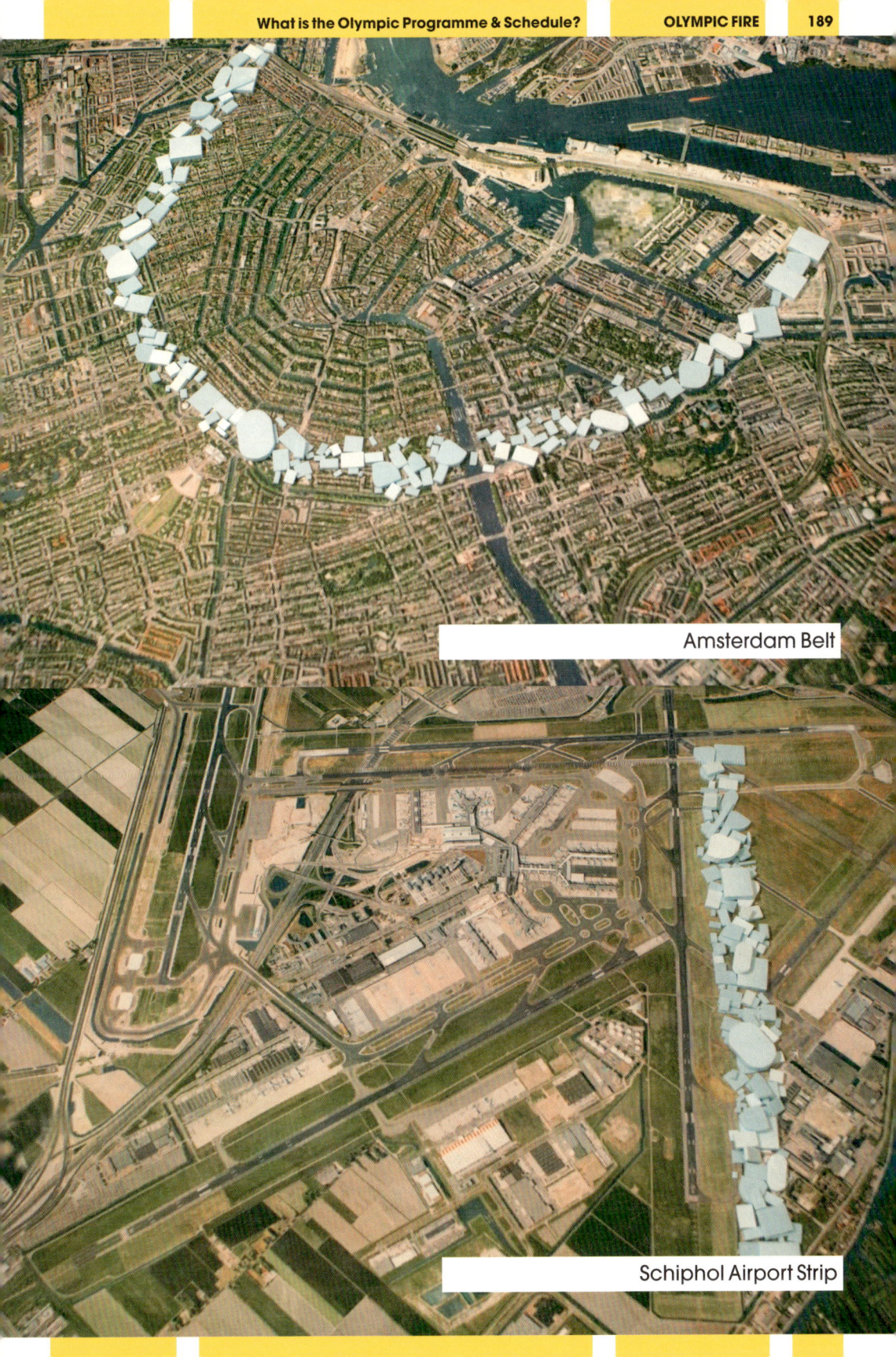

Amsterdam Belt

Schiphol Airport Strip

190 | OLYMPIC FIRE | What is the Olympic Programme & Schedule?

Coastal Strip

Rotterdam Wall

Amsterdam Dispersed

Schiphol Airport Hill

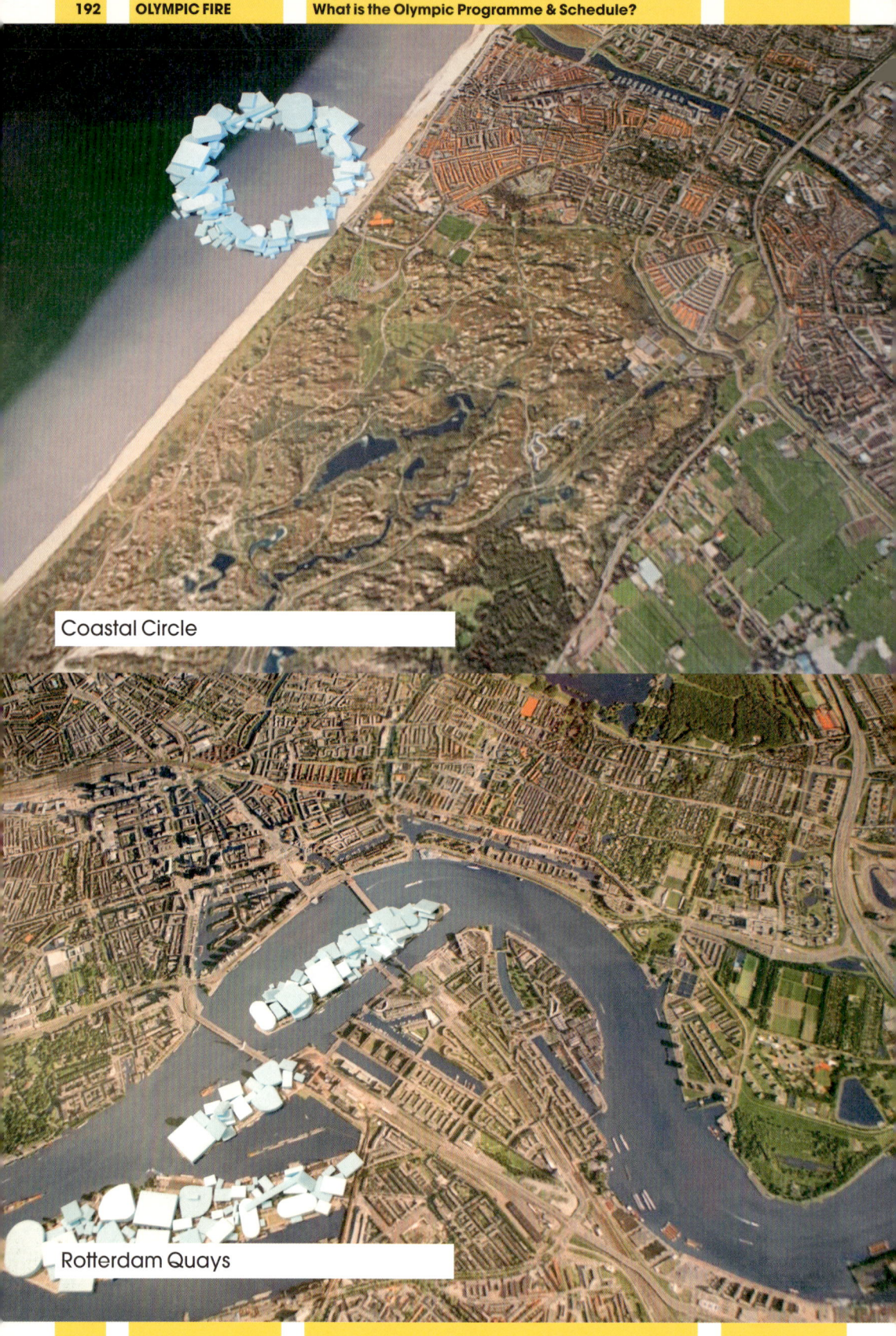

Coastal Circle

Rotterdam Quays

Amsterdam Bridge

Schiphol Airport Enfolded

'We must use the Games to put the Randstad on the world map'

Hans Mommaas interviewed by Harry den Hartog

Hans Mommaas is Professor of Leisure Studies at the University of Tilburg and Director of Telos, Brabant Center for Sustainability. He is the author of 'The Leisure Industry in City and Country. A Study of the Experience Economy' (De vrijetijdsindustrie in stad en land. Een studie naar de markt van belevenissen, SDU Publishers, 2000).

Involvement in the Olympic Games 2028: I am a member of the quality team that supports Twynstra Gudde Consultants and Managers, who will be studying the spatial implications and feasibility of an Olympic bid.

Plays an Olympic sport: No, nothing at the moment. I simply haven't got the time.

Memorable sports moment: I don't watch sports very much. Just the real highlights, like the Ronde van Vlaanderen recently. What particularly impressed me in terms of the Olympics was the opening ceremony for the Games in Barcelona in 1992. That set a new standard; it was a successful attempt to make a cultural statement. We must try to do the same thing in the Netherlands. An opportunity like that shouldn't be missed.

What can the Olympic Games offer the Netherlands?
That depends on how we approach the Games: just as an event in itself, or will spatial-economic development issues also be on the agenda? We can use the Games, for example, to pull the infrastructure within the Randstad [the urban agglomeration of Western Holland – HdH] out of its malaise. Moreover, the Games offer a chance to think about creating a new type of urban design and developing something better than, for instance, Rotterdam Alexander and the Amsterdam ArenA area. In the outskirts, the leisure infrastructure is currently comprised of separate bits and pieces: a climbing gym here and a golf course there. As an infrastructure it's all wrong, the result of uncontrolled growth rather than any planning. We can take advantage of the Olympic Games to introduce more coherence and quality. By connecting temporary and permanent sports infrastructure with other activities, we can create an attractive urban mix. For instance, sports can be combined with residential, work, cultural, shopping and public functions. With this new assignment it is important to design on a regional scale. The infrastructure should serve as support for a new urban network.

Where will this Olympic fire burn? Isn't it more sensible to spread the Games throughout the country rather than confining them to the Randstad?
I don't have any inflexible opinions on that. Concentrating the Games makes accessibility and security easier to organise. If we take the network approach, we could also spread the Games out. Besides having a central stadium in the Randstad area, it's of course also very well possible to organise activities in Brabant or elsewhere. In that case, many more regions could profit from the Games.

What does the Netherlands have to offer as a host country?
Our location in the delta area of Northern Europe. The Netherlands has a huge packet of well-connected services. We are a European hub. Moreover, the Netherlands has an impressive sports record. The most important thing, however, is our strong tradition of spatial and technical design.

So, the Netherlands is almost ready...
Very many things still have to happen first. We can design our networks in a sustainable and coherent way to make a good urban mix. The question remains of whether we are capable of finding the right administrative and organisational form. That is much more complicated. We will have to break through the various administrative levels in collaboration with market parties. In that respect,

the Netherlands is not at all ready. But we still have a bit of time…

What lessons can be learned from earlier Games?
In Barcelona, they managed to broaden the agenda of the Olympics into an extensive program in which the Games became an incentive for the revitalisation of the city. The Games were very strongly coupled with a spatial planning and cultural agenda, which also enabled other social partners, such as designers and artists, to become involved.

Can it also go wrong?
Certainly. Greece was left with a lot of white elephants. We have to prevent such a situation by opting for sustainable Games. There is a danger of ending up with stadiums everywhere, without anyone ever having looked into a well-coordinated program. You cannot finance big stadiums with sports alone. The Amsterdam ArenA is already hosting concerts and it has a boulevard with shops and entertainment. The combination of new sports facilities with functions such as working, living and leisure can lead to attractive municipal. The challenge is to design sports facilities in such a way that they can be reused.

As legacy of the Games, you mention a wider agenda and sustainability. Which do you value the most?
By that time, sustainability won't be a distinctive theme; in 2028 sustainability will be a basic premise that is no longer even be brought up. So a wider agenda is more important. We must play up our location in the delta area and put social cultural, ecological and spatial-economic aspects on the agenda and create new forms of urban living.

Finally, how old will you be in 2028 and where would you like to be when you are watching the Games?
By that time I'll be in my early 70s. I will come if the Games are rollator-proof. On the other hand, we live in a media economy. Thanks to digitalisation, it will soon be possible to follow all aspects of the Games in every corner of the world. Not that this will result in smaller Games; every concentration of communications media in the past has led to a greater desire for physical contact and gathering together. The Games will undoubtedly be an even bigger mass event than they are now. I don't know if I will still want to throw myself into such huge crowds at that age, so probably I'll just stay at home and watch it on screen.

'Ecologically sound Games in 2028: it goes without saying'

Liesbeth van Tongeren interviewed by Mieke Dings

Liesbeth van Tongeren is the director of Greenpeace Netherlands. Before this she was the director of an organisation for the homeless, refugees and battered women and the founder of a centre for peaceful conflict mediation. She has also worked for the Province of North Holland and the City of Amsterdam.

Involvement with Olympic Games 2028: Greenpeace is a worldwide organisation with 28 national offices. Our Chinese office is currently involved with the Games of 2008. We haven't yet thought about the Games of 2028 at all.

Playing an Olympic sport? I used to do gymnastics quite fanatically, until I grew too tall for some of the exercises, and consequently became too slow.

Most impressive Olympic Games: To be quite honest, I prefer doing sports myself, or watching other sports live. What never fails to impress me, though, is the mix of all those nationalities, which always makes me hope for more understanding through contact. We in Greenpeace have quite happy memories of the Games in Sydney.

Those were the first games where Greenpeace actively collaborated by developing the idea of Green Games in the bid, for instance. Greenpeace also formulated guidelines that served as the basis for legislation and monitored its enforcement. Did Greenpeace achieve what it set out to do?
It is inherent to our organisation to always want more drastic changes than can be realised in reality. The sheer size of the environmental problems demands it. Nonetheless we are quite happy with the fact that in Sydney so much attention was given to the climate and the environment. For quite a lot of issues, we have reached our goals. For instance, we succeeded in considerably reducing the use of PVC and we were able to give advice on sustainable energy sources. Also, the Olympic Village and sports facilities were not demolished after the games but instead were permanent. In public transport there were some structural improvements as well.

After Sydney's bid, the IOC decided that all candidate cities would henceforth have to make an extensive environmental plan. However, the IOC failed to regulate its implementation. How well did the next cities do?
Attention for the environment always has some effect, but with the next couple of Games we were not involved as intensively. Greenpeace always functions as a catalyser. This means that once we presented our agenda in Sydney we did not approach the next candidate cities about developing environmental plans, because we are not an executive agency. And we do try and encourage the organising committees to take a serious look at the environmental plans. If I were to roughly evaluate the Games after Sydney, I would say a lot more attention is being paid to the environment now than it used to be.

What is Greenpeace doing in Beijing right now?
Our office there has just opened and is now trying to establish a foothold in China, which means they have just started up their first projects. One of these projects is to find ways of making the refrigerating systems for food and beverages in China both CO_2 and CFK-friendly so that they will have no harmful effects on the climate or the ozone layer. The technique is available and if we succeed in introducing it in a large country like China, the effects may be enormous. So we are using the Games as a showcase to present an environmentally friendly way of refrigeration to China and the rest of the world.

Meanwhile China is building one power plant after the other. How can you win?
We can't really, of course. But what is in fact happening is that we in Western Europe are 'outsourcing' our environmental problems to countries like China. The electricity from those plants is used for a large part to manufacture products that we use over here. We may take steps to ensure that our air is clean and that our emissions don't get out of

control, but meanwhile we are buying those cheap products from China. So we need to approach the problem from more than one end. In the first place, coal-fuelled power plants are obsolete because now there are much more sustainable ways of generating energy, and in the second place we have to ask ourselves whether it is fair to shift our environmental problems to other countries. I don't think it is. By the way, the Netherlands is are also planning four or five new coal-fuelled power plants. We are now undertaking action to stop them from being built.

Would this be a subject for Greenpeace to put on the map via the 2028 Games?
These plants are being planned for long before 2028, but we are going to make sure that a choice is made for wiser alternatives now, while it still is possible. Whether we will be involved in the Games in 2028, and with what issues, is something I gladly leave to the team which will be in place then. These huge events always offer opportunities to draw attention to all sorts of unknown or unpopular subjects. But if by 2028 we have still not succeeded in making the organisers of such events realise that they should be friendly to the environment, then it will be getting pretty late in the day as far as climate change is concerned. Unfortunately, my guess is that we will still be tackling subjects such as climate, environment, deforestation and over-fishing. What we are aiming for by that time is to have realised fish reservations, an unconditional stop on the cutting down of primeval forests and to have made the transition to sustainable energy. Looking back, this development will have been inevitable, but whether it will be sufficient by that time is quite another matter.

Can the Netherlands be ready by that time to organise the most sustainable Games ever?
I think every country should be. The techniques and the know-how are available, also with regards to the damage that we do. That's why I am not primarily concerned with an event such as the Olympic Games, but rather with the entire system of our society and economy. The efforts of Greenpeace are aimed at bringing about real changes in our systems. The Games are of course a great opportunity to put items on the agenda, but you can also do that with a G8 Summit or any other major event. For our campaigns we are always looking a few years ahead and then we choose which issues to focus on.
What I would like to say to the IOC now and for the future, is that any organisation involved in this type of decision should make the environment a priority. We don't accept arsenic in our food, we don't want to wear clothes manufactured by slaves, and likewise it should be totally unacceptable in the public eye to organise any large event that has a huge impact on the environment.

Will Greenpeace assist the Netherlands in this, like it did in Sydney?
We are first and foremost a campaign organisation that wishes to kick-start things that are not on the agenda yet or are not high enough on the agenda. In the days of Sydney, that meant environmental issues in general, which is why we played a rather prominent role then, although we still mainly referred the organisers to the right third parties. I assume that by 2028 our country will have a flourishing industry for environmental advice, just like we have now for ICT. That has already started. And this industry will grow rapidly, since the problem of climate change is already affecting large outdoor events because of the unpredictability of the weather. Low countries such as the Netherlands have no option but to act. By 2028 Greenpeace will be referring the organisers of the Games to various consultancy firms. Right now we are also referring many organisations to websites like those of the National Institute for Public Health and the Environment (RIVM) and Milieu Centraal. Here they can find the techniques and knowledge that are already available. Meanwhile we are looking for new solutions to other problems. We are the catalyser, rather than the executive.

The games do offer a choice opportunity, however, for solving issues in a highly visible way, such as the construction of a reservoir for sustainable energy proposed by Rudolf Das [see elsewhere in this book – MD]. Such projects are there for the world to see.
If plans come up for creating artificial islands along the Dutch coast, we will certainly want to investigate what impact they have and offer advice about environmental and climate aspects. We are already citing Das's plan for the Falling Lake as a possible solution to the energy

problem, but we also say that there are enough techniques that can be applied right now. Saving energy without loss of comfort is already possible and the next step is to switch over to fully sustainable energy. A lot can be achieved with solar thermal power plants, like the ones that have already been built in California. If we built such power plants on a half of a percent of the Sahara Desert, they could supply all of Europe with sustainable energy. This is possible now.

How old will you be in 2028?
70.

Where would you prefer to be watching the Olympic Games then?
It is more likely that I will be walking in nature or watching my son doing sports than that I'll be watching the Games either in the stadium or on TV. I think it's a wonderful pastime for all those athletes and a great source of inspiration for amateurs, but it's really not my thing.

Can you think of a sports quote or slogan to make the country rally behind the idea of (Green) Games?
Sports are always nicer to practice than to watch from the sideline. So: be active!

WHAT K
OF OLYI
GAMES
WE IMA

KIND
MPIC
CAN
GINE?

A4 GAMES

AGRO GAMES

BRIDGE GAMES

DOWNTOWN GAMES

DYKE GAMES

ISLAND-AIRPORT GAMES

LIGHT & CHEAP GAMES

NS GAMES

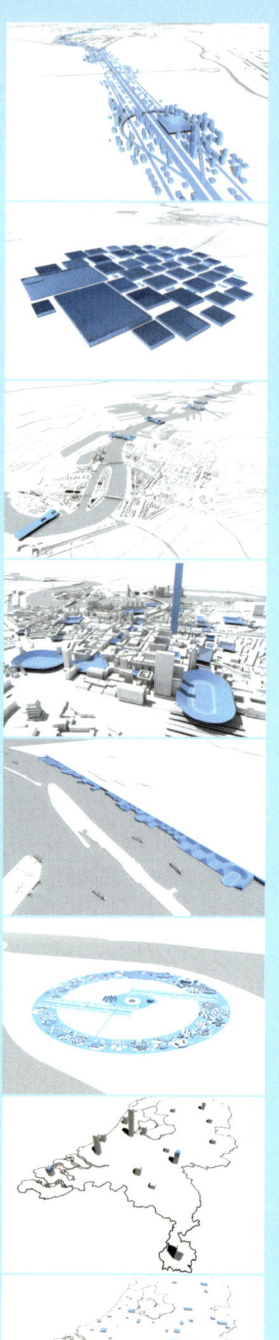

SOCIAL GAMES

SPHERE GAMES

SPORTS-MINDED CITY

STACKING GAMES

SUPERBOWL

TRAVEL GAMES

WALL OF SPORTS

WATER GAMES

A4 GAMES
NL WILL BECOME ONE CITY

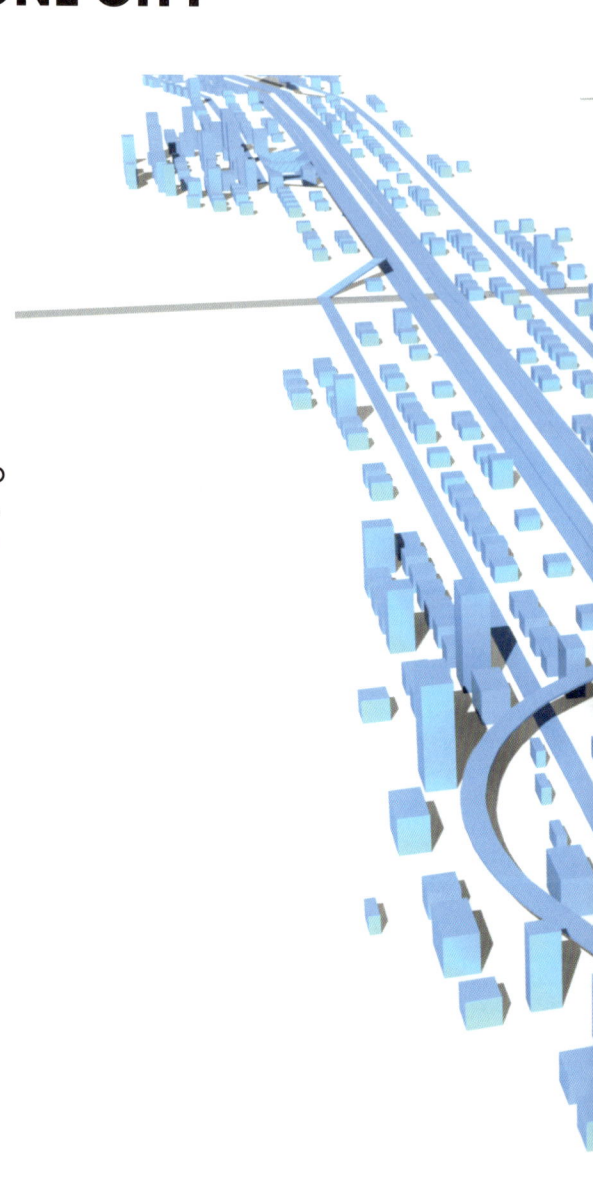

It's 2028.
Amsterdam, Leiden, The Hague and Rotterdam are no longer recognizable as separate cities. The urban agglomeration of Western Holland – known as the 'Randstad' in Dutch – is becoming one huge informal city governed by different yet adjoining public administrations. Sprawled out along the infrastructure without uniform regulation, this built-up area is subject to permanent gridlock. In the meantime, the Olympics are on the verge of being forgotten because their economic and spatial requirements have grown beyond the administrative capacities of a single city. In this vicious circle, the Randstad is the perfect location for testing a new regional Olympic ideal, while at the same time the Olympics are the last chance for the Randstad to catalyze its political and economic actors into overcoming their divisiveness and forming a supra-municipal identity. As the backbone of the area, the A4 highway can be developed into a facilitating and connecting framework incorporating infrastructure and programme at the same time.

Issues: miles driven, car ownership, population of hosting city, highway network
Goals: administrative and infrastructural reorganisation

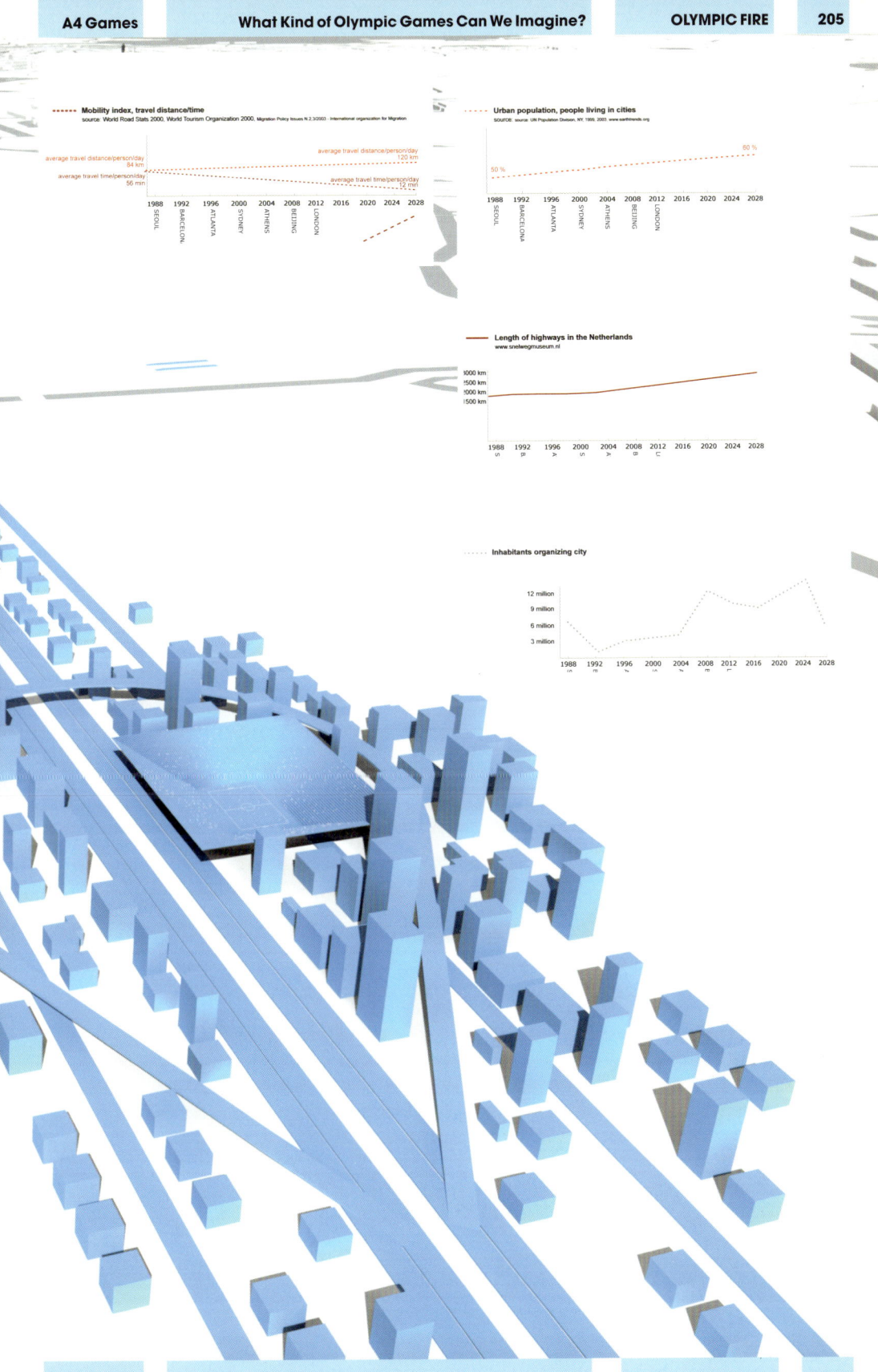

DURING THE OLYMPICS

Distribution of Olympic facilities along A4 highway between Amsterdam and Rotterdam

AFTERUSE

AGRO GAMES
NL WILL FEED THE WORLD

It's 2028.
The rise of living standards in newly developing countries has caused a continuous increase in energy consumption. Global organisations are not strong enough to renegotiate the situation as the world faces possible disaster. Finding new space to live, work and produce has become the main issue for survival. With the blurring of boundaries between the artificial and the natural, the values of sport and competition between equals are at stake. Yet this could provide the background for a new take on human life. Dutch territory has always been artificial; a brave, creative nation that has challenged natural conditions would be the best host for the prototype of the 22nd century. The combination of new agricultural production techniques with a variety of living conditions and programmes is proposed as a new landscape.
Issues: world population, demographics, GDP, food prices
Goals: new nature

Agro Games

What Kind of Olympic Games Can We Imagine?

OLYMPIC FIRE

211

related trend

Gross Domestic Product per capita
source: EconStats
price in trillion Dollars

related trend

Worldwide Calories Consumption
source: FAO, Rome, 2002

related trend

Worldwide urban population
source: UN Population Division, NY, 1999, 2003, www.earthtrends.org

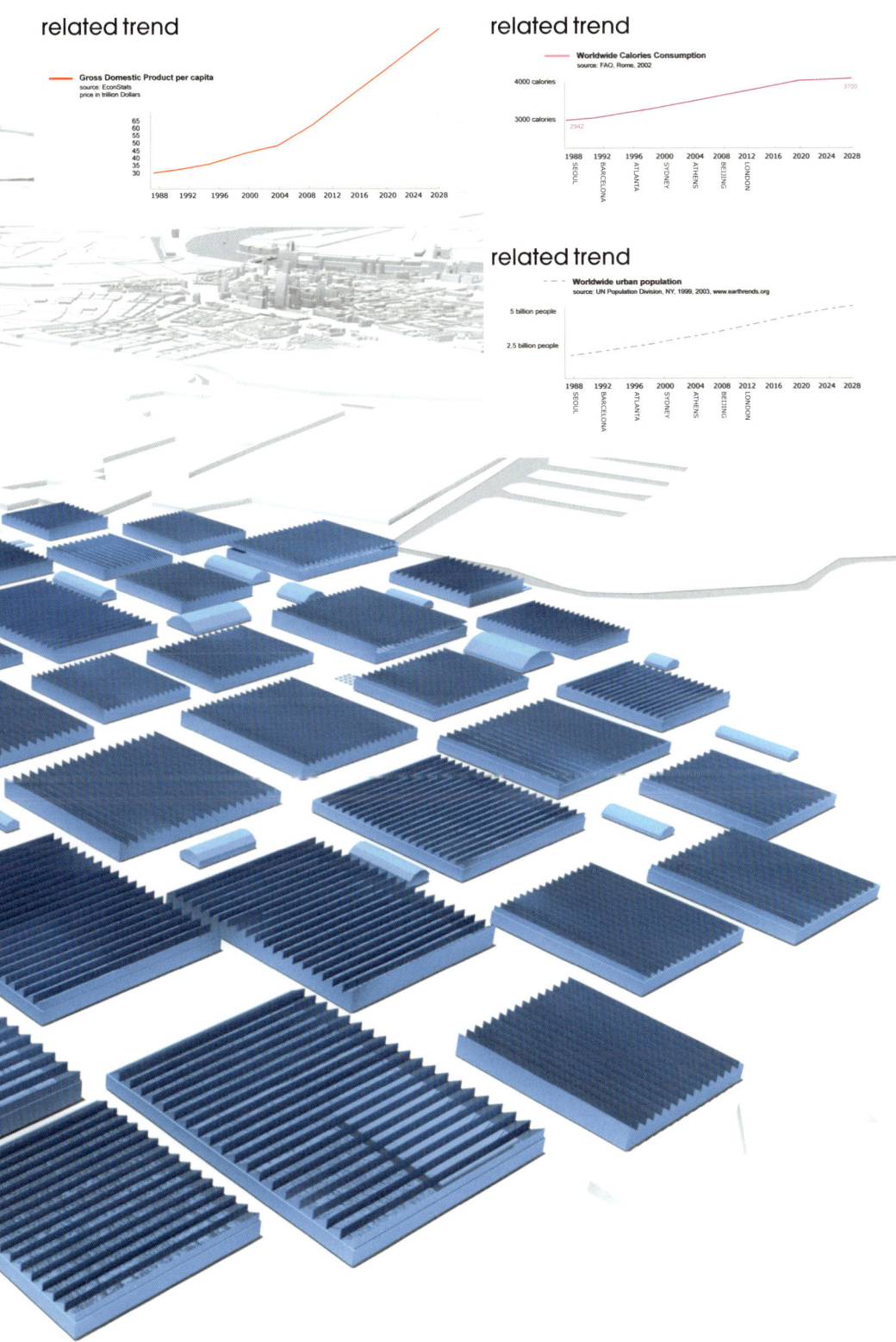

DURING THE OLYMPICS

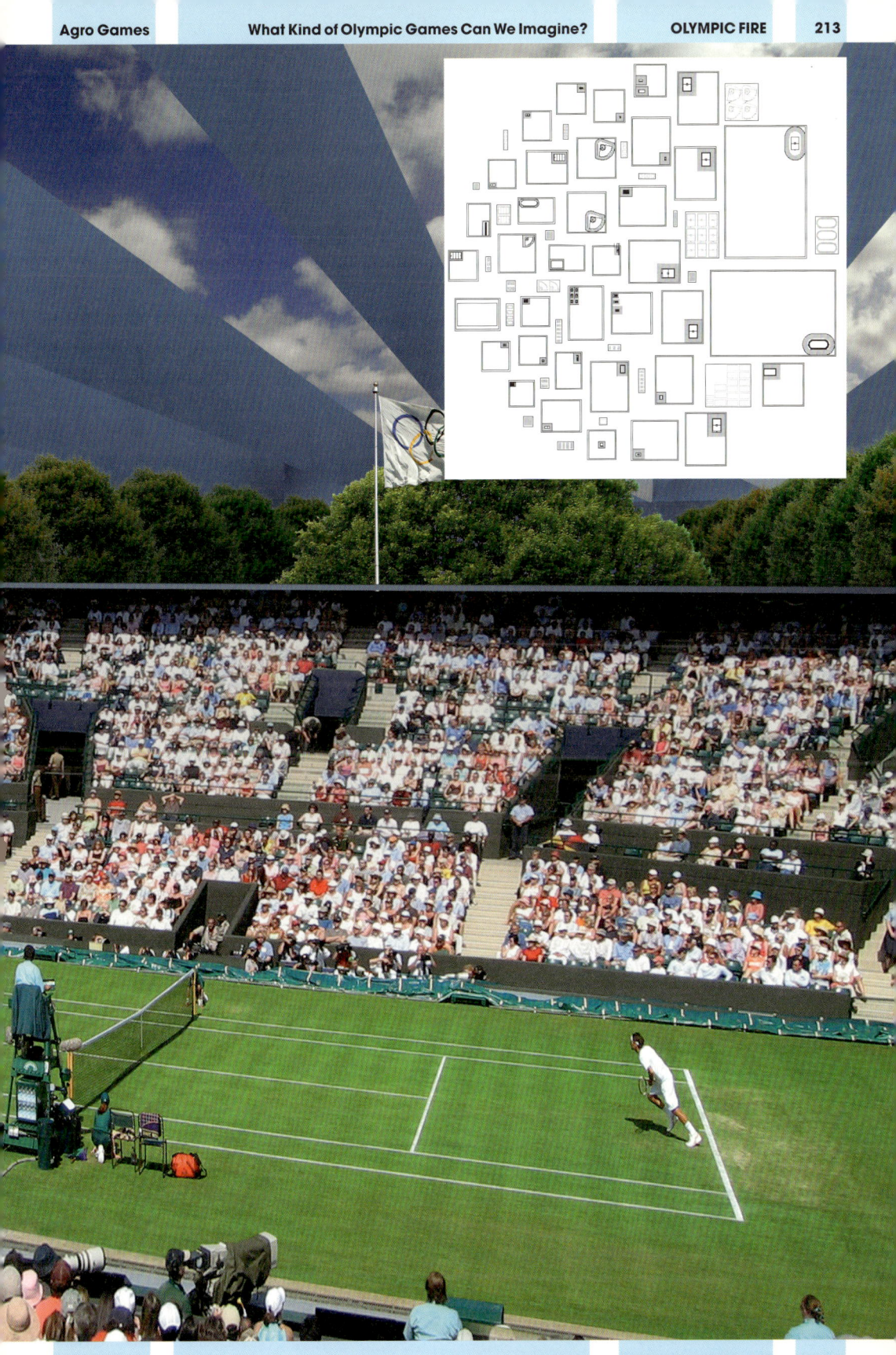

AFTERUSE

BRIDGE GAMES
NL WILL BRIDGE THE GAP

It's 2028.
More than half the world population lives in an urban area, which in most cases lacks the critical density to be considered a city. A city is a place of democracy; but since we now live in a post-democratic world that considers the city either a utopia or a vintage entertainment facility, a regeneration of the urban concept is necessary. The Games have lost their social potential in this process of individualization, yet the Games could be a chance to build a daring new espace sportif at the heart of a healthier city. The Netherlands, a country of waterways, will find this stunning new urbanity precisely in the most open part of the city – the river. It will offer to the world a prototype of social space that is also an infrastructure, drawing inspiration from its centuries of canal culture.
Issues: suburbanisation, oil prices, waste production
Goals: new public and connecting spaces in the city

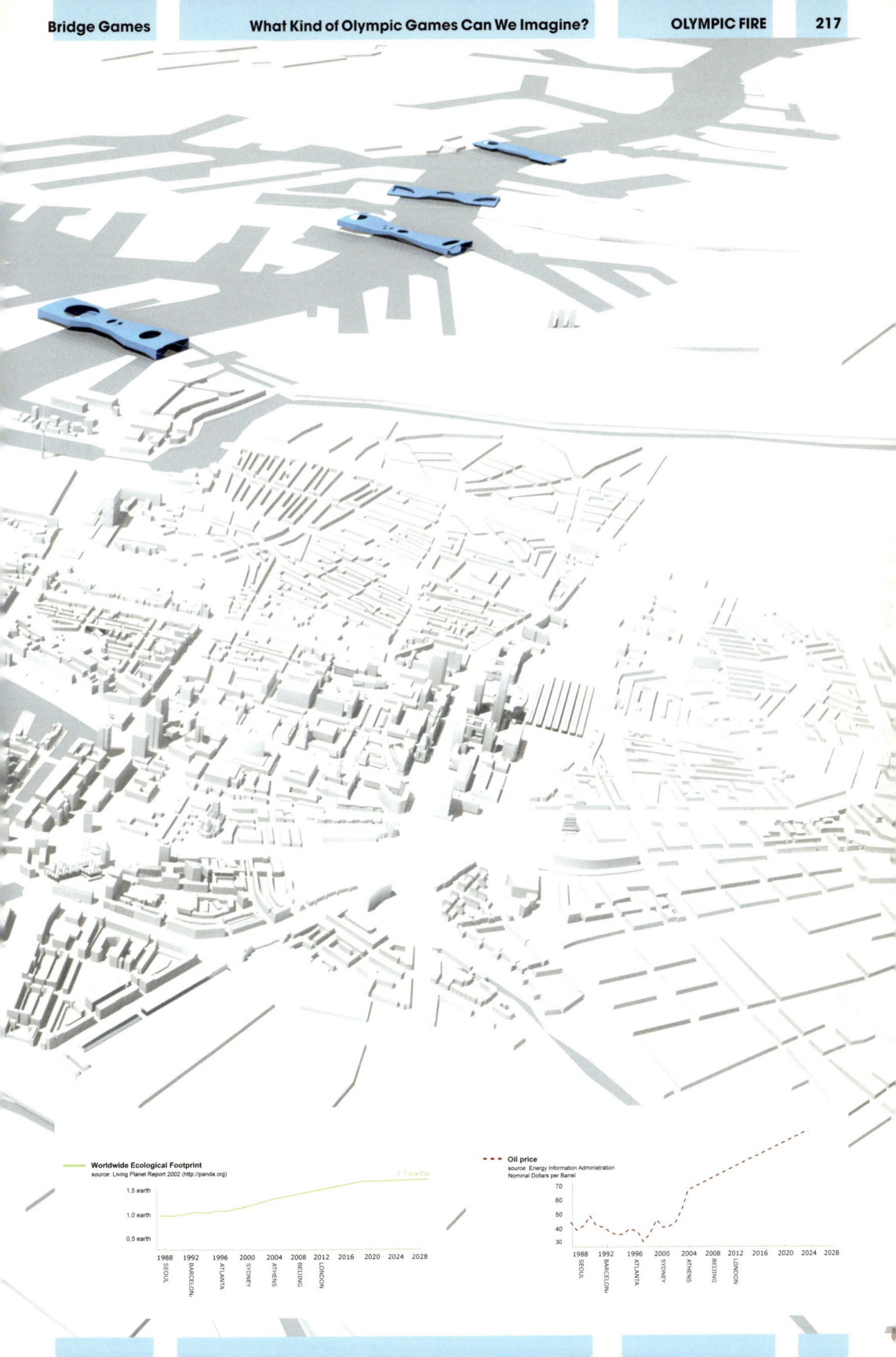

DURING THE OLYMPICS

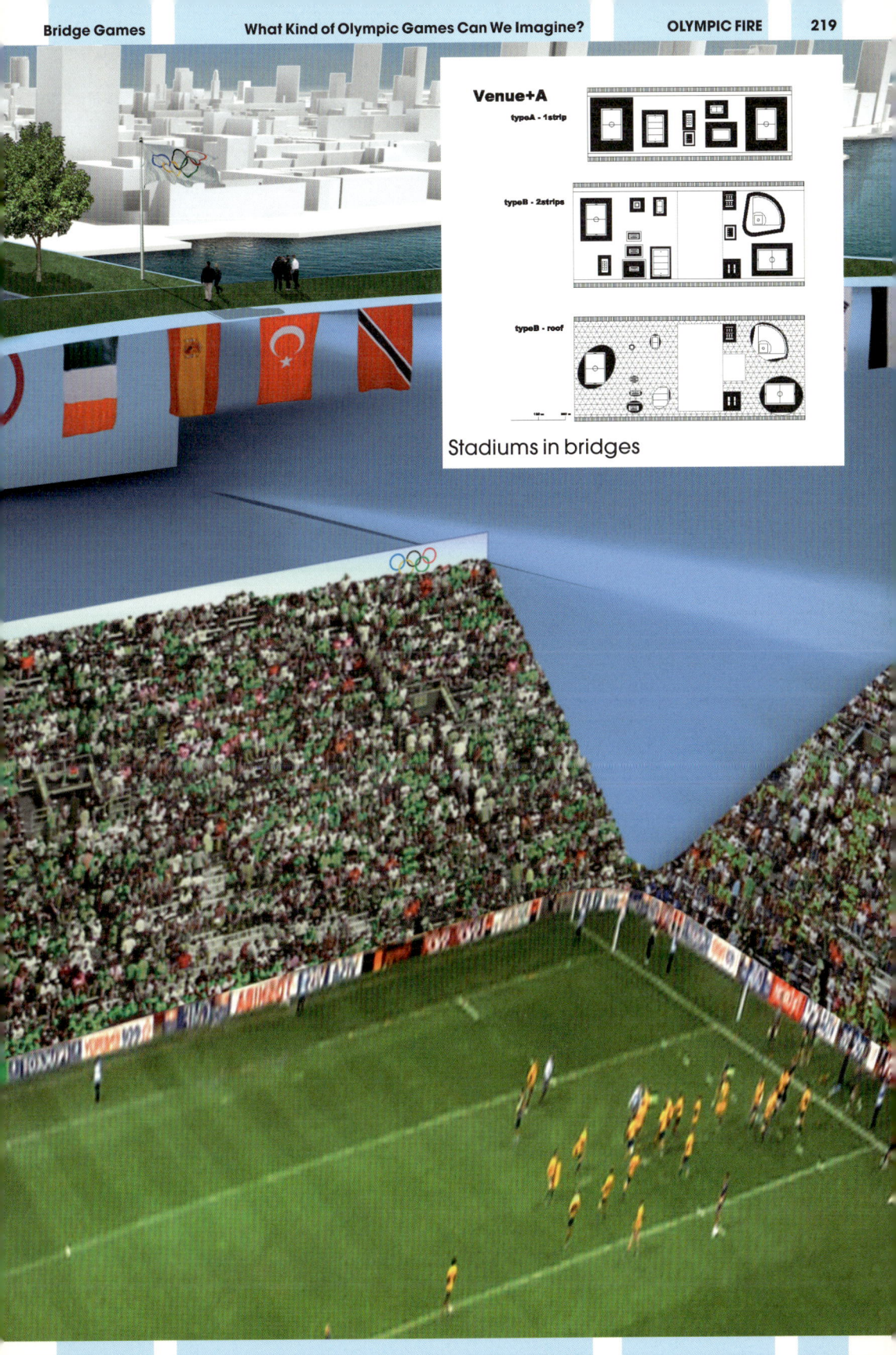

Stadiums in bridges

AFTERUSE

DOWNTOWN GAMES
NL WILL REJUVENATE THE CITY

It's 2028.
The games are so elitist that only very few people can afford a ticket. The difference in the share of GDP earned by the top 5% and that of the rest has dramatically increased, while the middle class undergoes a crisis, falling into poverty. In a progressive lack of perspectives, the economic elite thrives by exploiting the situation on a global scale. The city splits into a commercial, expensive downtown and low-income suburbia. The very idea of a vibrant downtown disappears in an increasingly clustered society. A strong host city should propose a radical act, putting forward the games as a catalyser for a new downtown life. The Netherlands, a melting pot much younger than most European countries, will challenge the idea of a lifeless elite downtown and equally lifeless elite games. Sports, and life with it, will return to the pavements.

Issues: food price, income discrepancy, Big Mac index
Goals: new city vibrancy

| Urban Games | What Kind of Olympic Games Can We Imagine? | OLYMPIC FIRE | 223 |

related trend

Gross Domestic Product per capita
source: EconStats
price in trillion Dollars

65
60
55
50
45
40
35
30

1988 1992 1996 2000 2004 2008 2012 2016 2020 2024 2028

related trend

World Income inequality
source: Gini, world distr of income, Xavier Sala

0.665
0.655
0.645
0.635

1988 1992 1996 2000 2004 2008 2012 2016 2020 2024 2028
SEOUL BARCELONA ATLANTA SYDNEY ATHENS BEIJING LONDON

related trend

Worldwide ageing population
source: UN population Division, NY, 1999, 2003, www.earthtrends.org

1 billion people
0.5 billion people

1988 1992 1996 2000 2004 2008 2012 2016 2020 2024 2028
SEOUL BARCE ATLAN SYDNE ATHEN BEIJIN LONDO

DURING THE OLYMPICS

Position of venues in Rotterdam

AFTERUSE

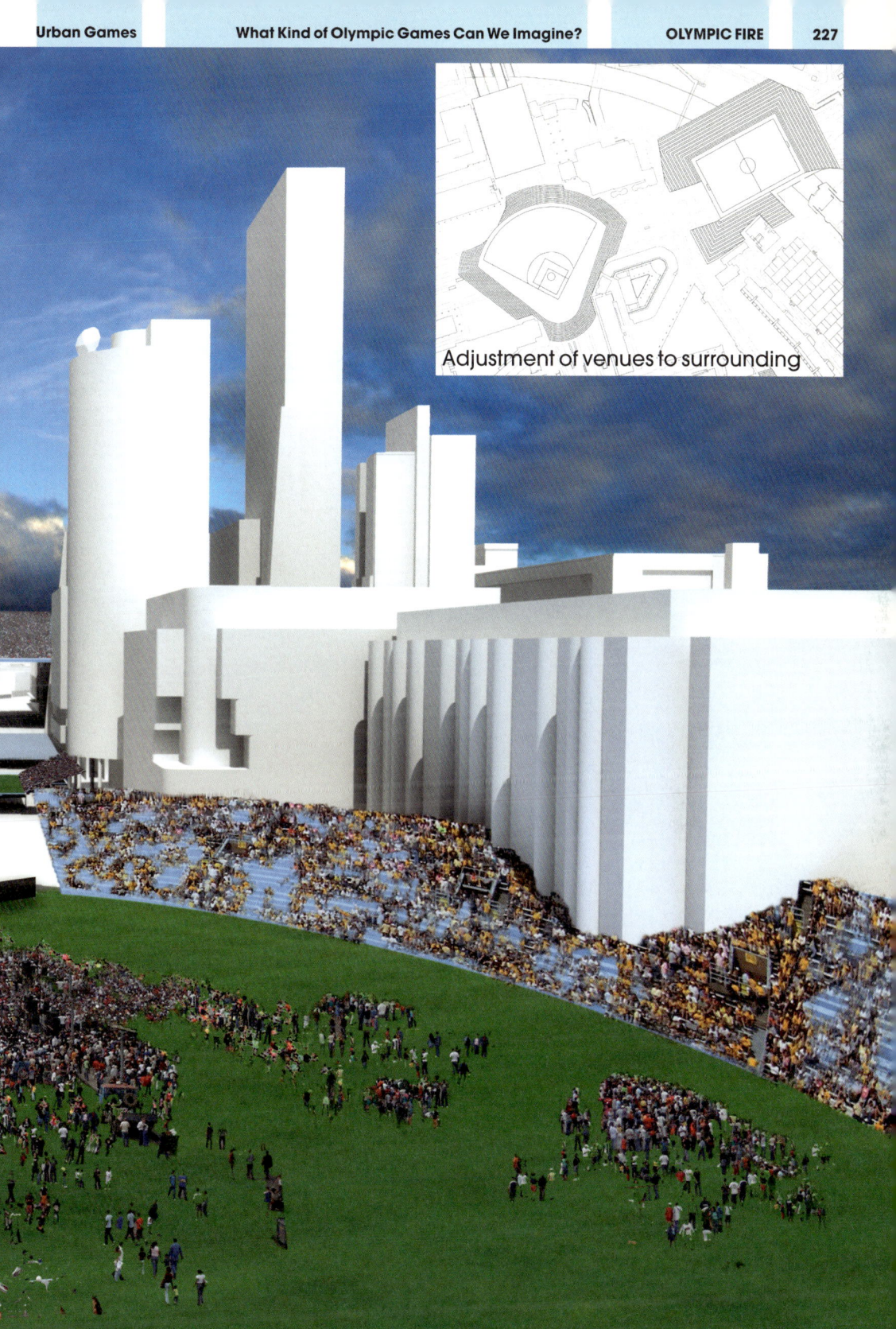

Adjustment of venues to surrounding

DYKE GAMES
NL WILL PROTECT US

It's 2028.
Global temperatures have increased, the sea is rising slowly and greater seasonal variations in sea level are occurring due to the new unstable condition of the polar ice caps. The progressively stronger seasonal behaviour of rivers makes waterways impractical during summer and adds new significance to sea ports. As a result, water management has become an increasingly significant element of the budget. In the context of this global shipwreck, sports are less and less interesting or heroic. Is it necessary to make a new pact with the sea and the natural elements in order to save the Olympics from doom? If the creation of polders in the Netherlands marked a spectacular major step forward in the relation between humanity and water, now the Dutch have the potential to stimulate a new 'glocal' (local initiative, global results) dimension of this old legacy.
Issues: environmental insecurity, river-level fluctuations
Goals: express Dutch potentialities, de-branding of Games

related trend

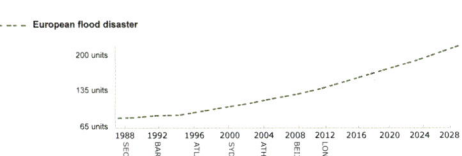

European flood disaster
200 units
135 units
65 units
1988
1992
1996
2000
2004
2008
2012
2016
2020
2024
2028
SEOU
BARC
SYDN
LOND

related trend

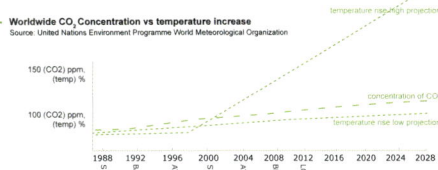

Worldwide CO_2 Concentration vs temperature increase
Source: United Nations Environment Programme World Meteorological Organization
150 (CO2) ppm, (temp) %
100 (CO2) ppm, (temp) %
temperature rise high projection
concentration of CO_2
temperature rise low projection
1988
1992
1996
2000
2004
2008
2012
2016
2020
2024
2028
SEOU
BARC
SYDN
LOND

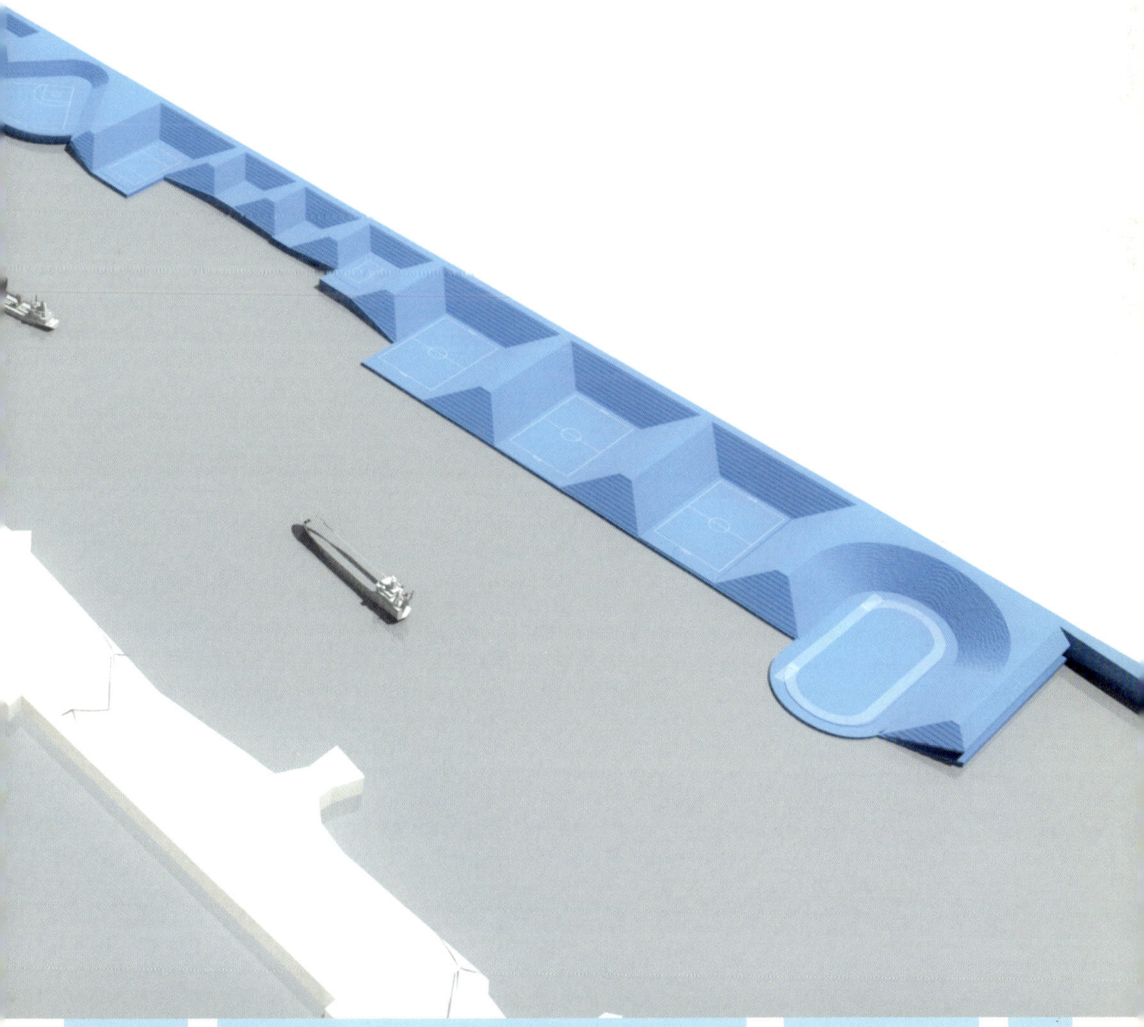

DURING THE OLYMPICS

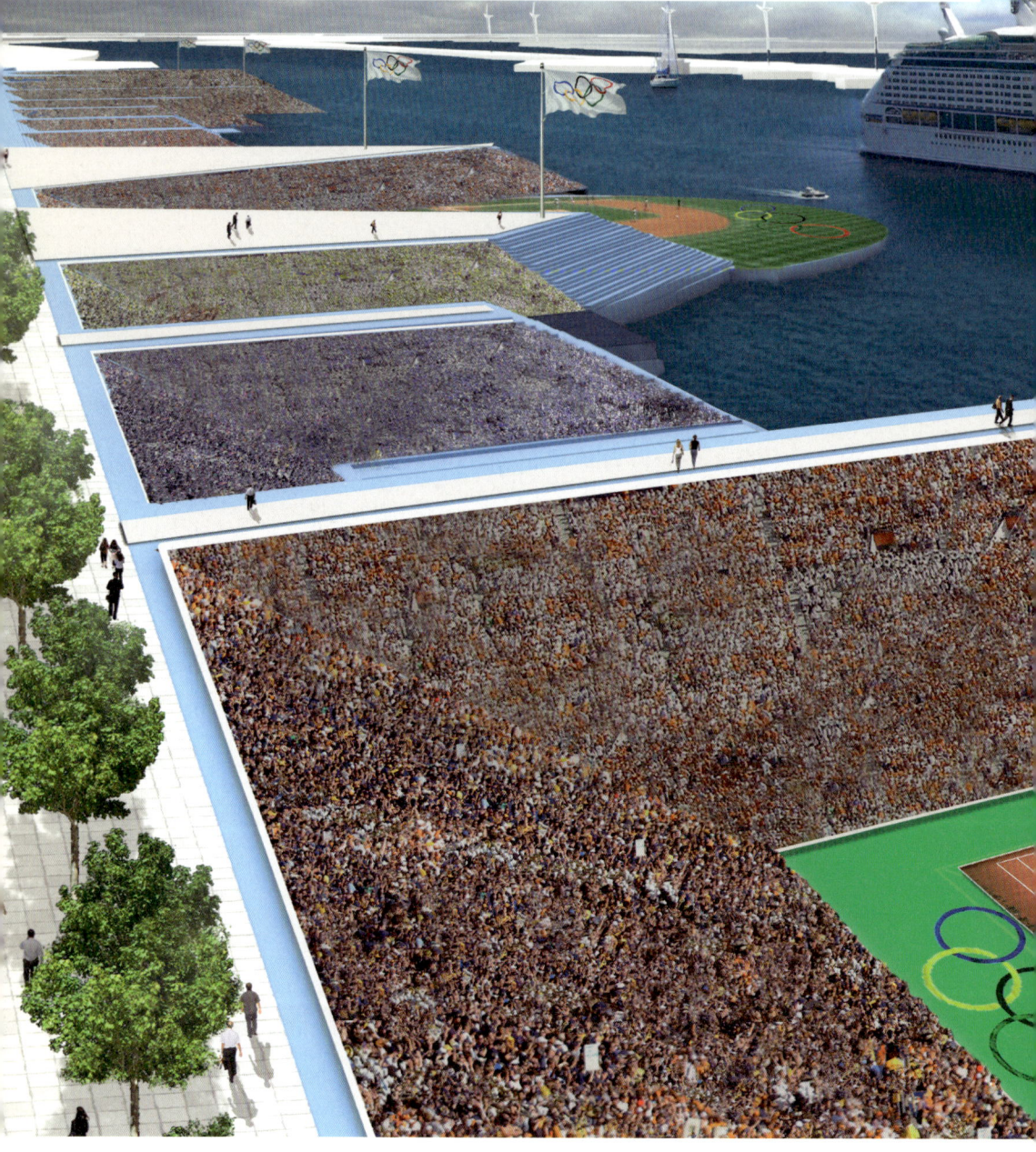

Plan of dyke along the Maas

Detail with stadiums

AFTERUSE

ISLAND-AIRPORT GAMES
NL WILL FIND NEW TERRITORIES

It's 2028.
The world has not managed to change the trends foreseen at the beginning of the millennium and we now live in a world of rising sea levels and altered sea currents. Now the only choice we have is to adapt or disappear, control the changes or not. In the meantime the Olympics have become bigger and bigger, so much so that at some point no one city alone could host them anymore. The huge economic power and influence of the Olympic Games have led to an increased demand for their political positioning, which has put severe strain on the relationship between the IOC and the host cities; the IOC has thus become unwilling to attach the Games to any national agenda. Neutrality, necessary for the survival of the Games, can only be guaranteed by developing a purely international agenda and therefore the Games will only take place on territory perceived as neutral. Masters at adaptation, the Dutch develop new coastal protections, cleverly using the existing sea currents to build barriers by taking advantage of the power of the sea instead of fighting against it. This new territory becomes the ideal location for the first truly international Olympic Games, without any national committee being involved and with direct air access. **Issues:** water level, insurance costs, Olympic boycotts **Goals:** new territories, new coast, global Games

Airport Island

What Kind of Olympic Games Can We Imagine?

OLYMPIC FIRE   235

related trend

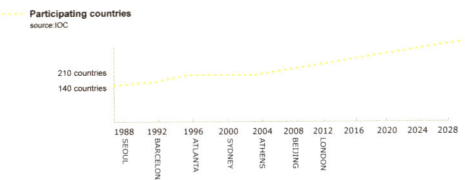

Participating countries
source: IOC

210 countries
140 countries

1988 SEOUL | 1992 BARCELONA | 1996 ATLANTA | 2000 SYDNEY | 2004 ATHENS | 2008 BEIJING | 2012 LONDON | 2016 | 2020 | 2024 | 2028

related trend

Worldwide CO_2 Concentration vs temperature increase
Source: United Nations Environment Programme World Meteorological Organization

temperature rise high projection
concentration of CO_2
temperature rise low projection

150 (CO2) ppm, (temp) %
100 (CO2) ppm, (temp) %

1988 SEOUL | 1992 BARC | 1996 ATLA | 2000 SYDN | 2004 ATHE | 2008 BEIJI | 2012 LOND | 2016 | 2020 | 2024 | 2028

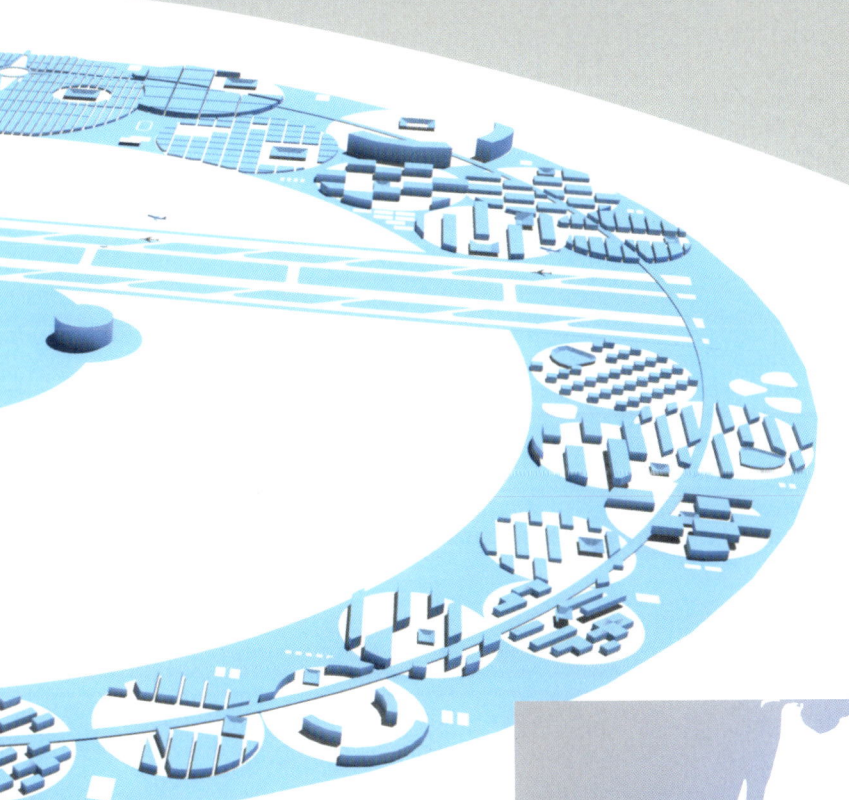

DURING THE OLYMPICS

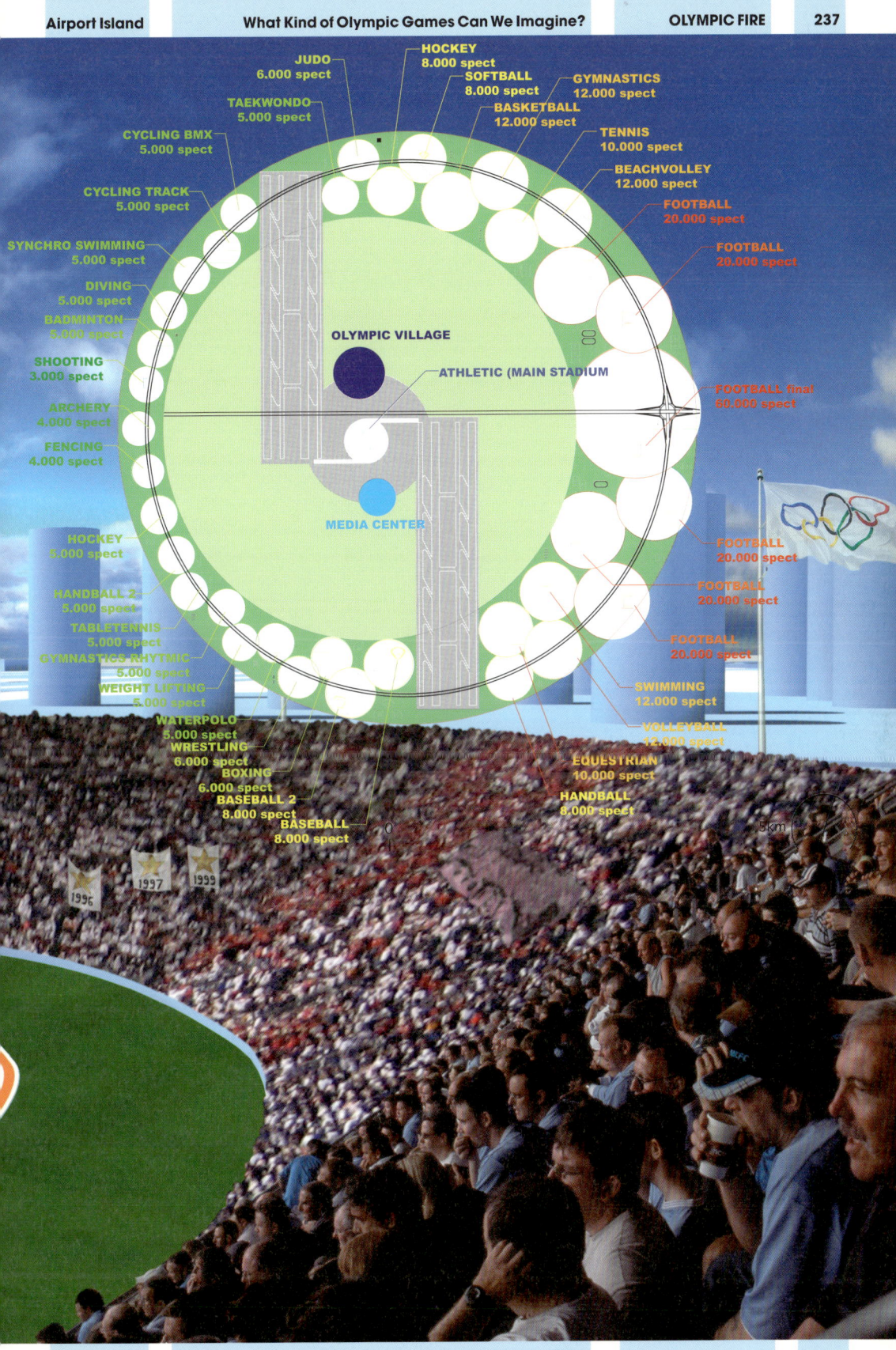

AFTERUSE

(ref. OMA/NACO; KM³ ISLANDS)

LIGHT & CHEAP GAMES

NL WILL RE-USE

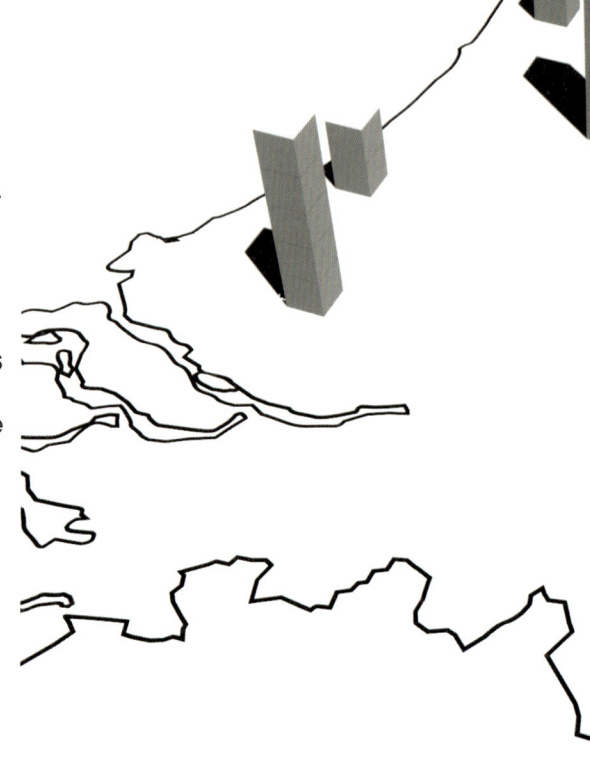

It's 2028.
As the Olympics have been growing at an even quicker pace than before, the backlash was inevitable. The general population has protested, taxpayers are refusing to pay, sponsorship deals have been cancelled. Now the Games need to find relevance by accepting the fact that they are only one expense on a list of many. In a last-ditch effort, the IOC changes the regulations: The cheapest bid with the lowest ticket price and lowest tax burden will win. The Games become a catalyst for improvement and renovation. With thorough research into existing facilities, including their shortcomings and an upgrade scenario, the Olympics inject energy into structures that already exist, thus avoiding the insertion of new structures, and retaining their pre-use as after-use.

Issues: cost of Olympics, white elephant, 16 days of luxury but years of debts

Goals: re-use all the facilities in the entire country, lowest Games cost, share Games services in many cities

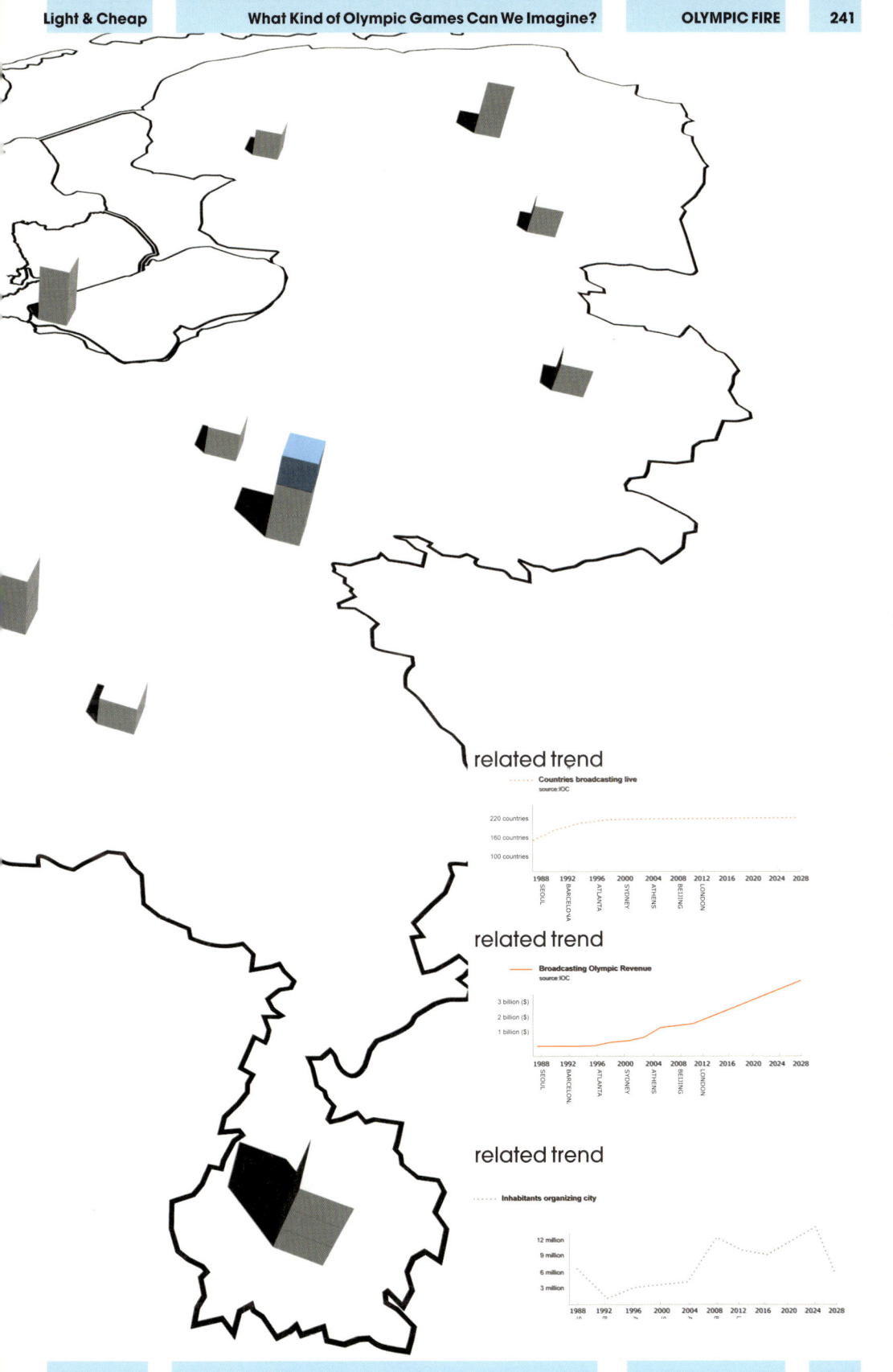

DURING THE OLYMPICS

Cost and revenue comparison of Olympic Games

AFTERUSE

Distribution of existing facilities which need to be upgraded to Olympic standards (white) and new facilities (blue)

NS GAMES
NL WILL LET EVERYONE TAKE PART

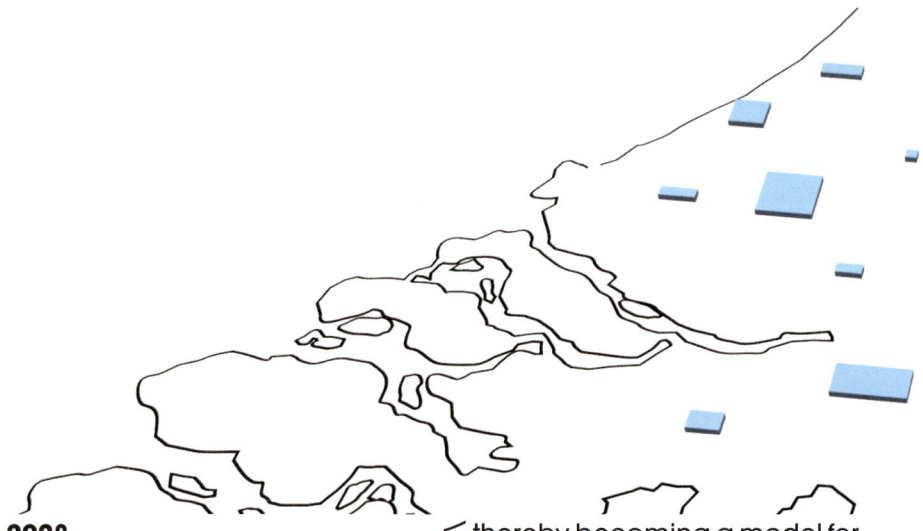

It's 2028.
The Olympics have finally run out of ever-larger cities to host the Games. An alternative would be to spread the events over a group of cities, moving to new, more specialised audiences while offering broader programming. More sports could be included; 48 events would cover all official and demonstration sports. Each city could bid for one sport that is suited to its local facilities, sports development, interests and population size. Accessibility will be the final factor in determining the location. In comparison with transport by road, water and air, railways have the best network and potential, considering the new investment in high-speed lines. The Netherlands is the perfect candidate for testing this strategy, due to its limited size, equal spread of population and dense infrastructure, thereby becoming a model for regional development. By placing new venues on or next to central railway stations, 100% after-use of these venues can be achieved. Of course the opening ceremony will be the biggest train ride in the world!

Issues: urban development, regional planning, built-up area, population of hosting city, participating sports, demonstration sports, infrastructure density, sports facilities per number of residents

Goals: connect infrastructure with sport facilities, more sports and more participation

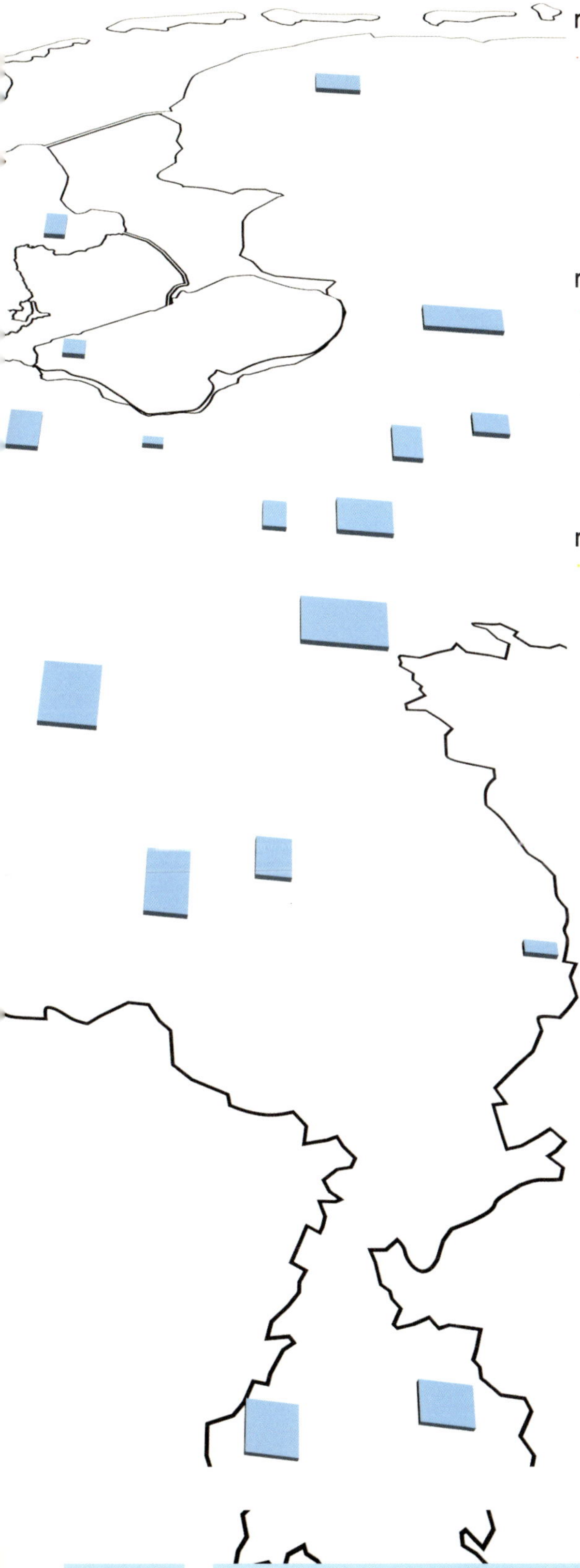

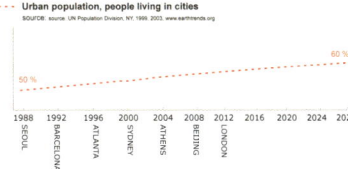

related trend

Urban population, people living in cities
source: source: UN Population Division, NY, 1999, 2003, www.earthtrends.org
50 %
60 %
1988 1992 1996 2000 2004 2008 2012 2016 2020 2024 2028
SEOUL BARCELONA ATLANTA SYDNEY ATHENS BEIJING LONDON

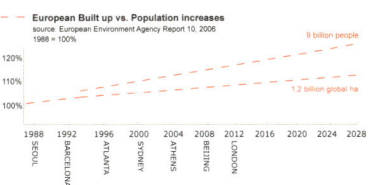

related trend

European Built up vs. Population increases
source: European Environment Agency Report 10, 2006
1988 = 100%
120%
110%
100%
9 billion people
1.2 billion global ha
1988 1992 1996 2000 2004 2008 2012 2016 2020 2024 2028
SEOUL BARCELONA ATLANTA SYDNEY ATHENS BEIJING LONDON

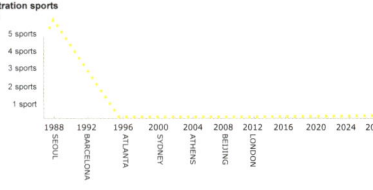

related trend

Demonstration sports
source:IOC
5 sports
4 sports
3 sports
2 sports
1 sport
1988 1992 1996 2000 2004 2008 2012 2016 2020 2024 2028
SEOUL BARCELONA ATLANTA SYDNEY ATHENS BEIJING LONDON

DURING THE OLYMPICS

Selection of 48 cities (Olympic and all demonstration sports) based on accessibility

AFTERUSE

Location of Olympic venues around 48 railway stations

SOCIAL GAMES
NL WILL REPAIR THE CITY

It's 2028.
Production has totally moved away from cities to where it's cheaper and easier; as a result, the difference between the investing rich and the producing poor has increased even further. The shrinking of production leaves new ghettos that are without economic means for investment and are ready to welcome new programmes. Meanwhile anti-global criticism against IOC policies has threatened the games, obliging the committee to identify more and more with social and local issues. The revitalisation of a host city could offer new meaning to the splendid ritual of the Games. As the Dutch are the first to experience changes due to their open, international economy, they are most concerned about these developments. A major repair act, an acupuncture for a city, would catalyze this unique mix of factors, and turn them into the strongest asset for the success of the future Games.
Issues: income discrepancy, GDP
Goals: sports as repair and rebirth of a community

DURING THE OLYMPICS

Areas with highest unemployement (red), youngest population (orange) and largest immigrant population (yellow) in Amsterdam overlaid

AFTERUSE

SPHERE GAMES
WELCOME TO NL!

It's 2028.
The developed world and the Netherlands are growing older, and retirees represent more than half the population. The working population can't produce enough to support the rapidly ageing population. Europe has tightened controls at its borders due to the political influence of a more conservative population and seems satisfied with managing the internal migration of its own poorer members. As it finally becomes evident that experimentation and innovation are the only way to withstand pressure from newly developing countries, there is a generally accepted feeling that a new population and new ideas are needed. In this drowning society, sports have acquired a newly significant role as the symbol of youth, body culture and health. The Olympics have once again become a ritual event, a celebration of youth, new ideas and competition and a catalyst for a new openness in the Netherlands. To avoid the suburbanisation which had threatened to destroy expanding cities in the past, new downtown suburbs are developed to house this new population.

Issues: demographics, density
Goals: celebration of body culture

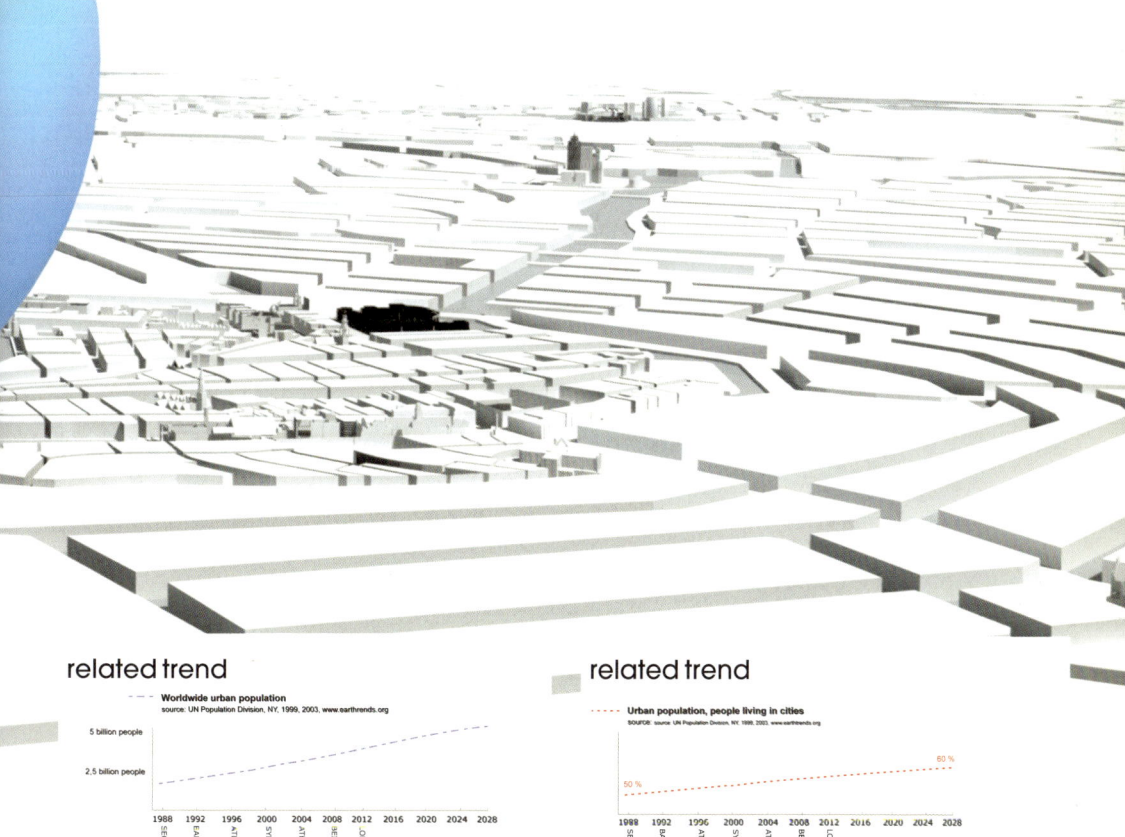

related trend — Worldwide urban population
source: UN Population Division, NY, 1999, 2003, www.earthtrends.org

related trend — Urban population, people living in cities
source: UN Population Division, NY, 1999, 2003, www.earthtrends.org

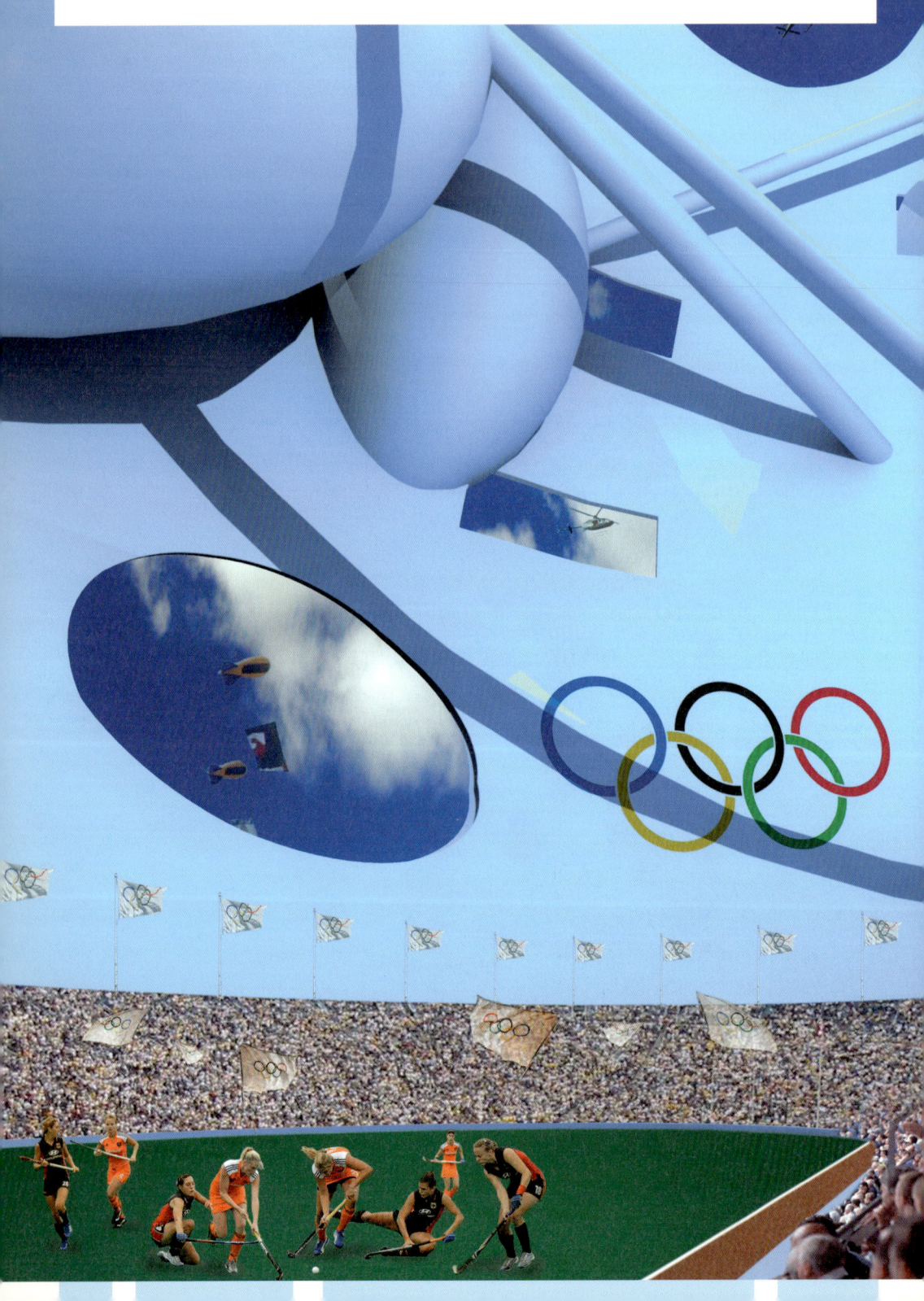

DURING THE OLYMPICS

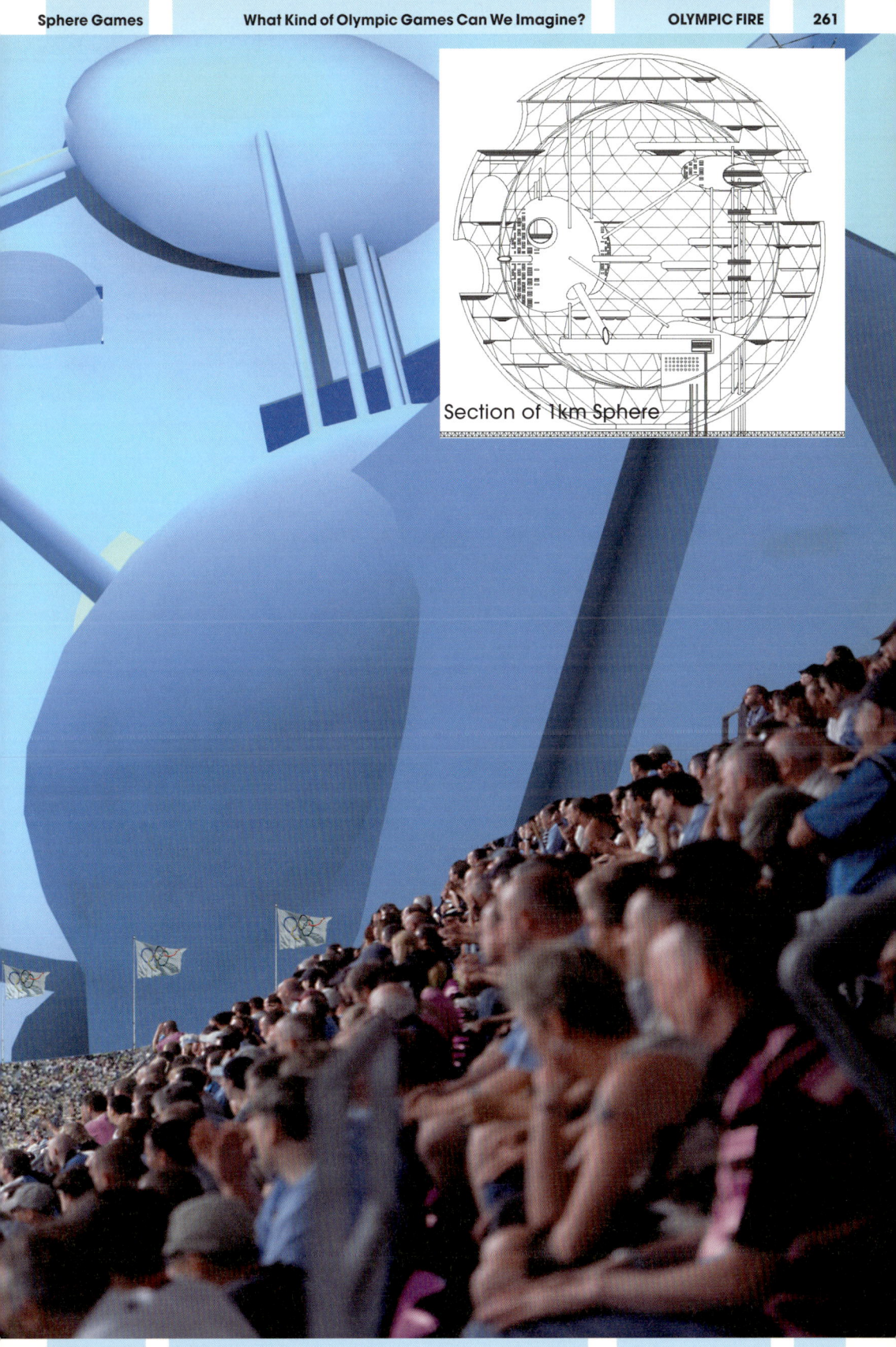

Section of 1km Sphere

AFTERUSE

SPORTS-MINDED CITY
NL WILL BE HEALTHY

It's 2028.

Obesity has only grown worse in all developed countries in the last decades and recently has been spreading to newly developed countries. Spectacular advances in medicine and bio-sciences have been reversed by the effects of an unstoppable obesity trend. At the same time a backlash is taking place against ever-larger venues for the Olympic Games being inserted in inner cities, leaving expensive sports ruins in their wake while bland suburban extensions continue to grow. Is it possible to imagine a new type of city, an Olympic city, where sports are more than a matter of health alone but also an intrinsic part of life? With our Dutch legacy of creating artificial landscapes, we can imagine a new 'Hill of Sports' as a recurring feature in the endlessly flat Dutch landscape, where 'Homo Sporticus' can live in a modern Olympia.

Issues: life expectancy, body mass index (obesity), calorie consumption, built area, cost of the Olympics
Goals: a new healthy society

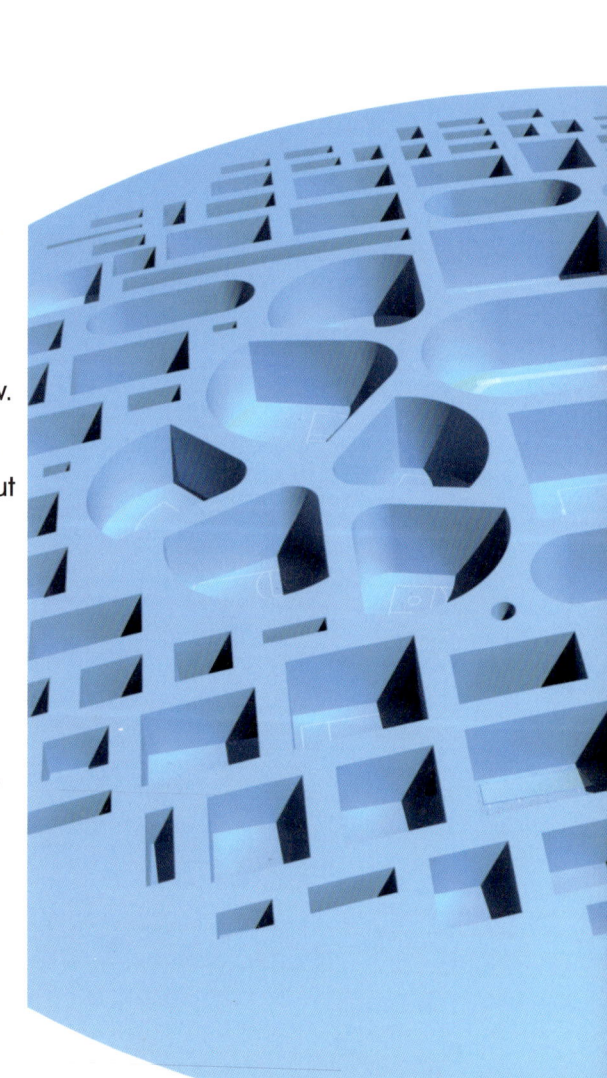

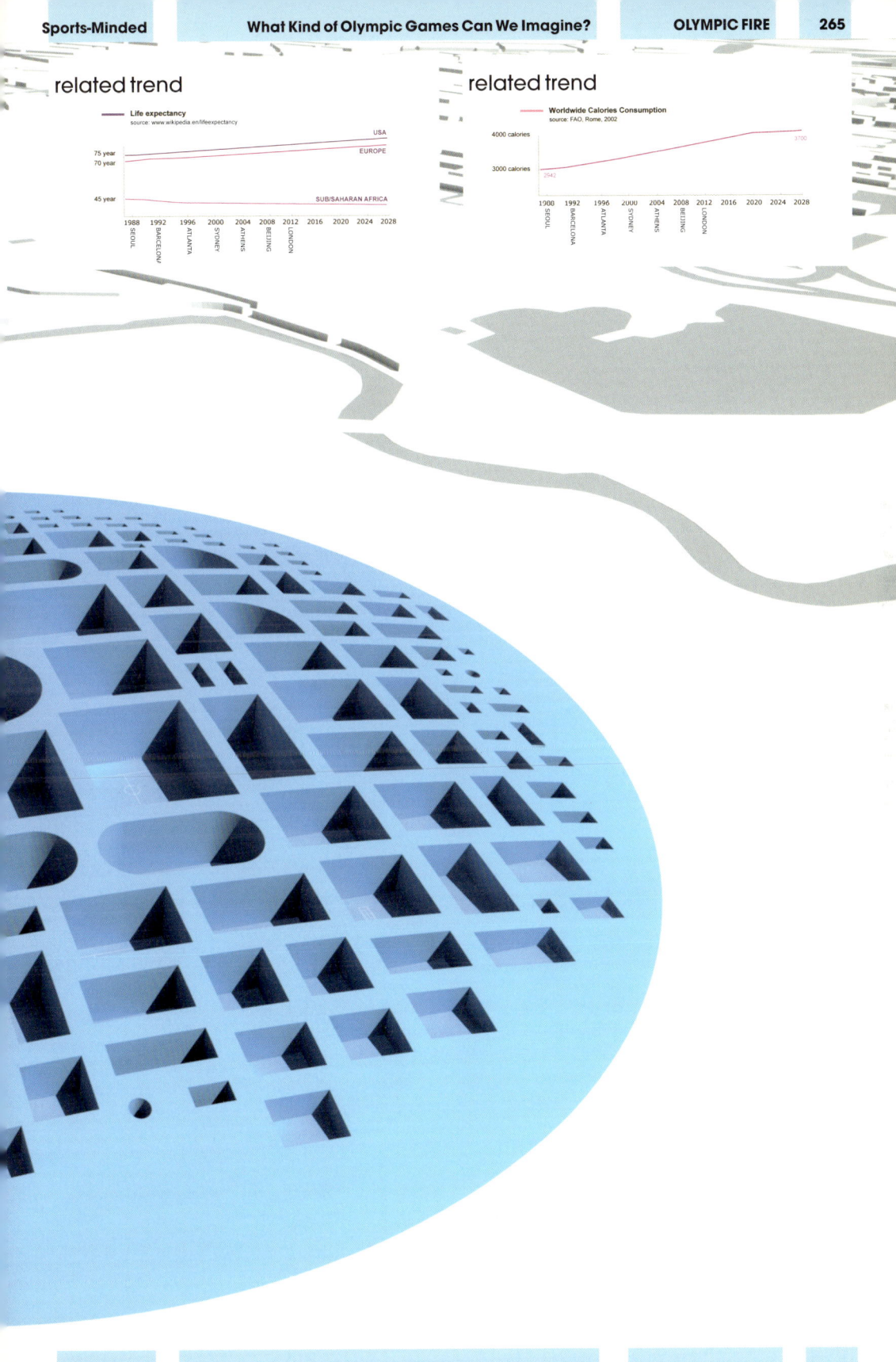

DURING THE OLYMPICS

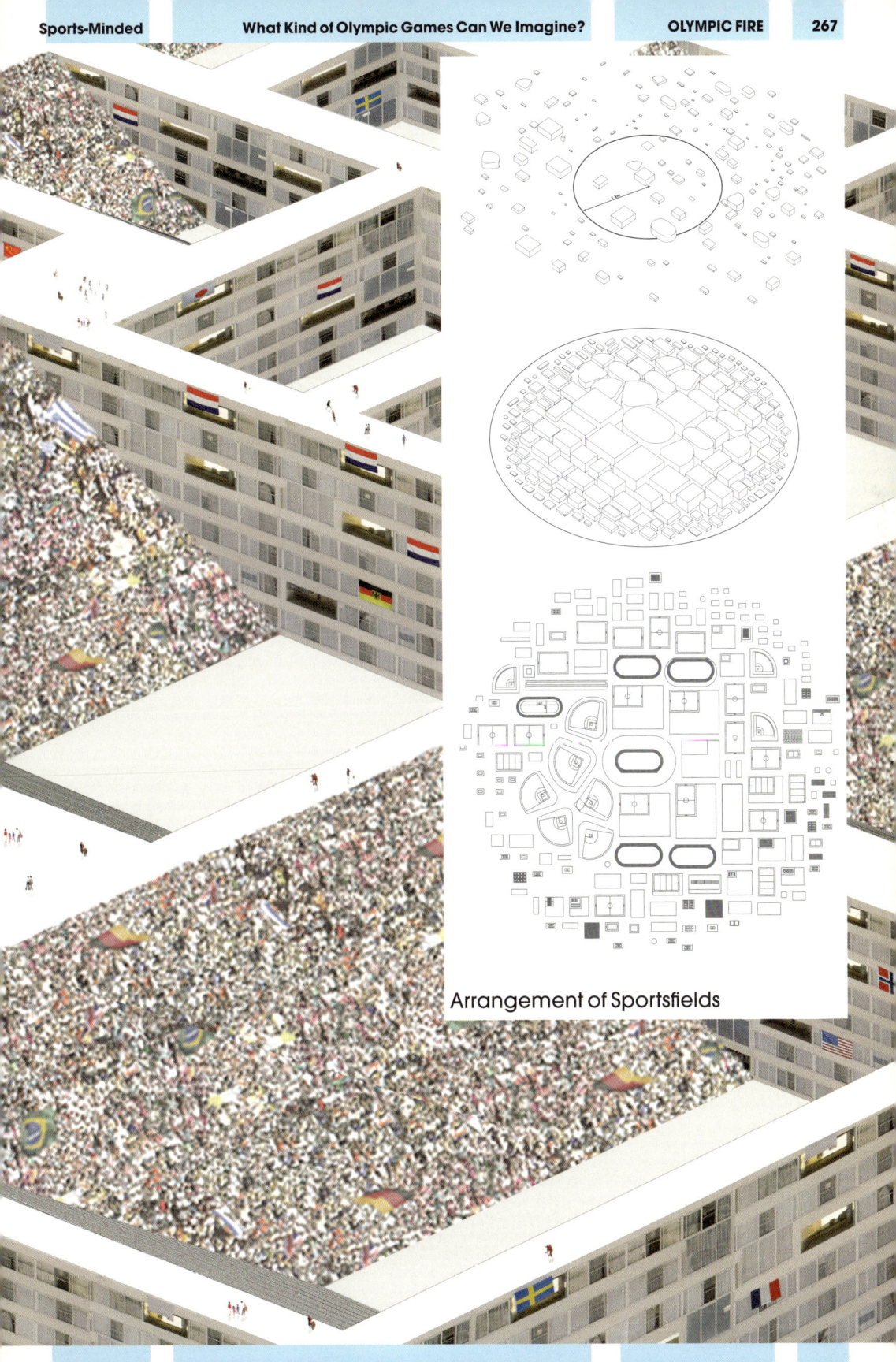

Arrangement of Sportsfields

AFTERUSE

STACKING GAMES
NL WILL DENSIFY

It's 2028.
Over the last 20 years the price of resources has hugely increased, leading to general political tension and security fears. All developed countries have accordingly made a concerted effort to minimise energy and land usage. In this situation the Olympic Games need to be hyper-secure, efficient and spectacular; they are therefore held in TV-studio-like, super-regulated, highly controlled buildings, allowing for the lowest land usage and energy consumption and best security: in short, the most guilt-free entertainment possible. Everybody is a voluntary prisoner of architecture, controlled and protected by design. Can the socially-oriented tradition and architectural creativity of the Netherlands lead to the invention of a new kind of social interaction here?
Issues: built area, density, CO_2 emissions, kilometres travelled per inhabitant, security costs, broadcasting revenues
Goals: a new and efficient society, a new social interaction

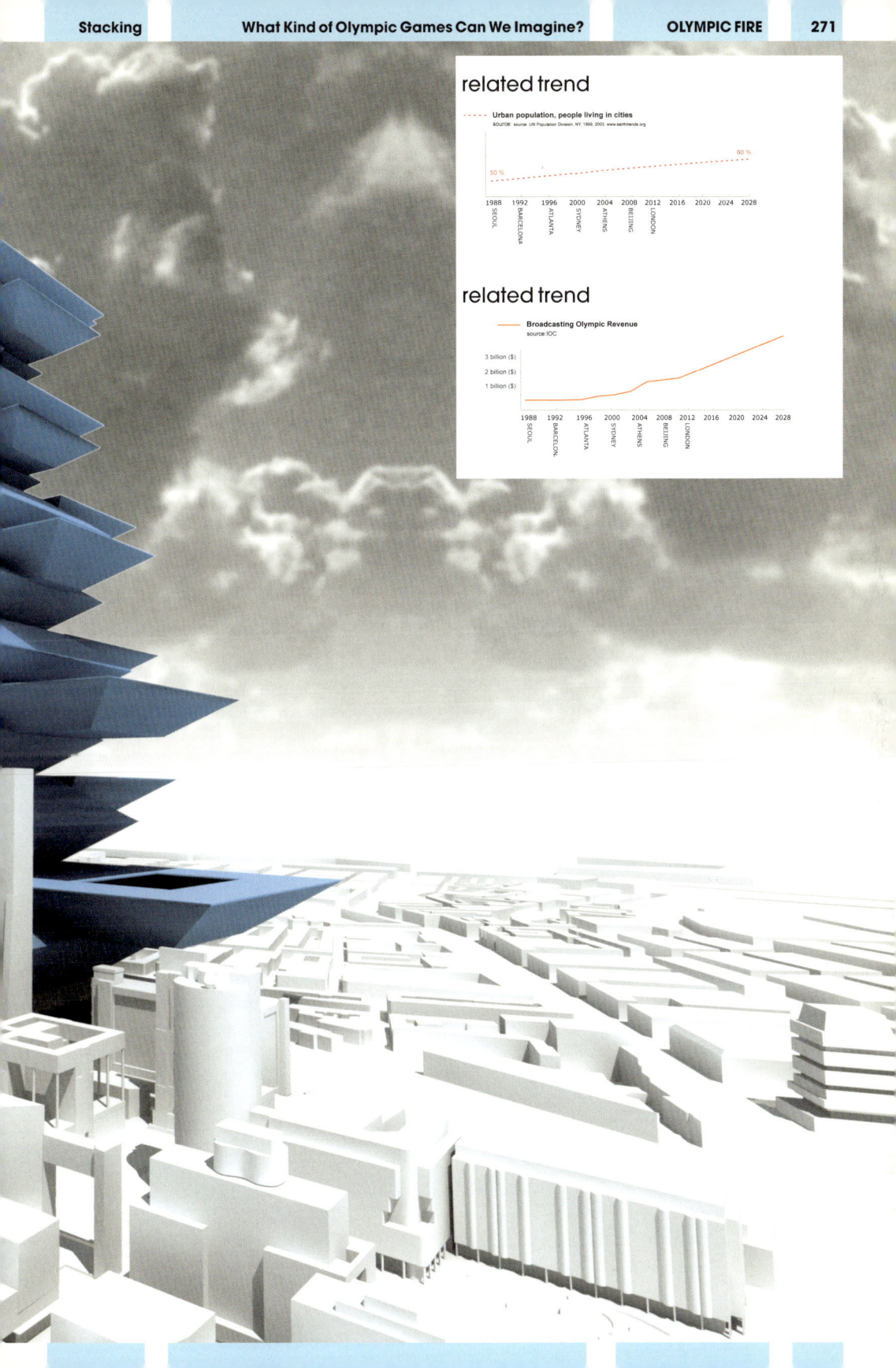

DURING THE OLYMPICS

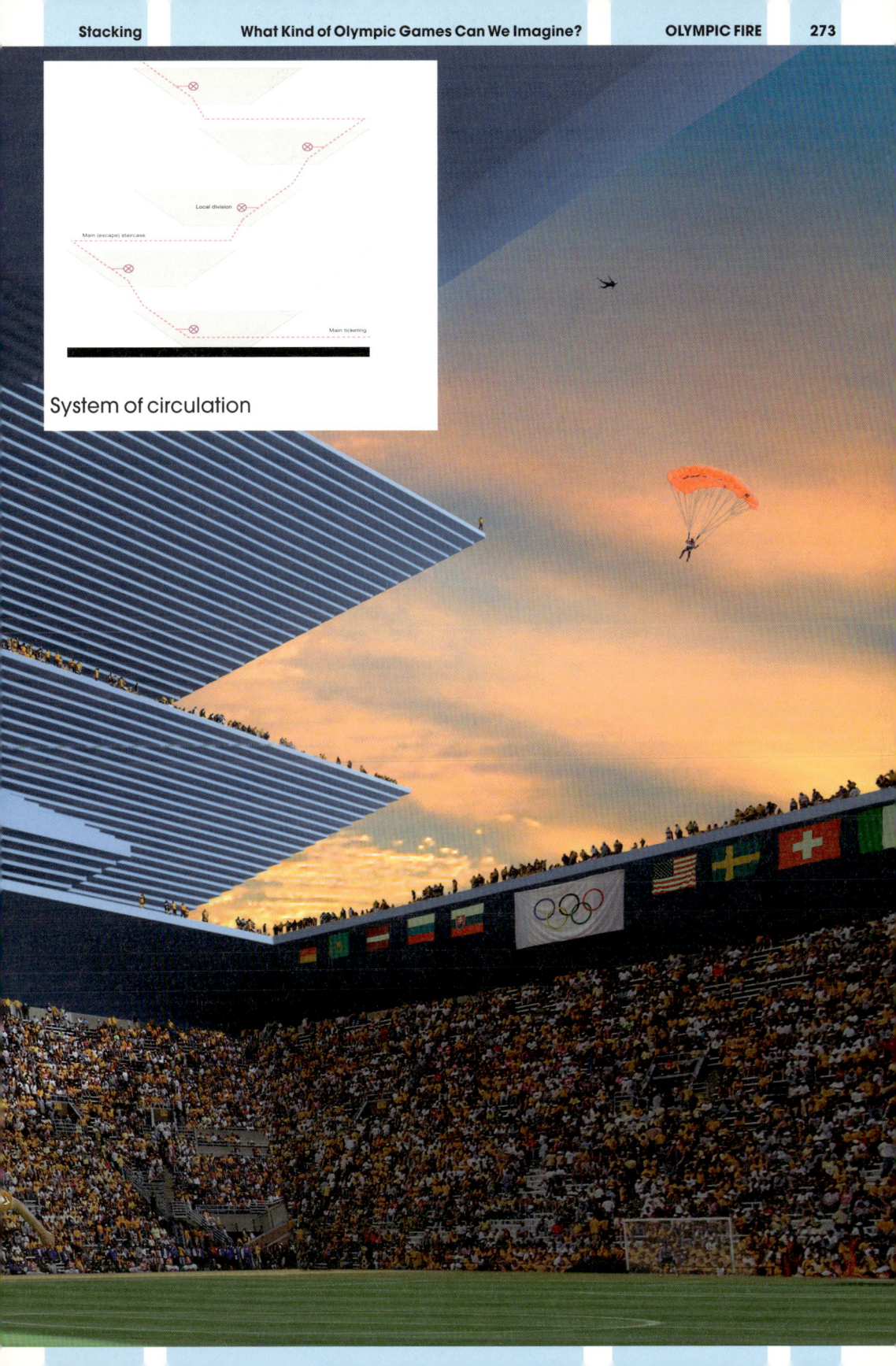

System of circulation

AFTERUSE

SUPERBOWL
NL WILL COME TOGETHER

It's 2028.
Thanks to collective international efforts and extreme measures, destructive ecological trends on the planet have been stopped. Once we were forced to renounce all unnecessary treats and live with a new frugality, human relationships were rediscovered to be at the centre of our lives. Now the IOC and the cities bidding for the Games wait for a chance to celebrate togetherness, and the sheer excitement of life itself, in a public space that aspires to gather the whole world in a single 'room'. The Netherlands, the most affected of all countries, has lived for the past 20 years in extreme caution, thus becoming an example of a sustainable society for the entire world. It will offer its daring, visionary interpretation of a highly technical and coordinated future by proposing the largest venue in the world, one that celebrates the Olympics more than any individual sport.
Issues: CO_2 emissions, energy use, ecological footprint
Goals: a new spectacularity

| Superbowl | What Kind of Olympic Games Can We Imagine? | OLYMPIC FIRE | 277 |

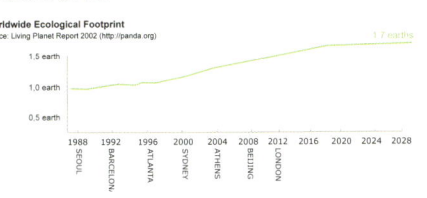

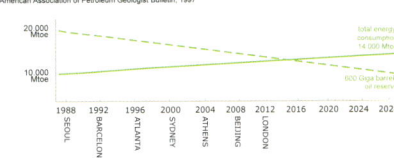

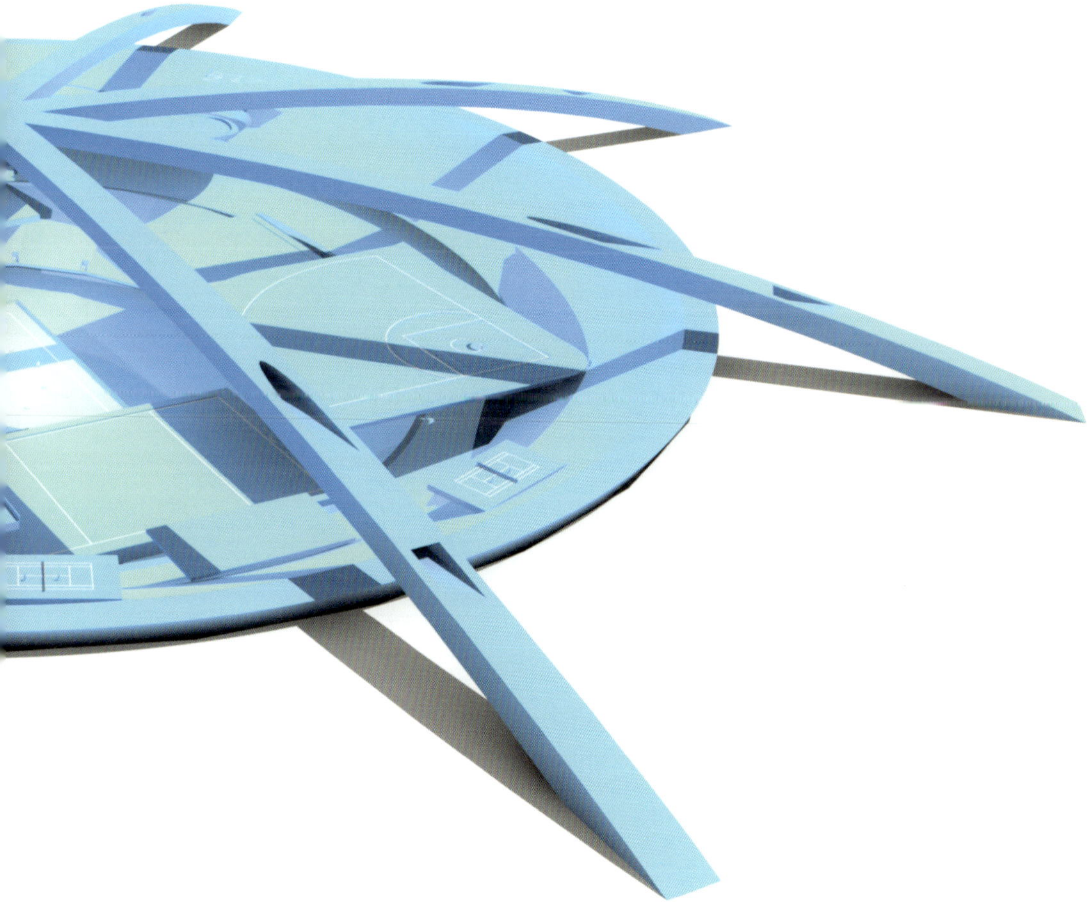

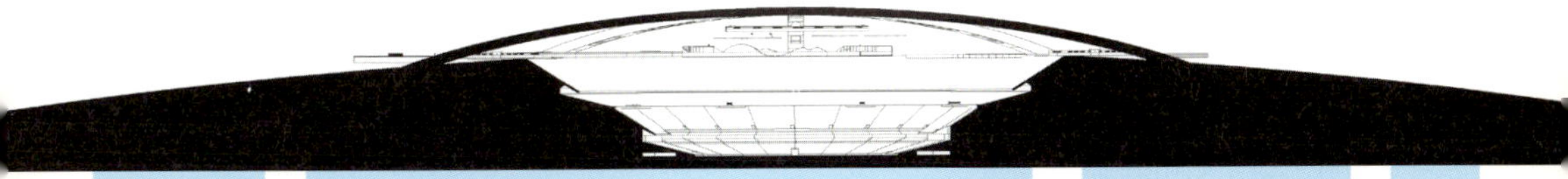

DURING THE OLYMPICS

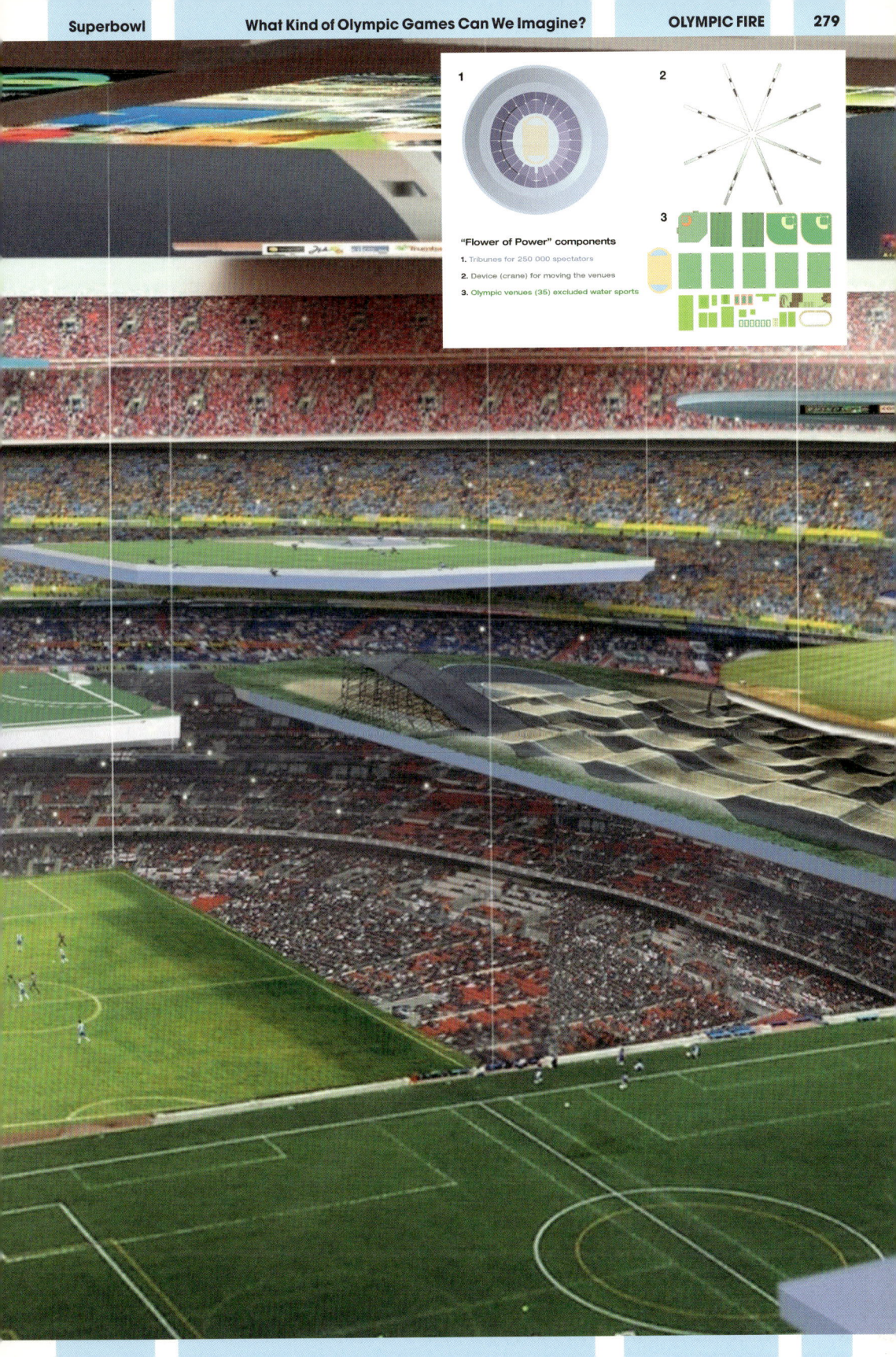

"Flower of Power" components
1. Tribunes for 250 000 spectators
2. Device (crane) for moving the venues
3. Olympic venues (35) excluded water sports

AFTERUSE

TRAVEL GAMES
NL WILL MOVE

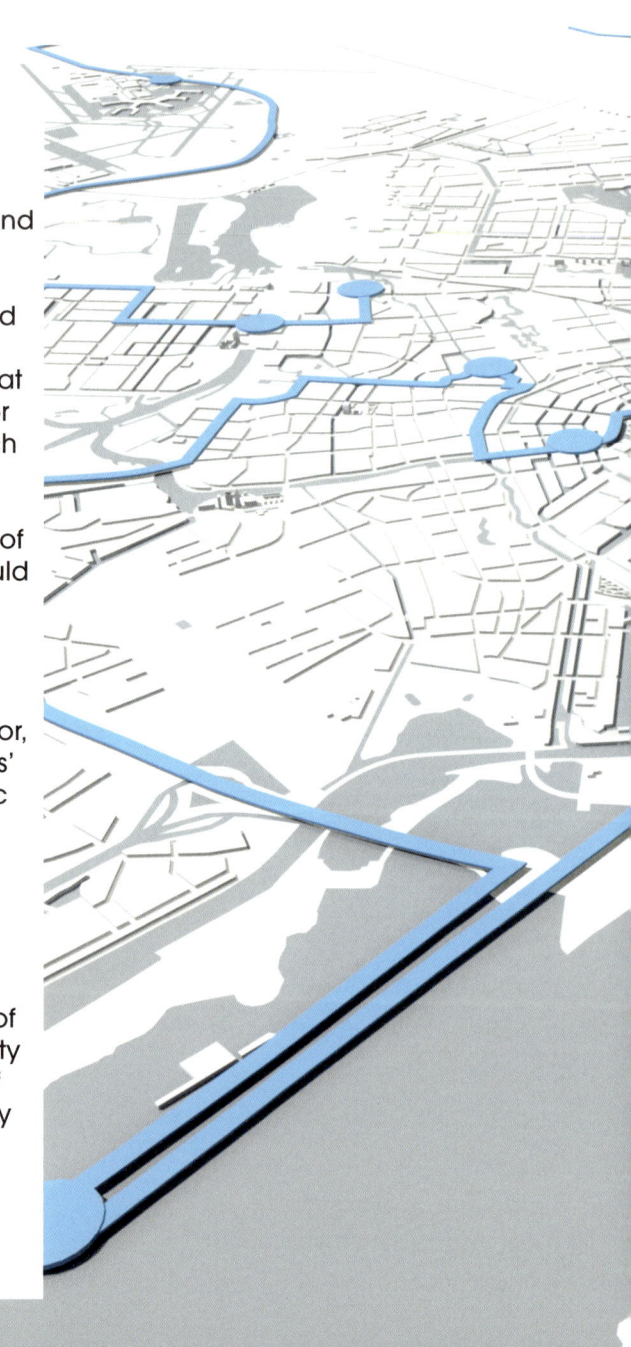

It's 2028.
The games have grown into a mammoth event with thousands of athletes involved and over a thousand scheduled matches. Taxpayers are enraged and sponsors are withdrawing their support, frightened by the narrow margin of profit. The very existence of the Games is now at stake. Furthermore, finding space for the Olympics in modern cities (which are necessary for the Olympic 'brand') has proven difficult. The organisation now accepts the idea of using ephemeral structures that could be reused, thus reducing the 8-year gap between bid and Games. The Netherlands, with its experience in hosting some of the largest festivals worldwide and its big transport sector, will design the first 'Moving Olympics' ever. Dutch engineering and logistic expertise will organise a stunning choreography for a completely ephemeral Olympic prototype, a travelling circus of sports, which will then be shipped off to the next Olympic city.
Issues: cost of Olympics, influence of the ephemeral in 21st century society
Goals: expose the playful aspect of the games, humanity's need for play

| Travel Games | What Kind of Olympic Games Can We Imagine? | OLYMPIC FIRE | 283 |

related trend

Inhabitants organizing city

12 million
9 million
6 million
3 million

1988 1992 1996 2000 2004 2008 2012 2016 2020 2024 2028

related trend

European Built up vs. Population increases
source: European Environment Agency Report 10, 2006
1988 = 100%

9 billion people
1,2 billion global ha

120%
110%
100%

1988 1992 1996 2000 2004 2008 2012 2016 2020 2024 2028
SEOUL BARCELONA ATLANTA SYDNEY ATHENS BEIJING LONDON

Road map of Trucks

Agriculture OG — 8.6 km / 6 min/truck
Highway OG — 8.4 km / 11 min/truck
Port OG
Railway OG — 12.3 km / 17 min/truck — 5.2 km / 11 min/truck
North IJ plein OG
Plaza OG — 1.5 km / 4 min/truck
Canal OG — 3.2 km / 8 min/truck — 9.1 km / 19 min/truck
Museum Park OG — 1,8 km / 5 min/truck
1928 Berlage OG
South Axis OG — 5.4 km / 11 min/truck — 10.9 km / 17 min/truck
IJ burg OG
Industry OG — 5.0 km / 7 min/truck
Bijlmermeer OG
23.0 km / 30 min/truck
Green Park OG — 7.2 km / 11 min/truck
8.1 km / 6 min/truck
Vinex OG — 12.3 km / 17 min/truck — Airport OG

DURING THE OLYMPICS

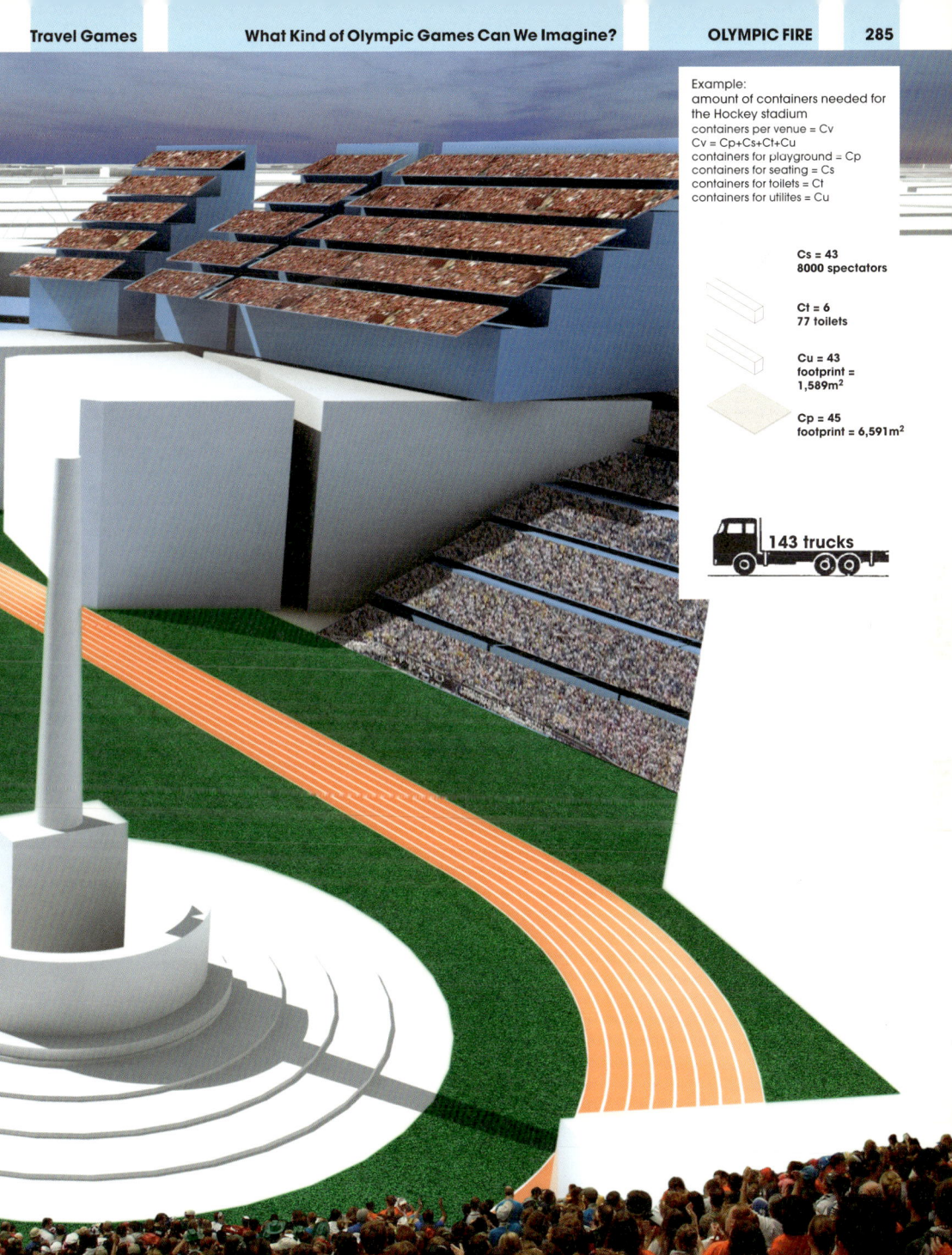

AFTERUSE

WALL OF SPORTS
HEALTH WITH A VIEW

It's 2028.
The Olympics itself has been the most powerful media to propagate sports, the host city and the event. But while stadiums are getting larger and more spectacular in themselves, they remain sealed off to the general public. With Olympic venues having an ever-larger impact on the cities they are hosted in and every city having a huge stadium, which is hardly ever filled to capacity, the general public resents having to pay for these inaccessible monsters. Is it possible to transform these closed fortresses into a device of the city? Positioned in the city all sports would be visible and everything would be visible while you are doing sports.
A cathedral to a new neutral and pragmatic ideology.
Issues: Olympic Media, NL city footprint
Goals: most open Olympics

Wall of Sports | What Kind of Olympic Games Can We Imagine? | OLYMPIC FIRE | 289

related trend

Increasing overweight children
source: Tackling Obesities, Government Office for Science, UK

- 25 % overweight
- 20 % overweight
- 15 % overweight

USA
England
Ireland
Japan
Germany

1988 SEOUL | 1992 BARCELONA | 1996 ATLANTA | 2000 SYDNEY | 2004 ATHENS | 2008 BEIJING | 2012 LONDON | 2016 | 2020 | 2024 | 2028

related trend

Life expectancy
source: www.wikipedia.en/lifeexpectancy

- 75 year
- 70 year
- 45 year

USA
EUROPE
SUB/SAHARAN AFRICA

1988 SEOUL | 1992 BARCELONA | 1996 ATLANTA | 2000 SYDNEY | 2004 ATHENS | 2008 BEIJING | 2012 LONDON | 2016 | 2020 | 2024 | 2028

DURING THE OLYMPICS

Venue Facade with Seats

AFTERUSE

WATER GAMES
NL WILL CLEAN UP

It's 2028.
The Olympics strives to put forward its fair-play values in an increasingly conflicted political environment, while the event itself is jeopardized by its size and cost. In a world that is swamped by garbage and is starving because of a lack of drinking water, inviting millions of people into your backyard seems a folly born out of vanity. The Netherlands, barely surviving without direct access to a freshwater source of its own, is on the delta of some of Europe's largest and most polluted rivers. This combined with local agricultural run-off leads to a desperate and untenable situation. By combining a new water treatment facility with a communal event like the Olympics, while at the same time smartly balancing the two budgets to the benefit of both, the Netherlands could gradually clean up the environment, giving new relevance and perspective to the host city and the Games. The cleanest Games ever!
Issues: drinking water price, water pollution, ecological cost of the Games
Goals: the games as ecological device, spectacle of the cleaning machine

DURING THE OLYMPICS

AFTERUSE

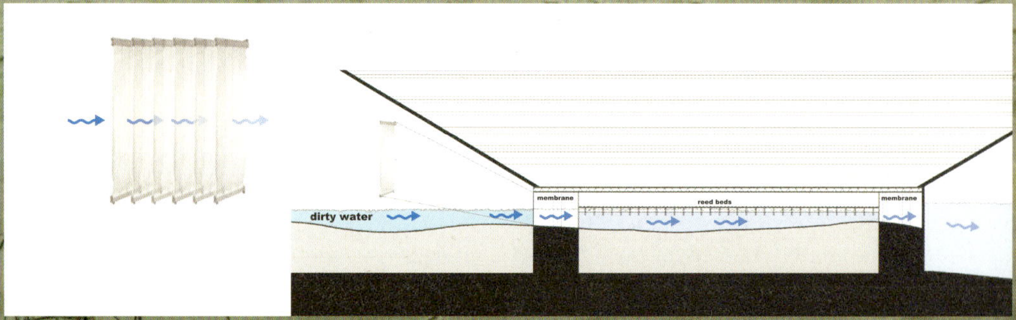

dirty water · membrane · reed beds · membrane

'If it is only about sports, than we should not want to organise the Games'

Henk Ovink interviewed by Mieke Dings

Henk Ovink is the director of Vision, Design and Strategy with the Directorate-General for Spatial Planning of the Ministry of Housing, Spatial Planning and the Environment (VROM).

Involvement with the Olympic Games 2028: On behalf of Minister Cramer of VROM, I am the government's commissioner for the spatial development of the Olympic Plan 2028. Our department conducts a study into the spatial possibilities and models for the Olympic Games in the Netherlands and we draw up design proposals for 2028 and later.

Olympic sport: I go in for bicycle racing and I used to play field hockey and practice gymnastics.

Most impressive Olympic Games: The other day I visited the restored stadium of the 1936 Games in Berlin, and again I was very impressed. Not just by the stadium itself, but mainly because those Games were so politically charged, as emphasised by Leni Riefenstahl's film Olympia. The way in which Nazi Germany used those Games to position itself is both fascinating and frightening. The 1992 Games in Barcelona are also an important example, because they were so successful in boosting the transformation of the entire region. Barcelona succeeded in making the Games into an overall development project instead of just a sports event.

Memorable sports moment: I have more vivid memories of the Winter Games than of the Summer Games, despite the fact that I played field hockey myself. The hockey final between the United States and the Soviet Union, somewhere in the early 80s I think, was terribly exciting. The tension was so palpable you could have cut it with a knife.

What would be ideal Olympic Games 2028 be like, in your view?
As far as I'm concerned the vision of Netherlands Sports Land is not the main motive, but only one of the motives. Our international competitiveness, the issues of sustainable growth, accessibility and quality of the living environment are the other ones. I hope that by embracing the Olympic Games we will generate the administrative power to tackle all of those issues energetically. My ideal Olympic Games 2028 serve as a binding force during the preliminary stages; put health, sports and sportsmanship on the map; provide an overall agenda for development during the realisation stage; and have a strong spin-off, especially with regards to our international competitiveness. If we fail to achieve this ideal, then we are missing opportunities. If it is only about sports, then we should not want to organise the games. That would be naïve.

Which issues in spatial planning should receive a boost from the Games?
In the Netherlands we still have a lot of work to do in public transport, which is difficult because there is no financial profit in that. It would be wonderful if the Olympic Games could provide a boost in this respect. We should also use the construction of Olympic facilities as a means to address larger issues, for instance in the fields of climate change and sustainable development. Building a bridge between Amsterdam and Almere is not the main issue; what is at stake is a broader vision of the future use of our land.

This is a high-scale vision and therefore we should approach the Games at the same high level. If the four major cities continue to compete with each other, we had better forget the whole thing. As a small country, despite the fact that a city presents itself as a candidate, we cannot afford to not fully support this higher approach. That is why in our studies at VROM we deliberately distinguish between a number of models, varying from organising everything on and in the Randstad to spreading the Games over the entire country, from using existing rural areas to the development of new land. I do think that, in terms of profiling, the emphasis should be on the Delta. After all, it is the land below sea level, our bond with the water, which is the source of our innovative powers. That is the image we should project internationally. Delta innovation, sustainability and mobility: those are the concepts to apply in order to have wonderful Olympic Games.

To what extent are these things already in place?
The high-scale level is already strongly developed here. We don't have one large metropolis, but rather a network of places, whether they are cities or landscapes. The presence of those networks, combined with the innovative power of the Delta, make our country very suitable for organising the Olympic Games. We can prove that it is irrelevant whether a city or country puts itself up as a candidate. China is also organising the games in a network form, but in its presentation it focuses on Beijing only. The moment our bid succeeds, we can jumpstart the discussion about the relevance of city bids.

Which lessons can we learn from previous Olympic Games?
Most of the previous editions focused too much on the period in which the Games take place instead of on the period afterwards. Our bid will have to be on two levels: one aimed at getting the Games, and one that addresses the period until 2040 and later. It is precisely in the period after the Games that the investments may pay off in achieving social goals. We have to offer a sustainable perspective. We could say: the Netherlands is realising the most sustainable Games ever. That would ensure that we are always ready in the period between 2020 and 2040. That is the best bid.

What is the first thing we should do?
First, we should try to envision the spin-off in the long run. Next, we have to create collectiveness and public support, because the administrative and organisational capacity in the run-up to such an event should be kept simple. Everyone, the business world, the people and the government, should start thinking "the Olympic Games, my idea as well." That can only be achieved with a vision of a sustainable future, a vision that will be an important trigger for early investments. The sports world is now developing the vision of Netherlands Sports Land and we at VROM are working on the spatial scenarios. If we manage to connect those two visions, we will have a powerful coalition.

How old will you be in 2028?
60.

Where will you be watching the Olympic Games then?
In any case in the most beautiful stadium of the world, but also at all those different places in the network that are needed to make the Games in the Netherlands a success.

Who will be the architect of this most beautiful stadium?
It would be nice if designers and students from all over the world would design the Games as teams, in workshops led by the Young Turks of today or in international competition rounds. So that we would not just end up with icons by a few famous architects, but a linking of the network of knowledge and expertise to specific tasks.

Can you think of a sports quote or slogan to make the country rally behind the idea of hosting the Olympic Games in 2028?
The way in which you hit the ball determines the way it spins. The bid is for the winner, the games are for everyone. When the Low Lands play for high stakes, the future will triumph.

OLYMPIC FIRE — Interview Ivo Opstelten

'No guts, no glory'

Ivo Opstelten interviewed by Mieke Dings

Ivo Opstelten is the Mayor of Rotterdam and has recently been elected chairman of the VVD [the Liberal national political party – MD]. Previously he was mayor of the cities of Utrecht, Dalen, Doorn and Delfzijl, respectively.

Involvement in the Olympic Games 2028: Rotterdam supports the NOC*NSF's study exploring the possibility of having the Games in the Netherlands in 2028. We contribute financially to the Olympic Plan; we have set up a steering committee, and the bench has decided to make an effort and offer expertise.

Plays an Olympic sport? I have practised field hockey, rowing and tennis, although tennis is not really an Olympic sport. Next January, when I retire as Mayor of Rotterdam, I intend to pick up rowing again with the veteran Eight.

Most impressive Olympic Games: Many Games have made a lasting impression ever since I became aware of them as a small boy in 1952 and kept track of everything in my Planta scrapbook [a special album published by Planta on the occasion of the Olympics of 1952 – MD]. I have always been an avid follower of the Games, partly because I played field hockey in Eindhoven and various Olympic athletes, one of whom was the Dutch decathlete Eef Kamerbeek, were living and training there.

Memorable sports moment: As a rower, I of course enormously enjoyed the Holland Eight's winning the gold medal in Atlanta with Nico Rienks as the stroke. Rienks had already won gold in the Two and now he did it again. The Holland Eight were very much the favourite, but they didn't get off to a very good start. I have tremendous respect for the fact that they managed to win in the end. Otherwise, I have enjoyed great moments in track and field, swimming, field hockey, volleyball, bicycle races and judo.

Which edition of the Games and which city would you take as an example for the Games of 2028?
Sydney. I went over there for the Hockey World Cup in 1990 – ten years before the Games. The Australians have managed to put all the facilities to excellent use. There are no deserted venues. Taking this as our cue, the Big 4 [the Netherlands' four major cities of Rotterdam, Amsterdam, The Hague and Utrecht – MD] have to really collaborate in order to coordinate the necessary facilities as best we can. We should also promote sports in general within the Randstad. Even if the Games do not come to the Netherlands in the end, there will be no harm done, because we still will have had the beneficial experience of making a tremendous concerted effort.

What would you like to accomplish in Rotterdam?
You name it. In essence, it is not so very difficult to realise the required facilities in Rotterdam. We are building a very large stadium next to the Kuip [a football stadium, home to FC Feyenoord – MD] for the finals of the Football World Cup in 2018; we will have a new Olympics-proof rowing course; we have field hockey facilities and we can accomplish a lot more: the CHIO [Concours Hippique International Officiel – MD] can accommodate the equestrian events, etc. And some facilities can be of a temporary nature.

Are there spots in Rotterdam which the athletes and the world community shouldn't miss?
Yes, for instance, Ahoy, our wonderful sports and convention centre, which we are expanding anyway. In combination with the new Kuip, this could become the focal point. We also should develop many things along the river, since the waterfront defines Rotterdam.

The architect Winy Maas, together with students, has designed a stadium that has a skyscraper as a tribune. Will Rotterdam allow such experiments?
Of course; this is a city were such things are possible and we have the guts to do them. Rotterdam is the only Dutch city whose skyline has international allure and we should use that to our benefit. This is why so many architects insist that we concentrate the Olympic facilities along the river. These studies by Winy Maas look very awesome and futuristic now, but we shouldn't forget that we still have twenty years to go. I think it's important to make many studies in order to be aware of what the Games may bring.

Do you feel that the city of Rotterdam is ready for an event like the Games, on an administrative level?
The important thing is that we, the bench of Mayor and Aldermen, have expressed our intention to make an effort on behalf of the Games. We will, however, stick to the agreements we have made with the other cities of the Big 4 and therefore will not claim the Games for ourselves, nor will Amsterdam. We will start by working together, and we will not decide which city will make the bid until 2016. All the same, we are not making preparations for Utrecht's candidacy here.

How will Rotterdam prepare itself?
There are many top sports events in Rotterdam, and more to come. This year the Champions Trophy for field hockey and the World Port Tournament for baseball take place here, and in 2009 we have the judo World Championships, in 2010 the World Artistic Gymnastics Championship and in 2011 the World Table Tennis Championships. These are all rehearsals. For 2012 we are trying to get the Pre-Olympics here, meaning that athletes on their way to London come here to practice. Amongst the Big 4, we have also discussed the possibility of organising the Olympic Youth Games, something we are very keen on. Together with Utrecht and Dusseldorf, we are on the shortlist for the start and prologue of the Tour de France in 2010. And, finally, we are already busy with the Football World Cup of 2018, a major but very attractive operation.

Do you think that the people of Rotterdam will want all these events?
Looking at all of the Big 4 cities, I think this will be less of a problem in Rotterdam. The people here like events, and sports. We have already earned the title 'Events City of the Year' a couple of times and I'm convinced we will earn it again. Of course we have to seriously study the financial aspects, as we don't want to rush forward in blind enthusiasm without knowing what the price tag is going to be. The Games mustn't become the prestige project of a few relatively inapt administrators and politicians, but should be supported by the top of the corporate world, politics, and organising cities. If we can demonstrate how the Games will boost our national economy, how they will improve infrastructure and facilities and how, on top of that, they will stimulate people to participate in sports more than before, then I think we will be taking a sensible and capable approach.

How will the athletes experience Rotterdam by then?
That is something you should ask the athletes who have recently run the marathon here. They are all Rotterdam-minded and love this city. It has to do with the atmosphere. The city not only looks good, but it has an international flavour, with warm-hearted people and the passionate attitude of 'actions speak louder than words' and 'getting on with it'. It is an attitude that athletes can relate to.

How old will you be in 2028?
I will be 84, it can't be helped.

Where would you prefer to watch the Games then?
Well, here in Rotterdam, naturally. I'd love to see the Holland Eight win again on the rowing course and I will go see the field hockey and gymnastics. The other day, Cohen [the Mayor of Amsterdam - MD] and I mused how we would be moving between events with our canes by then. I certainly intend to stay fit, so that at the age of 84 I might still row in a veteran Eight. Although not very fast anymore.

Can you think of a sports quote or slogan to make the country rally behind the idea of hosting the Olympic Games?
The Netherlands Dare! That has a typically Rotterdam ring to it, as we have the campaign 'Rotterdam Dares'. If you wish to organise the Games, you need some guts. After all: no guts, no glory.

WHAT K
OF STA
CAN W
IMAGIN

OLYMPIC FIRE 305

DRIVE-IN STADIUM

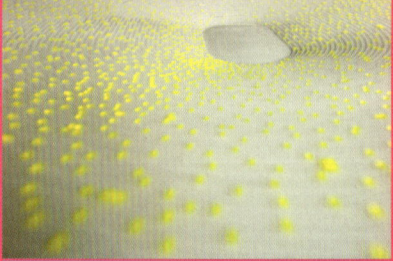

RESIDENTIAL STADIUM

PARTICIPATOR

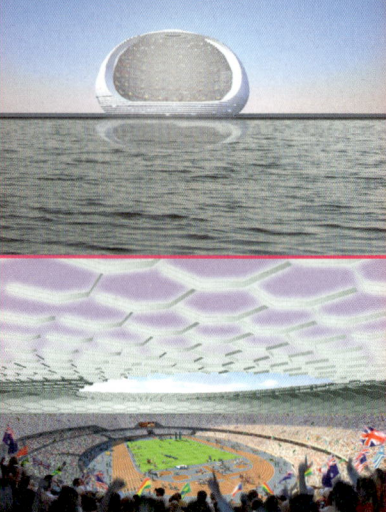

SUPERDUNE

DRIVE-IN STADIUM

What if we make a stadium where every spectator comes by car?
We provide the structure; the spectators and their automobiles form the building.

THE SPECTATORS
Finally nearing their destination... A gigantic woven structure slowly appears on the horizon. From the distance they can see ramps along its cantilevered exterior, granting access into the mighty edifice. Enjoying the amazing view, they spiral around and around to the top. The last turn takes them onto a landing, the parking platform. The parking ritual begins as a personal parking slot opens up for them. The car is installed and the guidance system manoeuvres the slot, car and all, into the perfect viewing angle.

THE FUSION
Together, the cars determine the stadium's final shape; their colours comprise the stadium's colours. The entire car becomes an extension of spectator admiration for the athletes. The ambiance of the stadium is created by the cars' headlights and horns. Charge, with 3000 Watts burning in your back! Honk the horn of joy; express the power of anger!

A web of roads forms the structure, leading the cars in and out in the fastest possible manner. The power of personality as a patch in the patchwork quilt of togetherness.
A giant car park where you stay in the car; the biggest Park & Ride ever.

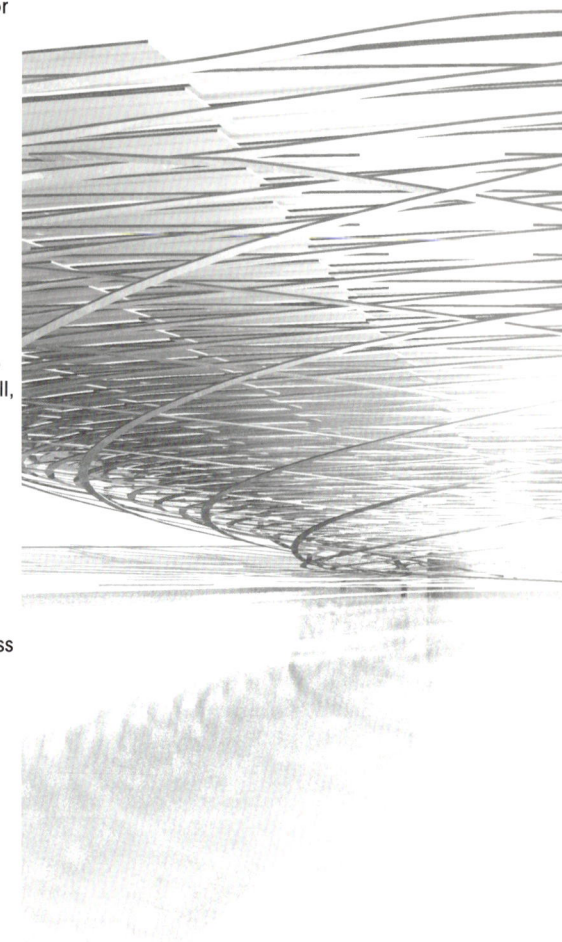

stadium layout

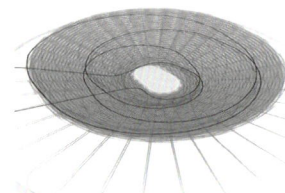

spiral routing in-out

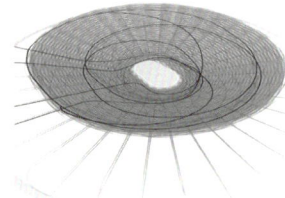

spiral routing in-out and high-level routing

secondary

routing + parking areas

routing + parking areas + spaces

parking spaces

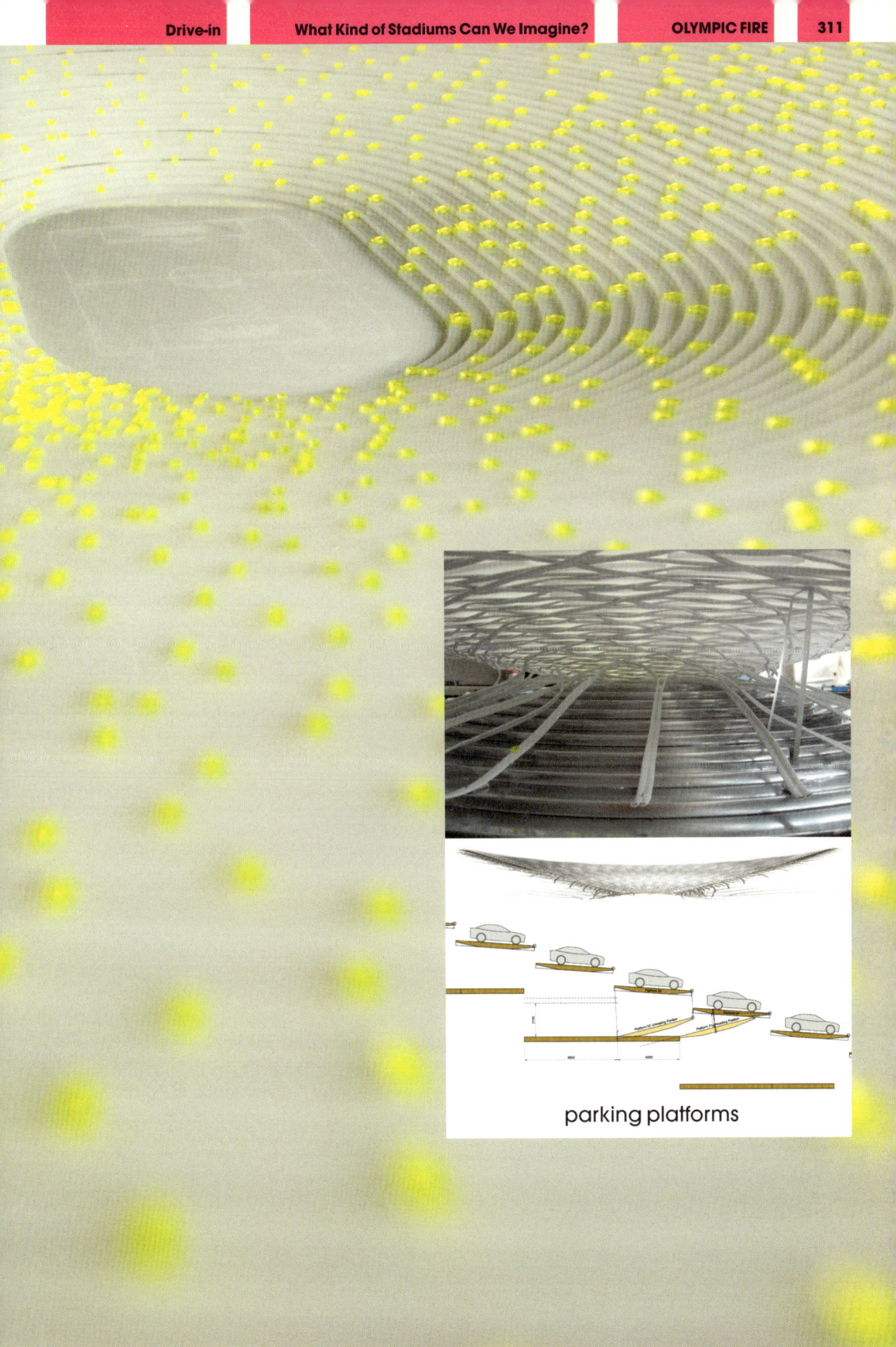

parking platforms

RESIDENTIAL STADIUM

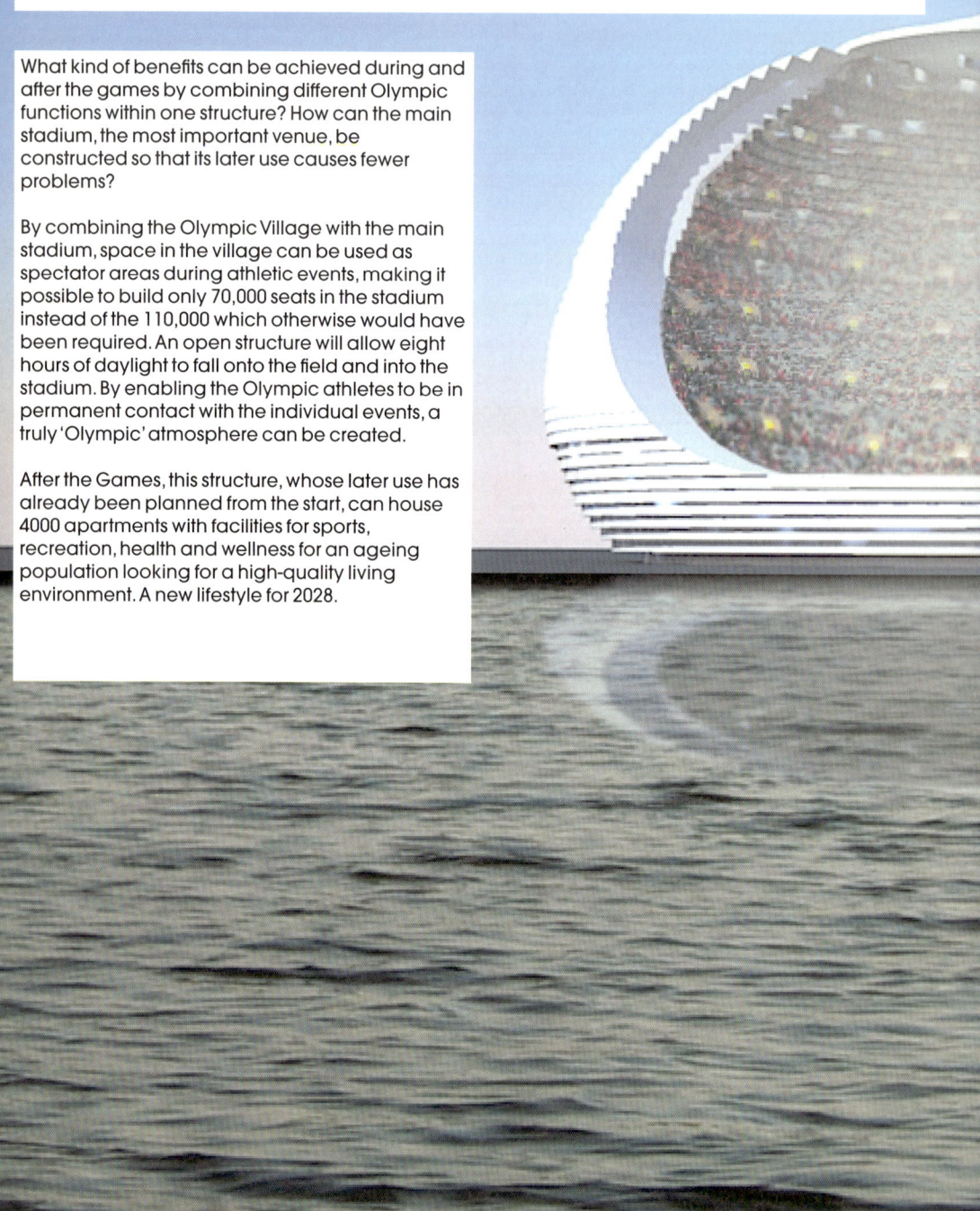

What kind of benefits can be achieved during and after the games by combining different Olympic functions within one structure? How can the main stadium, the most important venue, be constructed so that its later use causes fewer problems?

By combining the Olympic Village with the main stadium, space in the village can be used as spectator areas during athletic events, making it possible to build only 70,000 seats in the stadium instead of the 110,000 which otherwise would have been required. An open structure will allow eight hours of daylight to fall onto the field and into the stadium. By enabling the Olympic athletes to be in permanent contact with the individual events, a truly 'Olympic' atmosphere can be created.

After the Games, this structure, whose later use has already been planned from the start, can house 4000 apartments with facilities for sports, recreation, health and wellness for an ageing population looking for a high-quality living environment. A new lifestyle for 2028.

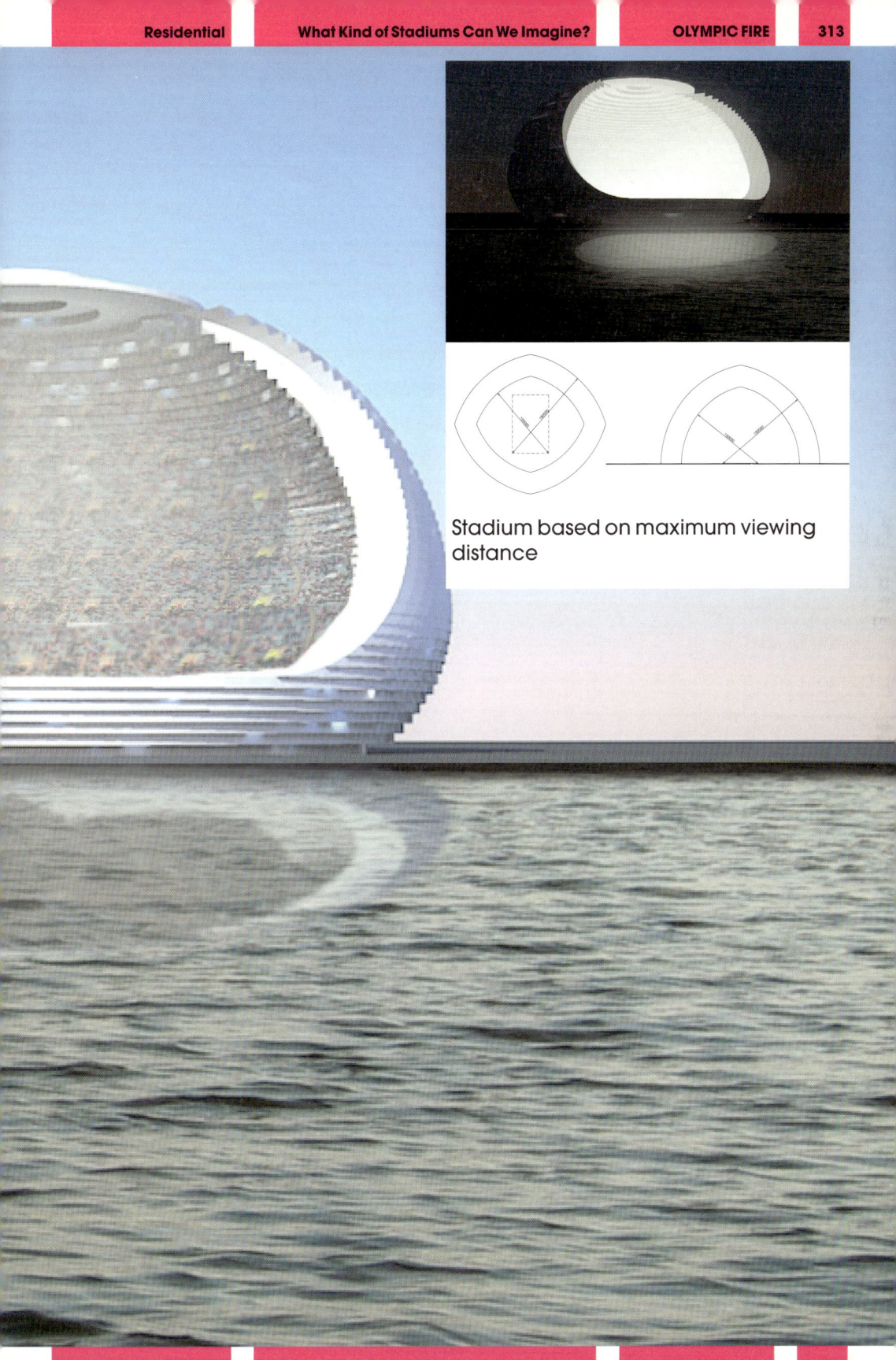

Stadium based on maximum viewing distance

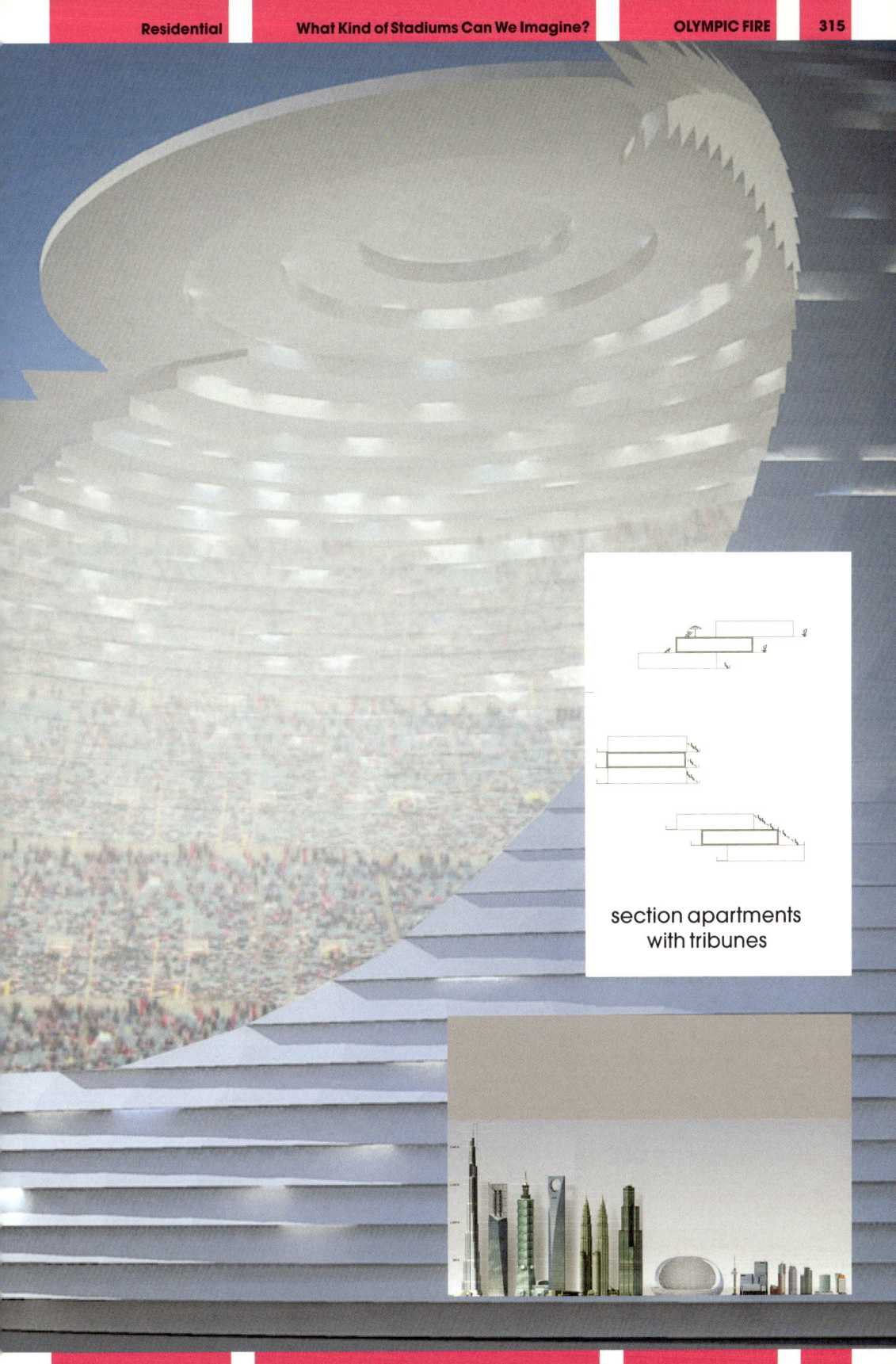

section apartments with tribunes

PARTICIPATOR

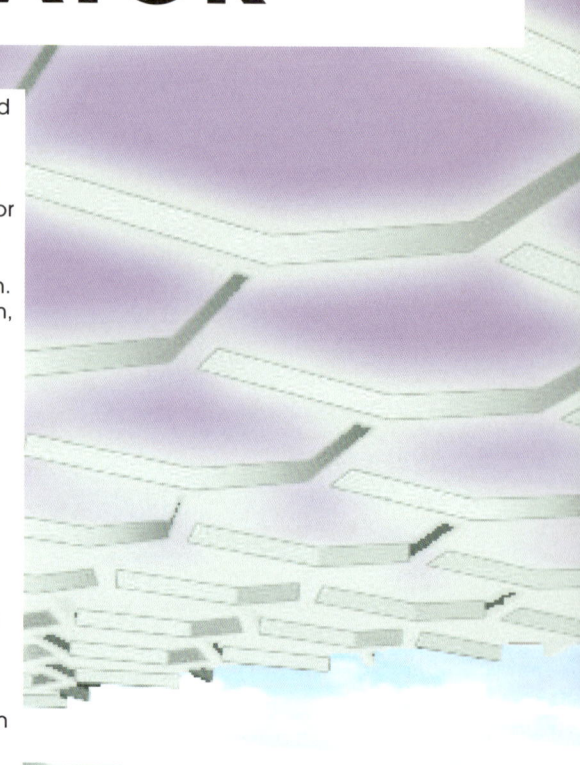

How can you participate in a competition instead of simply watching it?

The interactive 'Participator' shell reflects the way supporters react to the athletes' performances. For example, the Participator lights up when a world record is broken or a goal is scored and the supporters are yelling and jumping up and down. The shell, which can be put up over every stadium, illustrates the synergy of construction and 'opening'. Comprised of hexagons, its stiff construction provides support for the steps and landings at various levels. The lighting is incorporated in the transparent planes of the hexagons and is activated by the spectators themselves.

Everywhere you go in the stadium, from the entrance gate to your seat, the movements and sounds you make have an influence on the lighting in the shell. Seeing as you take part in this game with thousands of others, the Participator becomes a projection screen for the city: 'the wave' will also be visible to people outside the stadium, and competition will even arise between the spectators themselves.

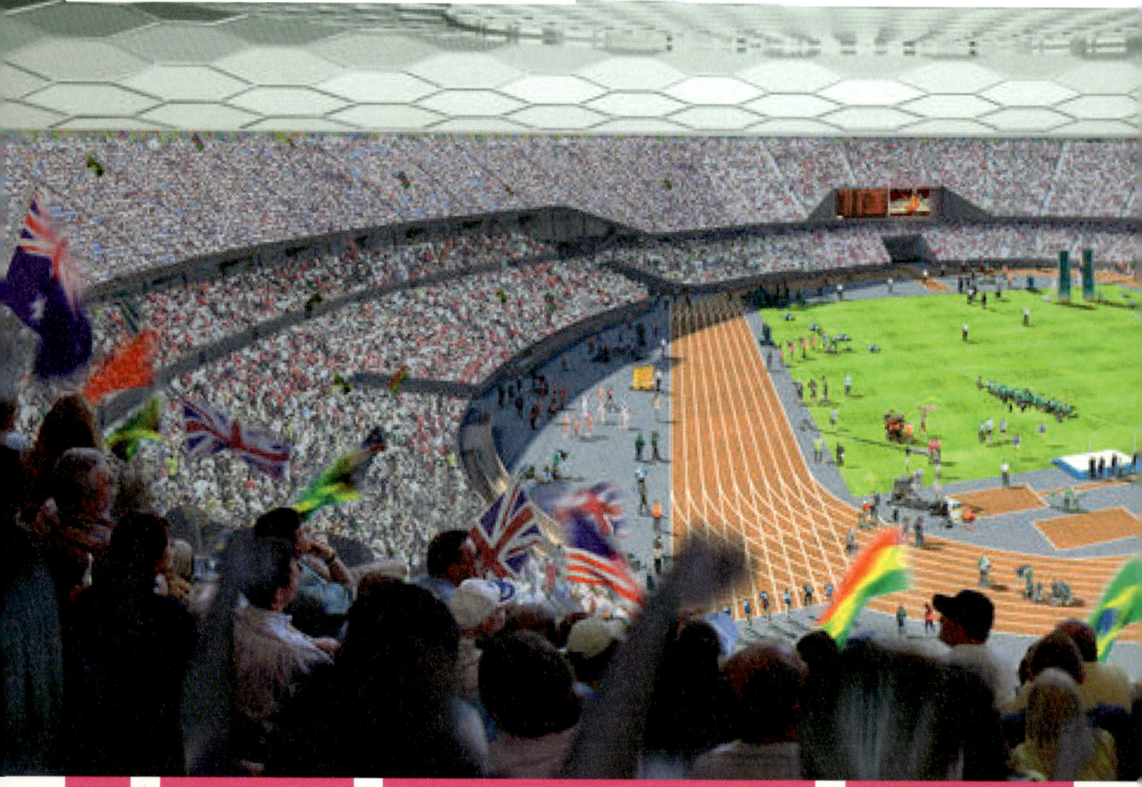

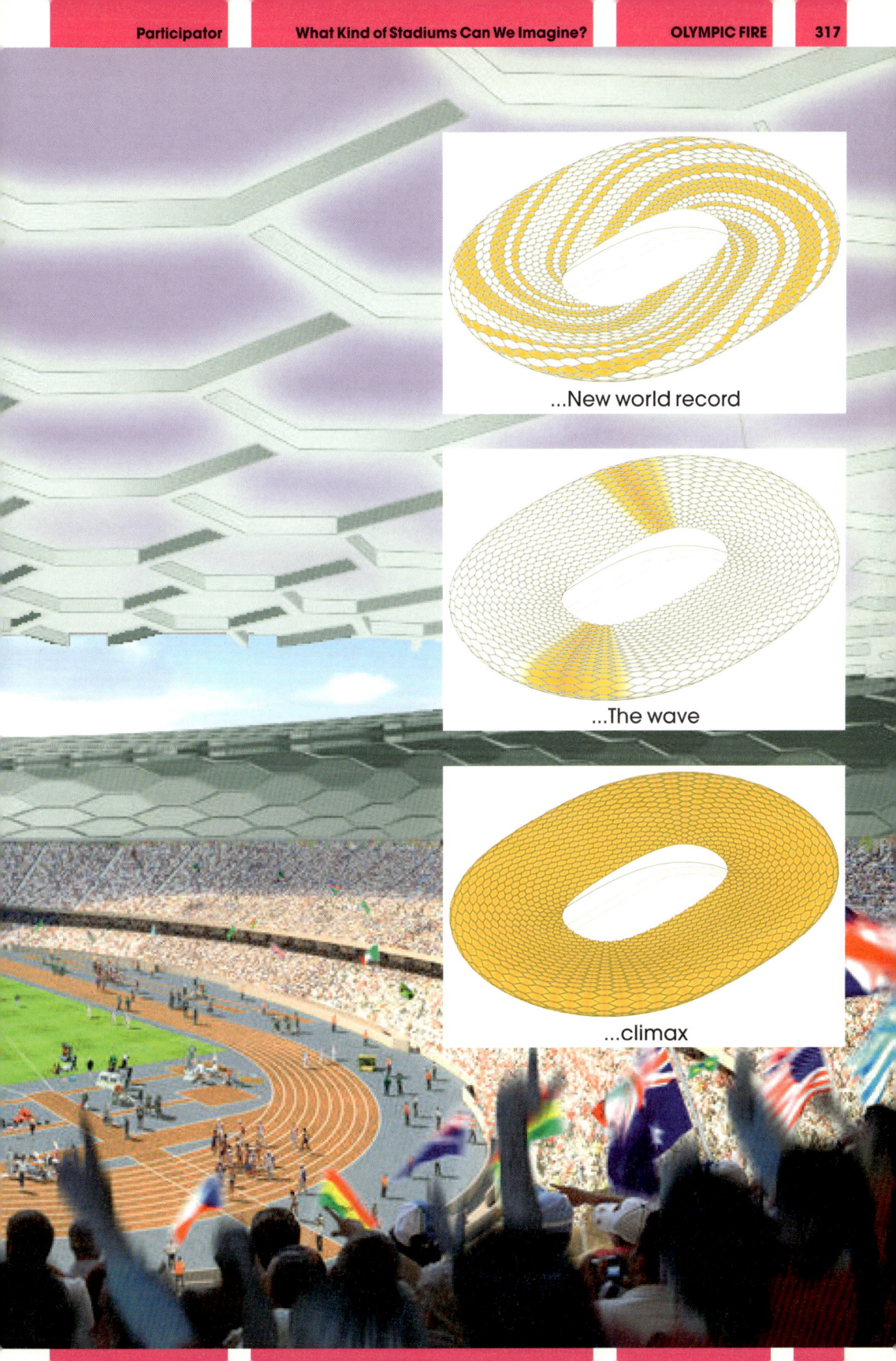

...New world record

...The wave

...climax

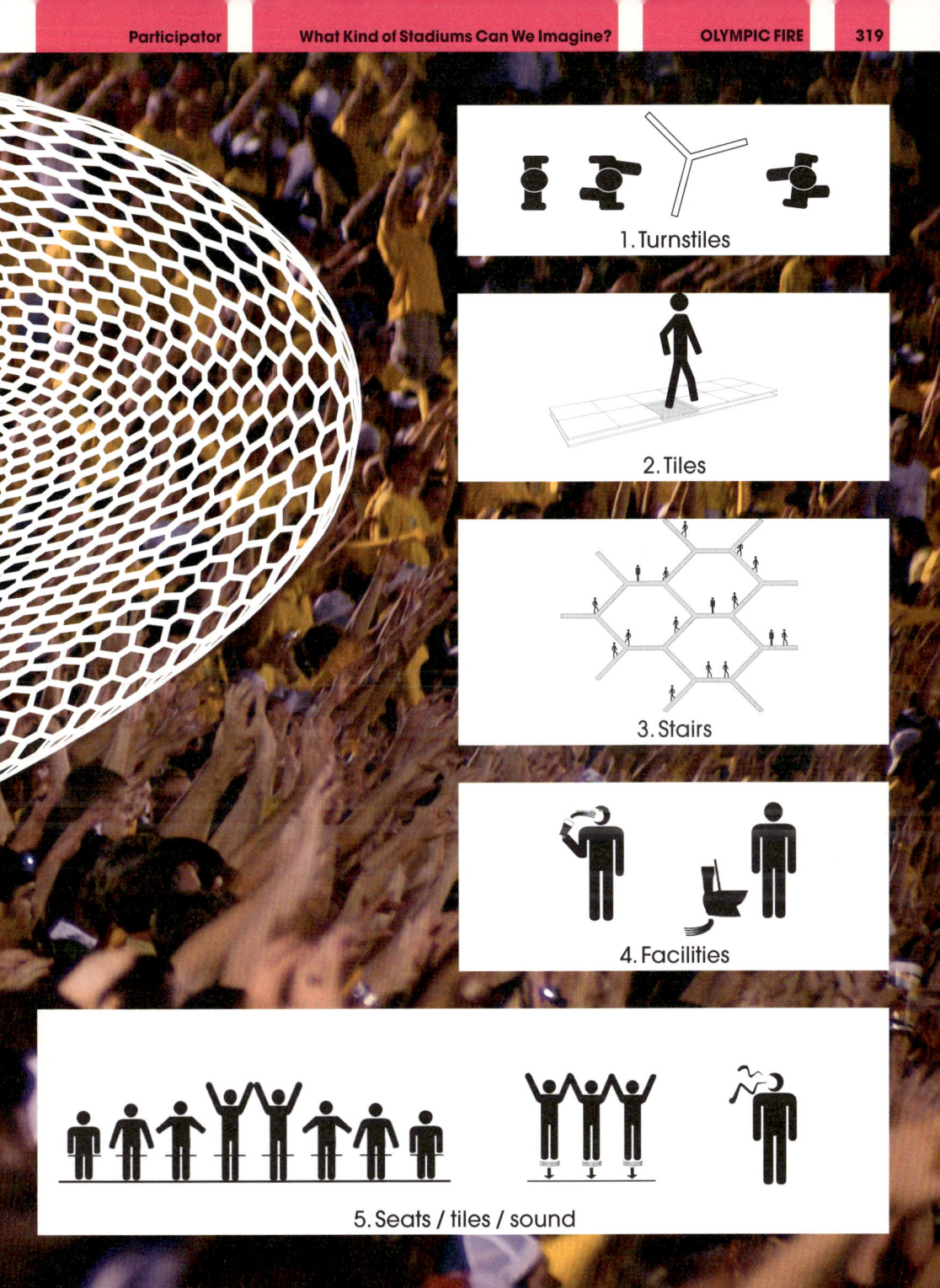

SUPERDUNE

In the foreseeable future, climate change will cause problems across the globe, such as rising sea levels and a greater prevalence of storms. An essential component of the Netherlands' defence against the sea is its coastline of dunes, which will need strengthening. The area from the Hook of Holland to The Hague is especially vulnerable in this regard. The Dutch have a long tradition of adapting nature and living in harmony with it and applying this knowledge worldwide. An international event like the Olympic Games would be the ultimate showcase for a local solution to a global problem.
Would it be possible to locate an Olympic Games programme in the sensitive but vital environment of the dunes?

The advantage is that nothing needs to be added to the dunes in order to facilitate their later use, but building with sand does indeed present some technical challenges. Such problems can be solved with a new innovation in bio-technology: BioGrout, a durable biochemical cementation of sand, comprises bacteria that naturally occur in the soil, producing calcite crystals that strengthen the soil. The result can be as strong as sandstone.

Tribunes can be formed from sand in the dunes and strengthened by spraying BioGrout on them. The extra Olympic programme takes place on stages surrounded by these strengthened dunes. The stadiums and dune pavilions form the Olympic landscape, a hybrid of the natural and the artificial. By only using sand that is already there, the dune landscape will slowly replenish itself and the stadiums will simply disappear after the Games.
What will be left over is a seawall with an Olympic past.

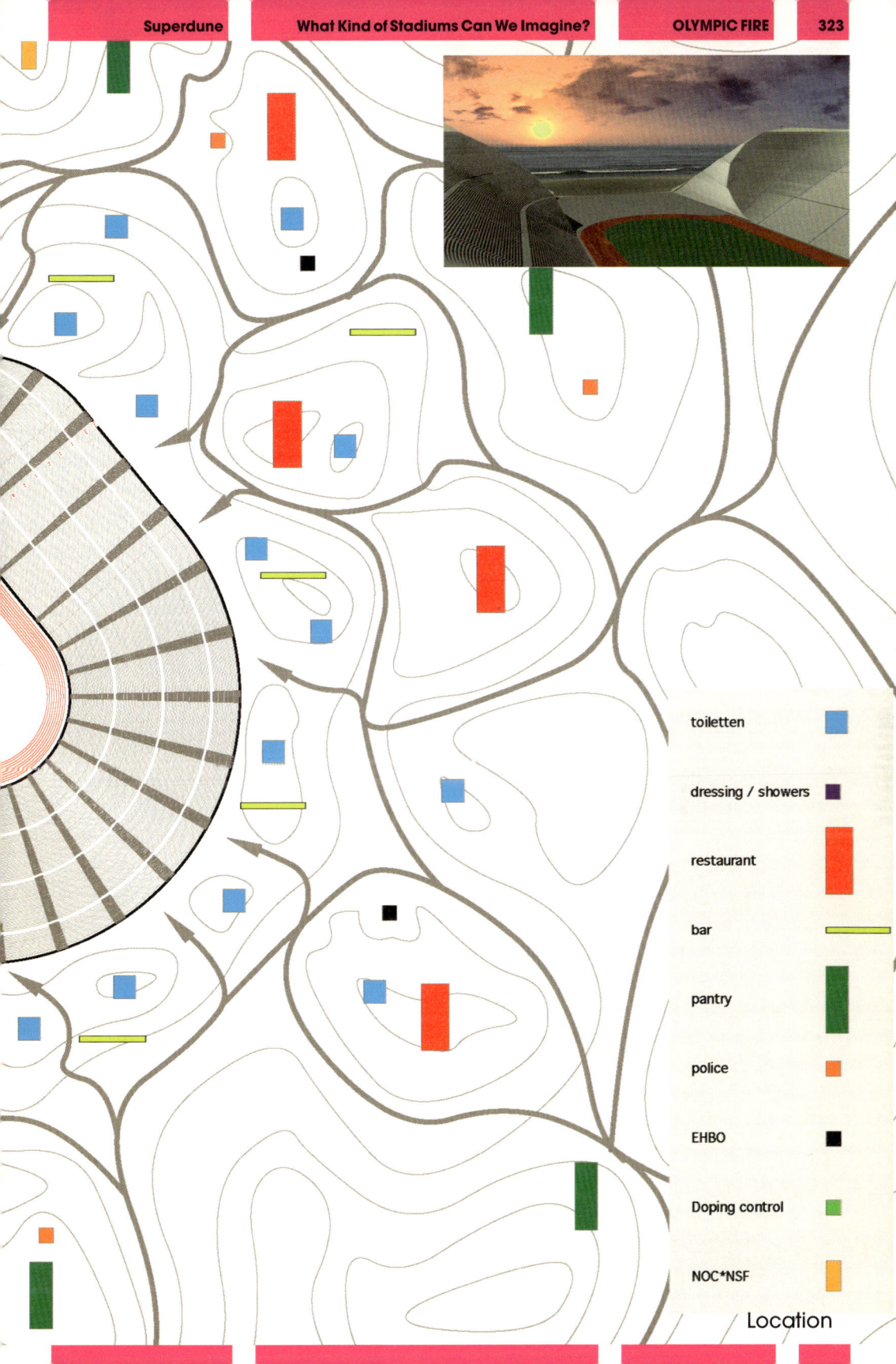

'We will have to "cast" sports and landscapes'

Dirk Sijmons interviewed by Mieke Dings

Dirk Sijmons is a partner with H+N+S Landscape Architects and a Government Advisor for Landscapes.

Involvement in the Olympic Games 2028: None. I have a necktie that says 'Amsterdam 1992'; I wore it the other day during a brainstorming session about the idea of the Olympic Games 2028 with NOC*NSF. I have also recently joined the quality team of the Ministry of Housing, Spatial Planning and the Environment (VROM) that supports the spatial feasibility studies for the Olympic Games coordinated by Twynstra Gudde Consultants and Managers. But through a mix-up in my schedule I missed the first meeting. So I don't know anything about it yet.

Plays the Olympic sport: I do a bit of walking; quite a noble sport that unfortunately never has become an Olympic event. Well, maybe Nordic Walking will prove to be a stepping stone towards the Olympic Games.

Most impressive Olympic Games: Munich 1972; not only because this was the first time that an Olympic Stadium was covered with such an immense canopy – by the architect Frei Otto in this case – but also of course because sports then became heavily politicised, with the hostage-taking and later death of those 11 Israeli athletes.

Memorable sports moment: The jump with which American athlete Bob Beamon – and we still haven't figured out how he did it – improved the world record long jump by 55 centimetres to 8 metres 90, whereas a jump of 8 metres 10 already qualified athletes for the finals.

What would your ideal Olympic Games 2028 look like?
Completely decentralised, with the sailing events on the Fluessen lake in Friesland and the Marathon in the Ardennes. If we take our lead from the Olympic Games in Tokyo or Los Angeles then we mustn't think too small. In fact, we are living in an urbanised delta that, with a bit of imagination, can be regarded as one huge city. The Games therefore should belong to all of the Netherlands, with some events even taking place across the border in other parts of the delta. Even if Amsterdam will be the name on the Olympic ticket, the games will be decentralised.

Which role does the landscape play in this?
Quite a large one. One of the biggest and longest advertising campaigns in the world is the one for France during the Tour de France, when cameras from helicopters show the French landscape from the 'Hell of the North' to the mountains of the Pyrenees. When I see those images I always feel like renting a little cottage there. So I think that here during the Olympic Games we should have the sailing contests, the equestrian events, the marathon and all those other long-distance sports take place at the finest locations. That way we will not be using the landscape simply as a backdrop, but showcase our country at the same time.

Which landscapes should definitely have to be part of the Olympic Games 2028?
The low landscapes that were formed during the Holocene, such as the coastal landscape from Groningen to Zeeland, and the river region. Because, like a fellow landscape architect of mine once said, across the river IJssel begins a landscape that continues until Moscow. While the landscape in the lower west of the land is quite interesting and differentiated, with polders, pastures, terps [artificial mounds peculiar to the Netherlands - MD] and islands. If we really want to do a bit of Holland promotion, these are the landscapes to focus on. Besides these, there are of course all sorts of special elements that lend themselves to specific Olympic events, such as the defence line of Amsterdam. This 135 km ring of 19th-century forts and defensive dikes – which is now on the UNESCO World Heritage list – would make a great location for a cycle race. We have until 2028 to analyse the landscape for such points and plan routes.

How would these landscapes be best portrayed? You already mentioned the helicopters of the Tour de France.
You can also capture the vastness of the landscape from well-chosen automobile routes. And we can help out our Minister of Transport if we make driving in traffic jams an Olympic sport! But of course we must also look for static points from which the Dutch landscape is best experienced, for building stadiums and such.

Could the landscapes also be meaningful to the athletes themselves?
I don't know whether they even assimilate anything or are so focused on their achievements that they don't care where they perform them. It would be interesting to look into that.

What kind of landscape issues have to be solved before the Olympic Games of 2028?
The greatest trick will be to build infrastructures that can be reused. For instance, a Randstad Round – providing a super-fast connection for the athletes between the Olympic Villages and the stadiums – may be an interesting gadget for the Olympic Games and will be very useful afterwards. As far as the landscape is concerned we will have to 'cast' the sports and the landscapes and then very meticulously map the bottlenecks of those landscapes and solve them. This also is very useful for the future.

Do you see any possibilities for addressing environmental issues?
We can of course try to organise CO_2-free Games by, for instance, installing solar panels on all the stadiums. However, everyone will still be flying here from all over the world and that carries a heavy CO_2 price ticket.

Unless we start investing in alternative transport between countries.
What I would very much like is for all these athletes to arrive here by old-fashioned ocean liners and then for us to receive them with cheers in the hall of the Holland America Line. On board these ships – which will of course have been built by Dutch shipbuilders – the athletes will have been training for weeks using all sorts of facilities. That would be a real breakthrough, I think.

How old will you be in 2028?
79.

And from where would you prefer to watch the Olympic Games then?
From the island of Texel, where the windsurfing event will undoubtedly take place. That is a spectacle I would like to watch from a number of beautiful spots on the beach and the dike.

Can you think of a sports quote or slogan to make the country rally behind the idea of hosting the Olympic Games 2028?
Chlorophyll [the pigment that makes plants green – MD] as the only drug permitted.

'I wouldn't be surprised at all if the Olympic Games withered away'

Abram de Swaan interviewed by Mieke Dings

Abram de Swaan is a professor emeritus in Social Sciences at the University of Amsterdam. He has written several books, including The People Society, an Introduction (De mensenmaatschappij, een inleiding [Bert Bakker, 1996]) and Words of the World, the World's Language System (Prometheus, 2002). He also writes columns in newspapers, including NRC Handelsblad.

Involvement in the Olympic Games 2028: None whatsoever.
Plays an Olympic sport? I am an enthusiastic karateka, but karate is not an Olympic sport. Then again, judo is.
Most impressive Olympic Games: I very much enjoyed the Games in Los Angeles in 1984. They were so brilliantly organised, almost Hollywood style. A man came flying into the stadium propelled by two small jet engines.
Memorable sports moment: I don't have any.

In Olympian Heights (De Olympische hoogte [Meulenhoff, 1985]) you wrote about the social and cultural implications of the Games coming to Amsterdam in 1992. Can you explain why, in the end, the Games didn't come?
There wasn't much time; Amsterdam didn't start making its plans until 1985. Besides, there was a lot of opposition from within cultural and intellectual circles in Amsterdam. Some people really took issue with the plans and even went to Lausanne or Geneva to argue against the Games being held in Amsterdam. That didn't go down well. But I think it was primarily the relatively small size of the city and the fact that it had started planning so late and also had very strong competitors.

You already argued in favour of Randstad-wide Games, with Amsterdam as their cultural centre, in 1985. How do you feel about this now?
My main motive for writing Olympic Heights was the fact that the Bijlmer district [a high-rise suburb of Amsterdam, built in the early 1970s – MD] was really going to seed at the time. The district, intended for the Amsterdam middle-class, was on the verge of collapse, caused by the unprepared migration of many Surinamese people and other immigrants after 1974. Despite fierce protests by the Provos [a group of activists who 'provoked' the Dutch authorities in the 1960s – MD] and all sorts of people wanting to preserve the city, the subway line had just been constructed, which is now the Bijlmer's lifeline. At the time I felt that one of the problems was that although there were many people living there and there was now even a subway line, the Bijlmer district was not sufficiently populated to support a decent infrastructure of shops, theatres and other facilities. I felt we could boost the Bijlmer by making it the location for the Olympic Village and stadium. Now we have the Arena there [the stadium of FC Ajax, also used for pop concerts and other large events – MD]. My second motive for writing about this was the wish to consider the Netherlands as one very large city, the Randstad, a horseshoe-shaped area extending from Eindhoven to Rotterdam, The Hague, Leiden, Haarlem and Amsterdam. An area that was as big, as vast and as densely populated and had as much potential as London or Paris.
So, I was concerned with giving a boost to both the Bijlmer and the Randstad. The Bijlmer no longer needs it, and I don't think any place in the Netherlands does, come to think of it.

The Bijlmer may not need a boost anymore, but the Randstad is still far from being a reality.
That would be the only consideration then, that the Randstad has still not been realised. But thirty years of administrative deliberations failed to accomplish this. There are all sorts of administrative layers though: district councils, city councils, intercity consultation platforms, provinces, and

then of course the national government and the European Union. I don't think it would be wise to add yet another administrative layer shortly before the Games. It should be the other way around. But this will never succeed, because it would be a measure that would need the approval of the existing administrative bodies – which they will never give because they are much too content with their current positions. Such a measure could be put to effect to strengthen the position of Almere as part of the Randstad. However, they don't have the administrative force to organise something like the Games either.

No Olympic Games for the Netherlands, then.
I don't see any reason for them. Maybe the Olympic Games will even cease to exist. It's not that I dislike sports; I believe it is a wonderful form of organised competition, an outlet for our natural propensity to compete. It is, however, becoming increasingly difficult to deal with all the political protests. The idea of international reconciliation as a motive is pure rhetoric. The Games have never led to any reconciliation, certainly not in the recent past. Besides, the Games are already struggling with the threat of terrorism, and this won't go away, because complex societies simply are extremely vulnerable and if it isn't Al Qaeda taking advantage of this vulnerability, then it will be another group. Another reason why it would be better to do away with the Games is the advent of digital media, which make it possible to watch any sports events anywhere in the world. So what's the point of having the Games at one specific location? It would be better to spread them over the entire world. This has the added advantage of not having to receive the tourist masses, who only go to the Olympic cities to party. Instead we could organise smaller events and be a little bit more particular about which tourists we want.

In your book you argued in favour of a strong link between sports and culture. Is there any potential in this idea to transform the Games into something new?
Yes, I was in favour of that at the time, seeing as the Games once began as an event with a strong cultural element, but this soon became ridiculous and implausible. Now we have a wonderful opening ceremony each time. But it lasts only half an hour and then it's over. There is no point in transforming the Games into a cultural event.
So my advice would be: don't do it, come up with something else. For instance, a succession of festivals and events in the area of sports and culture that each draw a crowd of, say, 100,000. That would make the whole thing manageable in terms of hotels and transportation – you would have a relatively continuous stream of visitors instead of a one-time peak. I can also imagine combinations like we have at the Arena now, with a football match one day and a pop concert the next.

That goes against the idea that the Games, because of their scale, can give a healthy boost to solving the spatial issues in our country that have been dragging on for years now. With such permanent events there would be no sense of urgency.
I see that, but I think it will be no small task even to organise the transportation for events that are only one tenth the size of the Games. Let's first get the trains and subways to the level where they should have been a long time ago: very frequent connections between the larger Dutch cities and high-speed railways to Berlin, Milan, Marseille, London and Copenhagen. Planes are fast becoming outmoded. Who wants to take off their belt and shoes and be shunted someplace packed together like cabin cattle for hours? Cars are becoming obsolete as well. I am in favour of investing in railways so that people from all over Europe can come and visit our beautiful events. But when I see the bungling with the North-South Line [a new subway line in Amsterdam – MD], the Betuwelijn [a railway for freight trains from Rotterdam to Germany – MD] and the high-speed railway, I am not very optimistic.

How old will you be in 2028 and where will you be watching the Games if they do take place in Netherlands, albeit against your wishes?
I will be 86 then and I certainly intend to still be around. But I won't be at the opening ceremony; I will sit snugly in my study, reading a book or writing an essay.

Finally, can you think of a sports quote or motto to steer our land away from the Games?
Don't do it. Come up with something new!

'Olympic Village in the city centre adds to the atmosphere'

<u>Stephan Veen</u> interviewed by Mieke Dings

Stephan Veen is Senior Vice President for Corporate Clients with Rabobank Nederland and a former top field-hockey player. As captain, he scored three times in the finals at the Games in Sydney.

Involvement in the Olympic Games 2028: I am a member of the 'Club of 28', a group which, under the auspices of NOC*NSF, advises, checks and guides the progress of the Olympic Plan. The club consists of 28 very different people – from the business world, government, sports world, media, etc.

Plays an Olympic sport? I still practice the sport that I played in the Olympics myself: field hockey. Only now I do so as a senior member.

Memorable sports moment: Having taken part in the Games myself, of course I remember my own sports moments best. But if you ask me about a memorable sports moment of someone else, I would say Carl Lewis, who won four gold medals in Los Angeles in 1984: for the long jump, the 100 and 200 metres, and the 4 x 100 metres.

Most impressive Olympic Games: I took part in the Games in Barcelona (1992), Atlanta (1996) and Sydney (2000). Of these, I found the Games in Barcelona the most impressive. It was not our best achievement – we finished fourth, while in Sydney and Atlanta we won gold – but they were my first Games and the atmosphere was really great.

Do athletes experience anything of the cities where the Games take place?
To a certain degree. Our matches were spread over two weeks, so we had little opportunity to see the city. Athletes who finished earlier and had reached their goals, would often go sightseeing. On our days off, we would usually stay in the Olympic Village and sometimes we would watch other events. Not very often though, because those were gruelling weeks for us.

What did you personally think of Barcelona, Atlanta and Sydney?
Barcelona is a beautiful city in itself, of course. And then there was the added energy that had gone into transforming the city, which reflected on the Olympic Village in the city centre. That was magical. In Atlanta I had the impression that the Games had been organised rather quickly and that daily life would swiftly resume afterwards. It felt like the Games were less of a 'happening' there than they were in Barcelona. Sydney was again quite different because the Olympic Village was in Homebush Bay, some 15 kilometres outside of the city. Most of the events were concentrated there, and this density had its advantages. On our days off we would, for instance, take a bicycle and go watch athletics or water polo. In Barcelona we wouldn't, because the sports venues were often at some distance from the city.

Were the Olympic Villages very different?
Absolutely. In Sydney we were living in freestanding, temporary houses, which was rather cosy. In Atlanta we had apartments in buildings four or five stories high, which were not bad either. The flats in Barcelona were about the same height, but they were in the city itself, in the harbour district. We also had a large patio in front of the flat, where we could relax. That was a bonus. But in the end we were of course focused on the sport. The environment did play a part, but it didn't make us run any faster.

Doesn't the environment have any influence at all on achievements?
It's hard to say. Of course you sense a better atmosphere in some places. For instance, we have played tournaments in India or Moscow where we would be staying in a remote hotel on the city's outskirts. That's not very cosy, but I can't say it really bothered us or influenced tournaments in a negative way. I think that atmosphere and surroundings are mainly important factors in attracting tourists.

Does it make any difference what a stadium looks like?
I don't think so. The IOC stipulates that the stadium must have at least 15,000 seats and I don't think its shape makes any difference. I doubt whether Pieter van den Hoogenband will swim any faster because they have built a nice 'water cube' in Beijing. The aesthetics are mainly of interest for the organising city and the Games themselves. Personally, though, I feel less comfortable in stadiums that are relatively open because there's more wind there, which irritates my contact lenses. And I find it more intimate and more exciting when the crowd is close to the pitch in a stadium.

Which Dutch stadium do you prefer?
The Wagener Stadium, the field hockey temple of the Netherlands. Besides, the Netherlands doesn't have that many large hockey stadiums. For the 1998 World Championships field hockey, Utrecht's Galgenwaard Stadium was altered to accommodate 20,000 hockey fans. If we do get the Games, those are the sort of solutions we should be looking for.

Do we have to reinvent the field hockey stadium for 2028?
Within the Club of 28 we tend to think of stadiums that can be used later as multifunctional venues. A field hockey stadium, for instance, can be altered to become a tennis court or a swimming pool, or both. Such multifunctional venues remain economically interesting afterwards. Flexible stadiums are a possibility as well. In Sydney, for instance, they had built smaller stadiums that were extended with add-on tribunes to a capacity of 15,000 for the duration of the Games only. We could do something like that with the Wagener Stadium, even though it will take quite a lot of renovation before it is up to IOC standards. We have to come up with clever constructions.

Where in the Netherlands would you like to see the 2028 Games take place?
I don't think we should aim for a single city, but the whole country. There's enough going on in the field of sports and we should make use of these existing activities. For instance, if bicycle racing is popular in the Brabant region, we might consider having that province organise the bicycle events. Other sports could likewise be distributed across the country. All these locations are perfectly accessible from one Olympic Village – our country is not that big, after all. We would have to improve the infrastructure, though.

The Olympic Village must be in the centre of the city of course, as in Barcelona.
I personally think that a city does add a little extra touch, but it is not a condition per se. The athletes spend most of their time in the Olympic Village anyway.

How do you think the athletes will experience the Netherlands?
We are a very well-organised country and the Dutch in general – after airing some healthy criticism – are quite enthusiastic about this sort of large-scale sports event. We are also quite open-minded and we easily engage in conversations with others. I think the athletes will be aware of this open attitude.

How old will you be in 2028 and where would you prefer to be watching the Olympic Games then?
I will be 57 then and I'll be watching my favourite sports wherever they take place. Naturally, I will want to watch the field hockey, but many other sports as well. I am sure that many Dutch will feel the same way by then.

Can you think of a sports quote or slogan to make the country rally behind the idea of hosting the Olympic Games in 2028?
Netherlands Sports Land. That's the one.

WHAT IS NEXT?

What is Next? **OLYMPIC FIRE** 331

What is next?

This book started out with as many questions as there are Olympic rings; four of them, 326 pages further along, have now been answered. Yes, we can play with a grand idea which taps our potential. The preparations for Olympic Fire, made in a concerted effort between Architecture, Sport, Business and Government, have shown that the most important aspect of that potential is having the courage to speculate. Thinking ahead, extrapolating, innovating, designing – without these qualities, the entire enterprise of proposing ourselves for the Olympic Games would be pointless. What's more, the Games stimulate these qualities. That was their purpose 112 years ago and it still is the case. Athletes and organisations share the capacity to set themselves a goal. No matter what new developments put the Games in a contemporary perspective, they are about a capacity that goes beyond the issues of the day. Yes, we have a sense of possibility.
That brings us to the answer to the second question. Yes, we know what to do with the value we have in common with the rest of humanity. As the greatest international gathering known to man, it is also an opportunity for the host country to show its best side to the world. This can be done by offering splendid sports facilities, architectural gestures of unprecedented beauty, or impeccable organization. But what it primarily comes down to is a value esteemed by all people throughout all ages: hospitality. Thinking about the Olympic Games also means imagining what a warm welcome will look like.

That exercise alone could give a tremendous boost to our national self-awareness. But hospitality includes much more than readiness to offer pleasant surroundings in which people can feel at home. It also means the opposite: showing how the Netherlands can contribute to the phenomenon of the Olympic Games in a way that can be done nowhere else. Precisely because of the boldness which has characterized the disciplines of urban planning and architecture in the Netherlands for so long, daring rhetorical games turn into concrete deeds. In these disciplines, the sense of possibility becomes the sense of reality. These are disciplines which are capable of thinking beyond the obvious and the clichéd. The proposals in this book make it clear that the programme of the Olympic Games is weighty enough to simultaneously encompass a programme for social renewal. This means creating models that start with sport but move on to such topics as the sustainable economy, new forms of water management, an integrated policy on feelings of insecurity, a vital public domain, smart solutions for a small-scale approach, and so forth.

Arriving at the third and fourth questions, we can therefore say: yes, we have found inspiration that gives direction to our deeds. Yes, we are motivated to embark upon a project that brings out the best in us. Lately it has become more and more clear that the Olympic Games are not only a goal but a beginning, a dot on the horizon by which to steer a course. There are so many reasons for doing this exploration: talent seeks an outlet; collaboration requires a project; union is strength; government seeks legitimacy; development requires a goal; investment requires a motive; idealism requires a mission. For all of these, the Olympic Fire is a positive incentive. At a time in which the desire for such an incentive is unusually great, perhaps it will offer extra hope.

The question remains, however, of whether we have the courage to set ourselves a deadline for our success. The work that has been accomplished in this collective project of the Berlage Institute, Academy of Architecture, MVRDV, Ministries, Cities, Provinces and the Netherlands Architecture Institute has been rooted in the thought that there had to be a time limit, an ultimate goal, which might be set for 2028. That goal is the key to the concrete, for only a deadline makes it necessary to practice.

It is just like participating in the Olympic Games themselves: the Netherlands is putting its all into qualifying. As every athlete knows, this usually requires several attempts. Olympic Fire; playing with the future, is precisely such an attempt. The coming period will show whether we have met that qualification. And if so, then the real work begins. Four questions have been answered; before the fifth can be dealt with, these answers must first be demonstrated. We hope this book fulfils that role.

CREDITS

This book is published in conjunction with the exhibition 'NL28 Olympic Fire' held at the Netherlands Architecture Institute from 31 May to 21 September 2008.

How did we come to do this?
During the Olympic Winter Games in Torino in 2006, the Dutch Olympic Committee (NOC*NSF) organised a panel of experts to discuss a new approach toward sports in the Netherlands and the possibility and spatial consequences of organizing a Summer Games in the Netherlands. A presentation on the 'Sportcity' by Winy Maas generated collective enthusiasm to study these topics in greater depth. A collaborative research project was accordingly set up at the Rotterdam Academy of Architecture and Urban Design and the Berlage Institute, the results of which have been presented in the exhibition at the NAI and in this book.
The project comprised four studios: In the fall of 2006, the Rotterdam Academy of Architecture and Urban Design initiated a research project on the history of the Olympic Games, presented in 'What can we learn from previous Olympics?'
In the spring of 2007, a collaborative studio at both the Academy of Architecture Rotterdam and the Berlage Institute investigated the potential of an Olympic Games programme and spatial ideals: 'What is the Olympic Programme & Schedule?'
In the fall of 2007, a design studio on 'black elephants' at the Academy of Architecture Rotterdam resulted in proposals for reusable stadiums: 'What Kind of Stadiums Can We Imagine?'
In the same period at the Berlage Institute, a research studio on possible Dutch applications led to a series of proposals: 'What Kinds of Games Can We Imagine?'
The material has been reviewed by the visiting critics mentioned below and edited by MVRDV in collaboration with DJS, SIA and NAI.

RESEARCH
This exhibition and book present the results of the 'Bid 1.0 & 2.0' workshops conducted at the Berlage Institute and the Rotterdam Academy of Architecture and Urban Design from 2006 to 2008. This research is based on an initiative of Winy Maas, with the support of Herbert Wolff (NOC*NSF Amsterdam), Lukas Verweij (director of the Rotterdam Academy of Architecture and Urban Design) and Rob Docter (director of the Berlage Institute).

Tutors at the Berlage Institute: Winy Maas and Marc Joubert with Tihamér Hazarja Salij, Young Wook Joung and Daliana Suryawinata
Tutors at the Rotterdam Academy of Architecture and Urban Design: Winy Maas and Marc Joubert with Tihamér Hazarja Salij, Young Wook Joung, Daliana Suryawinata and Anton Wubben
Berlage Institute participants:
Bid 1.0: Tsungren Chang, Botsung Chiu, Kwak Daewon, Julica Grzybowski, Seung Jeong Hong, Tsu En Hsu, Eun-Kyung Lee, Kyo-Suk Lee, Chia-Ying Lin, Alex Martinez, German Ramirez, Fairuz Reza Razali, Tsai-Ching Tsai and Mika Watanabe
Bid 2.0: Han Ju Chen, Jeong Eun Choi, Maria Giudici, Wanyu He, Kuniyoshi Katsu Sebastiano Manservisi. Alessandro Martinelli, Lukas Narutis and June Young Park
Rotterdam Academy of Architecture and Urban Design participants:
Bid 1.0: Jaap Baselmans, Elma van Boxel, Lieke Genten, Richard van Herwijnen, Rene Toet and Evgeniya Mednikova
Bid 2.0: Jimmy van der Aa, Joost Clymans, Dik Houben, Jan Houweling, Froukje van de Klundert, Tanja Lina, Leo Glastra van Loon, Paul Michielsen, Michiel Raats, Marc Taks, Maarten Tenten and Ronald van de Wel

VISITING CRITICS
Bid 1.0 at the Berlage Institute and the Rotterdam Academy of Architecture and Urban Design
Pier Vittorio Aureli (Berlage), Ole Bouman (NAI), Anna Joke Breimer, Maurits de Hoog (dRO/City of Amsterdam), Chris van Langen (AVBR), Friedrich Ludewig (Foreign Office Architects), Vedran Mimica (Berlage), Marcel Sturkenboom (NOC*NSF), Nico Tillie (dS+V/City of Rotterdam), Roemer van Toorn (Berlage), Wilco Verhagen (dS+V/City of Rotterdam), Lucas Verweij (AVBR), Martien de Vletter (NAI) and Herbert Wolff (NOC*NSF)
Bid 2.0 at the Berlage Institute:
Miguel Robles Duran (Berlage), Salomon Frausto (Berlage), Marco Kooiman (Topcity Amsterdam), Chris van Langen (AVBR), Friedrich Ludewig (Foreign Office Architects), Vedran Mimica (Berlage), Hiromasa Shirai (LSE, London), Saskia van Stein (NAI), Marcel Sturkenboom (NOC*NSF), Nico Tillie (dS+V/Gemeente Rotterdam), Roemer van Toorn (Berlage), Peter Trummer (Berlage), Martien de Vletter (NAI) and Herbert Wolff (NOC*NSF)

Guests: Miguel Robles Duran, Geke Hop and Marcel Witvoet
Bid 2.0 at the Rotterdam Academy of Architecture and Urban Design:
Pier Vittorio Aureli (Berlage), Rein Jansma (Zwarts Jansma Architects), Chris van Langen (AVBR), Ron van Sluys (HOK Sport Architecture), Saskia van Stein (NAI), Dirk Termijn (Termijn Management & Advies BV), Lucas Verweij (AVBR) and Herbert Wolff (NOC*NSF)

PUBLICATION
Concept: Winy Maas (MVRDV), Marc Joubert (DoepelJoubertStrijkers) and Tihamér Hazarja Salij (Space Intelligence Agency)
Book Editors: Marc Joubert (DoepelJoubertStrijkers) and Tihamér Hazarja Salij (Space Intelligence Agency)
Editorial Board: Ole Bouman (NAI), Salomon Frausto (Berlage Instituut), Marc Joubert (DoepelJoubertStrijkers), Chris van Langen (AVBR), Winy Maas (MVRDV), Tihamér Hazarja Salij (Space Intelligence Agency), Saskia van Stein (NAI) en Anton Wubben (MVRDV)
Texts: Ole Bouman (NAI), André Bolhuis(NOC*NSF), Marc Joubert (DoepelJoubertStrijkers), Winy Maas (MVRDV), Tihamér Hazarja Salij (Space Intelligence Agency) en Marcel Sturkenboom (NOC*NSF)
Text and Image Editing: Marc Joubert (DoepelJoubertStrijkers), Tihamér Hazarja Salij (Space Intelligence Agency) and Saskia van Stein (NAI)
Interviews: Mieke Dings and Harry den Hartog
Images Sports Fields: Dieuwertje Komen Fairuz Reza Rezali and Saskia van Stein
Photography models: Dirk Vroemen
Digital Presentation: Eline Wieland, Marino Gouwens (Wieland & Gouwens) with Twan Haanen
Artistic Impressions: Marcin Gajewski
Additional Contributors: Maria Giudici, Wanyu He, Kuniyoshi Katsu, Kyo-Suk Lee, Alessandro Martinelli, Fairuz Reza Razali and Dirk Verhagen
Logo NL28: Thonik in collaboration with Enchilada
Translation & Copy-Editing: Jane Bemont and Leo Reijnen (articles and interviews only)
Graphic Design: Sander Boon
Lithography and Printing: Drukkerij Die Keure, Bruges (B)
Paper: Arctic Volume, 150 grs
Production: Marcel Witvoet, NAi Publishers, Rotterdam
Publisher: Eelco van Welie, NAi Publishers, Rotterdam

© 2008 NAi PUBLISHERS
All rights reserved. No part of this publication may be reproduced, stored in a retrieval system, or transmitted in any form or by any means, electronic, mechanical, photocopying, recording or otherwise, without the prior written permission of the publisher.

For works of visual artists affiliated with a CISAC-organization the copyrights have been settled with Pictoright in Amsterdam.
© 2008, c/o Pictoright Amsterdam
It was not possible to find all the copyright holders of the illustrations used. Interested parties are requested to contact NAi Publishers, Mauritsweg 23, 3012 JR Rotterdam, the Netherlands. info@naipublishers.nl

NAi Publishers is an internationally orientated publisher specialized in developing, producing and distributing books on architecture, visual arts and related disciplines.
www.naipublishers.nl

Available in North, South and Central America through D.A.P./Distributed Art Publishers Inc, 155 Sixth Avenue 2nd Floor, New York, NY 10013-1507, tel +1 212 627 1999, fax +1 212 627 9484, dap@dapinc.com
Available in the United Kingdom and Ireland through Art Data, 12 Bell Industrial Estate, 50 Cunnington Street, London W4 5HB, tel +44 208 747 1061, fax +44 208 742 2319, orders@artdata.co.uk

Printed and bound in Belgium

ISBN 978-90-5662-628-0

With thanks to:
NOC*NSF, International Olympic Commitee (IOC), the Academy of Architecture Rotterdam, Berlage Institute Rotterdam, Made by Mistake, Family Rovers, Janssen-Fritsen, Lucas Verweij, Dieuwertje Blok, Mieke Dings, Rob Docter, Katrien Franken, Tijmen Hordijk, Mirjam Stolwijk, Dirk Verhagen, Dirk Vroemen

With special thanks to:
NOC*NSF, City of Rotterdam, City of Amsterdam, Province of Flevoland, Netherlands Ministry of Housing, Spatial Planning and the Environment (VROM), Netherlands Ministry of Health, Welfare and Sport(VWS), Koninklijke BAM Groep, Embedded Fitness, de E-fitzone, Janssen-Fritsen, Rotterdam Atletiek, Shipmate